SCIENCE ESSENTIALS

GRADES 3-4

School Specialty Publishing

Copyright ©2005 School Specialty Publishing. Published by American Education Publishing™, an imprint of School Specialty Publishing, a member of the School Specialty Family.

Send all inquiries to:
School Specialty Publishing
8720 Orion Place
Columbus, Ohio 43240

ISBN 0-7696-6048-7

2 3 4 5 6 7 QPD 13 12 11 10 09

Section 1
Dinosaurs

Name _____

Keeping Up With the Dinosaurs

Directions: Read the dinosaur facts below. Then, write true or false in the blanks before the sentences at the bottom of the page.

Paleontologists believe that the first true **dinosaurs** evolved on Earth about 225 million years ago and became extinct, or disappeared, about 65 million years ago. All true dinosaurs were land-living creatures. The gigantic prehistoric sea creatures, such as ichthyosaurs, mosasaurs and plesiosaurs, were not really dinosaurs. Pterosaurs were not really dinosaurs either. They were flying reptiles that looked like lizards with wings.

The word dinosaur means "terrible lizard," but dinosaurs were not lizards. Modern science now links dinosaurs to **birds**. Today's birds are thought to be the closest relatives to the dinosaurs. Crocodiles are also thought to be more distant relatives of the dinosaurs. Scientists believe all animals and plants living on Earth today are descendants of creatures that lived when dinosaurs roamed the earth.

True or false?

1. ___ The first dinosaurs evolved on Earth about 65 million years ago.

2. ___ Ichthyosaurs were true dinosaurs.

3. ___ Dinosaurs were not lizards.

4. ___ Scientists believe birds are related to dinosaurs.

5. ___ Some dinosaurs were flying reptiles.

Challenge:
Think of your favorite bird. List some ways this bird is like, or similar to, a dinosaur.

_____

_____

Name _____

Nippers, Rippers and Grinders

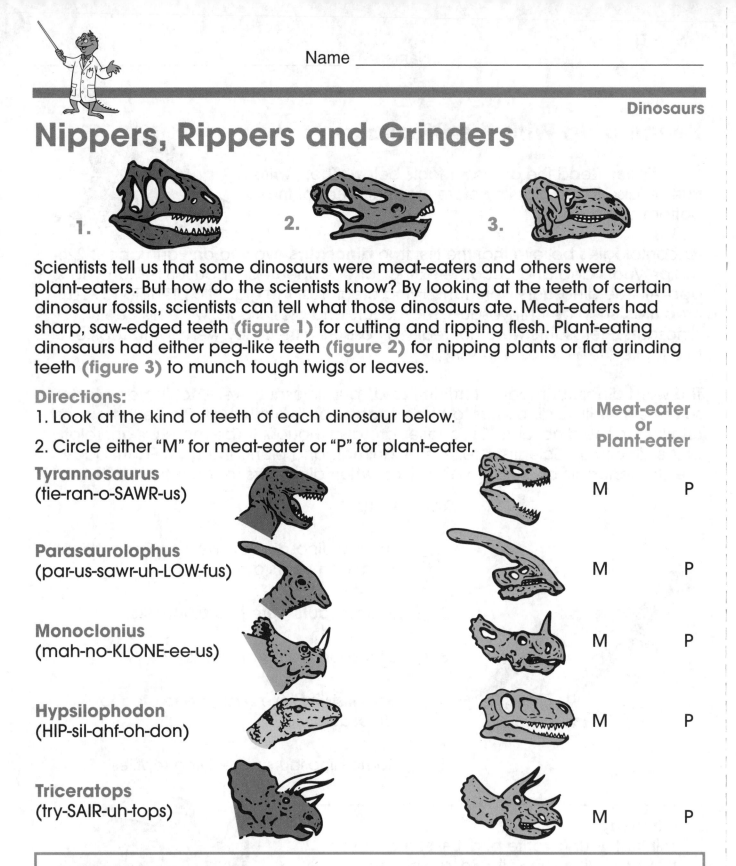

Scientists tell us that some dinosaurs were meat-eaters and others were plant-eaters. But how do the scientists know? By looking at the teeth of certain dinosaur fossils, scientists can tell what those dinosaurs ate. Meat-eaters had sharp, saw-edged teeth **(figure 1)** for cutting and ripping flesh. Plant-eating dinosaurs had either peg-like teeth **(figure 2)** for nipping plants or flat grinding teeth **(figure 3)** to munch tough twigs or leaves.

Directions:

1. Look at the kind of teeth of each dinosaur below.

2. Circle either "M" for meat-eater or "P" for plant-eater.

Meat-eater or Plant-eater

Tyrannosaurus
(tie-ran-o-SAWR-us)   M   P

Parasaurolophus
(par-us-sawr-uh-LOW-fus)   M   P

Monoclonius
(mah-no-KLONE-ee-us)   M   P

Hypsilophodon
(HIP-sil-ahf-oh-don)   M   P

Triceratops
(try-SAIR-uh-tops)   M   P

Fantastic Fact
The **Tyrannosaurus,** whose name means "king of the tyrant lizards," was the largest meat-eater. It weighed over 8 tons and was over 50 feet long. Its teeth were over 6 inches long and had edges like a steak knife.

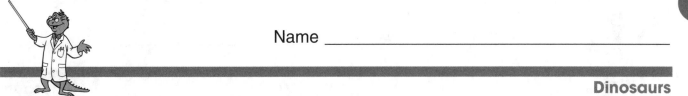

Name _____

Prehistoric Sea Creatures

While dinosaurs were living on the Earth, large prehistoric sea creatures were living in the sea. These large creatures were not fish. They gave birth to live young.

Directions: To find out what the three prehistoric sea monsters below looked like, follow the correct path. The correct path will also give you some interesting facts to help you answer the questions at the bottom of the page.

Plesiosaurs
(PLEEZ-ee-uh-sawrs)

Ichthyosaurs
(IK-thee-uh-sawrs)

Pliosaurs
(PLY-uh-sawrs)

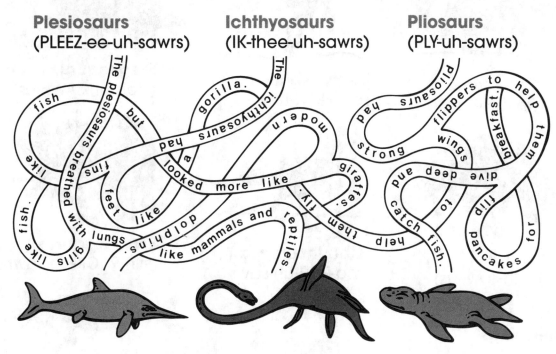

Directions:

Circle True (T) or False (F).

T   F   Plesiosaurs breathed with gills.
T   F   Ichthyosaurs looked very much like giant dolphins.
T   F   Most prehistoric sea creatures laid eggs.
T   F   Reptiles breathe air with their lungs.
T   F   Pliosaurs were meat-eating sea creatures.
T   F   Ichthyosaurs were big fish.

Fantastic Fact
A young girl found the first complete **Plesiosaur** fossil! Eleven-year-old Mary Anning was walking along the southern coast of England looking for small fossils to sell in order to earn money for her family when she found the fossil.

Name _____

Dinosaur Names

Did you know that most dinosaur names tell us something about the animal?

Directions: Look at the pictures below. Write the correct letter next to the dinosaur name.

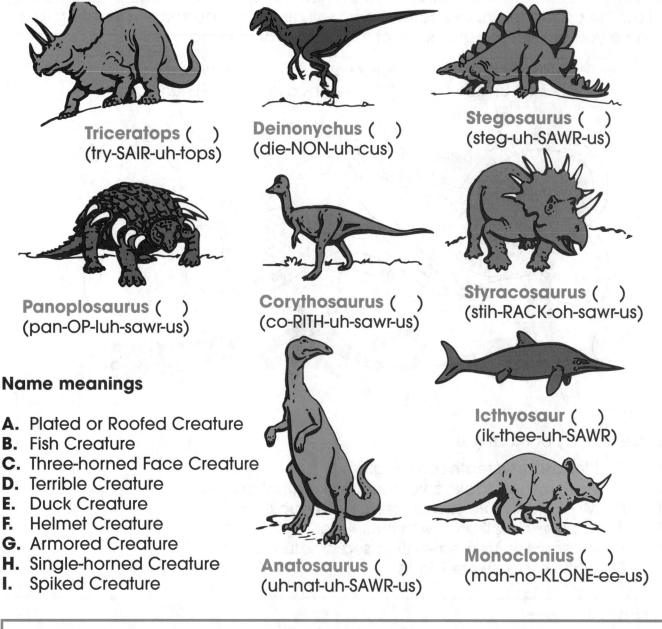

Triceratops ( )
(try-SAIR-uh-tops)

Deinonychus ( )
(die-NON-uh-cus)

Stegosaurus ( )
(steg-uh-SAWR-us)

Panoplosaurus ( )
(pan-OP-luh-sawr-us)

Corythosaurus ( )
(co-RITH-uh-sawr-us)

Styracosaurus ( )
(stih-RACK-oh-sawr-us)

Icthyosaur ( )
(ik-thee-uh-SAWR)

Anatosaurus ( )
(uh-nat-uh-SAWR-us)

Monoclonius ( )
(mah-no-KLONE-ee-us)

Name meanings

A. Plated or Roofed Creature
B. Fish Creature
C. Three-horned Face Creature
D. Terrible Creature
E. Duck Creature
F. Helmet Creature
G. Armored Creature
H. Single-horned Creature
I. Spiked Creature

Fantastic Fact
The eggs of a dinosaur were not always safe from other dinosaurs. The **Oviraptor** (ov-uh-RAP-tur), or "egg thief," had a birdlike beak which it used to crunch large dinosaur eggs.

Name _____

Dinosaur Defense

How did the plant-eating dinosaurs protect themselves from the attacks of the fierce meat-eating dinosaurs? One way was to travel in groups. But they also had other ways to defend themselves. For example, some had horns and some could run very fast.

Directions:

Look at the plant-eating dinosaurs below. Find the features of their bodies that gave them protection from their enemies. Explain in the space provided.

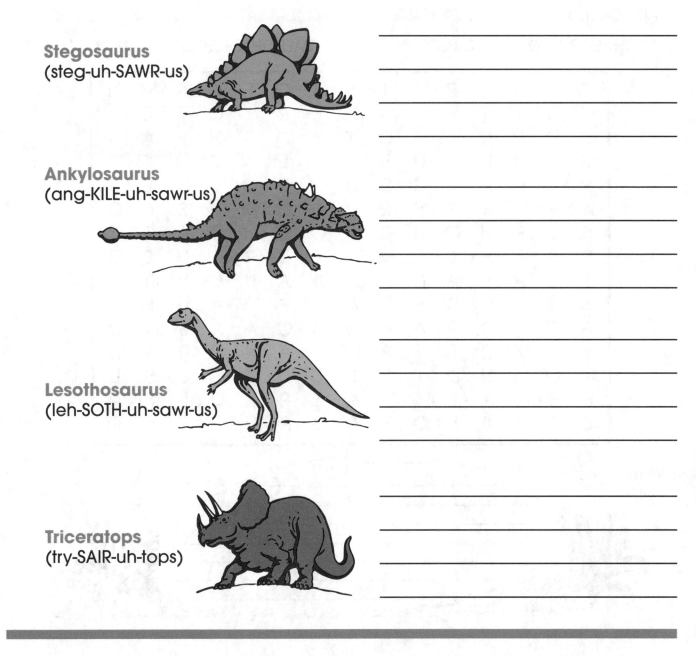

Stegosaurus
(steg-uh-SAWR-us)

_____
_____
_____
_____

Ankylosaurus
(ang-KILE-uh-sawr-us)

_____
_____
_____
_____

Lesothosaurus
(leh-SOTH-uh-sawr-us)

_____
_____
_____
_____

Triceratops
(try-SAIR-uh-tops)

_____
_____
_____

Dino-Find

Directions: Find the hidden words in the puzzle below. The words may be written forward, backward, up, down or diagonally. Circle the words. When you have located all the words, write the remaining letters at the bottom of the page to spell out a message.

ALLOSAURUS	BIRD HIP	FOSSIL	PLANT-EATER
APATOSAURUS	COELURUS	JURASSIC	PLATED
ARMORED	DINOSAUR	MEAT-EATER	SAUROPOD
ARCHAEOPTERYX	DIPLODOCUS	PALEONTOLOGIST	STEGOSAURUS

```
S D B U R L I S S O F I S M N
G U I T H I S P E R I O T E T
J D R U A S O N I D S H E A S
U A D U L D L O S E W S G T I
R E H A A S O U C R O V O E G
A E I R E S R P D O M U S A O
S C P H O U O F O M N O A T L
S R T H L A M T E R R I U E O
I C A E A N D E A A U U R R T
C R O O D E T A L P P A U E N
A C N D R A I N S C A A S M O
E X Y R E T P O E A H C R A E
T O T H D I P L O D O C U S L
R E T A E T N A L P E D E S A
E R A L L O S A U R U S T S P
```

Hidden message: _____

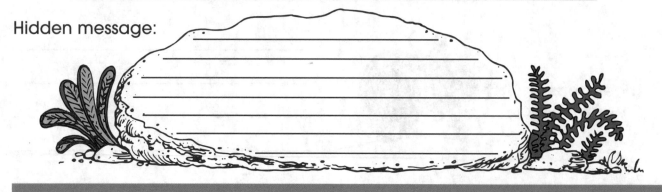

Name _____

How Long Were the Dinosaurs?

Dinosaurs varied greatly in size. Some were up to 90 feet long!

Directions: Use a dinosaur encyclopedia or other reference materials to find the lengths of some dinosaurs. Write the names of the dinosaurs along the bottom of the line graph. Color in the lengths (in feet) with different colored pens or crayons.

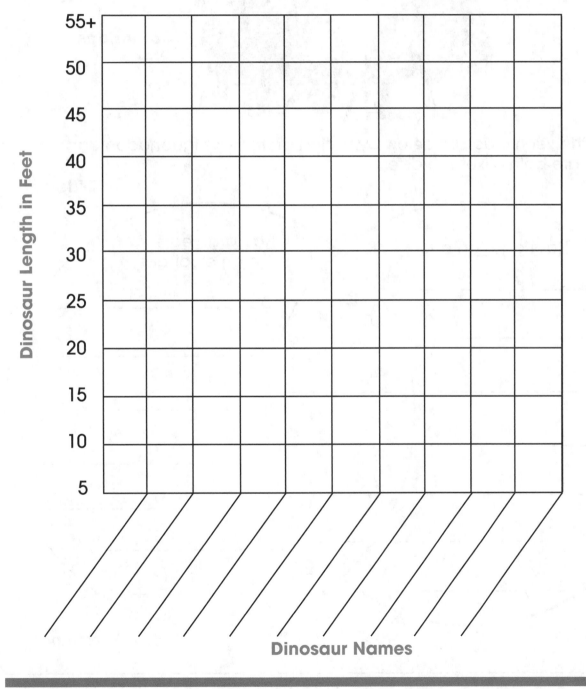

Dinosaur Length in Feet

55+
50
45
40
35
30
25
20
15
10
5

Dinosaur Names

Name _____

Dinosaur Diagram

A Venn diagram can be used to compare things. First, look at the picture to notice ways the two dinosaurs are the same. Then, look for how they are different.

Iguanodon

Triceratops

Complete the Venn diagram below by writing more ways Iguanodon and Triceratops are both alike and different.

Different　　　　　　　　　　　　**Same**　　　　　　　　　　**Different**

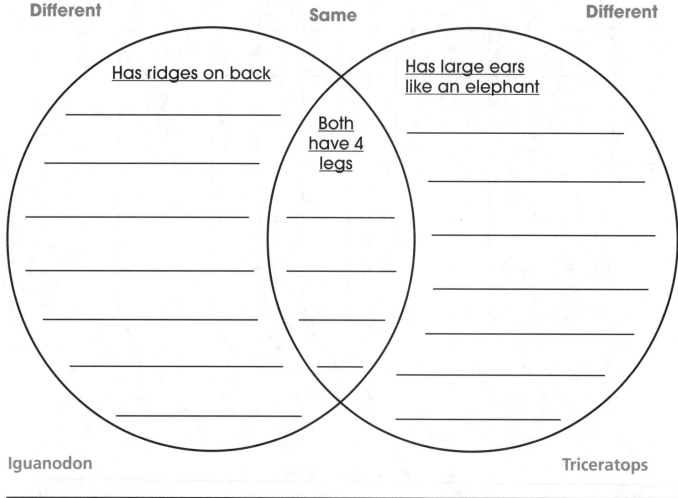

Has ridges on back

Has large ears like an elephant

Both have 4 legs

Iguanodon

Triceratops

Name _____

A Dinosaur Tale

Directions: Study the dinosaurs illustrated below. Then, complete each category with words that you associate with these animals. A few examples are already written under each heading. Use the words to compose a poem or short story about these dinosaurs.

Nouns	Verbs	Adjectives
tail	walk	huge
teeth	run	spiked
head	eat	sharp

Title: _____

_____

_____

_____

_____

_____

_____

Get a Clue!

Directions: Read the 16 clues below about a certain dinosaur. Use a science book or other resource materials and your own logical thinking to guess the name of the dinosaur. When you are finished, write your own clues about another dinosaur. Give it to someone else to see if he/she can guess the answer.

I am a dinosaur.

1. My name means "three-horned face."

2. My skull was 7 or 8 feet long.

3. I had a beaked mouth like a parrot.

4. I ate plants.

5. I walked on all four legs.

6. I was 30 feet long.

7. I weighed up to 10 tons.

8. I was one of the last dinosaurs to live.

9. I had 3 claws on my front feet.

10. I lived in Canada and the U.S.

11. I had a thick neck frill.

12. I had 3 horns on my skull.

13. I am the best-known horned dinosaur.

14. I used my horns for protection.

15. I had a small hoof on each toe.

16. I was named by O.C. Marsh in 1889.

I am a _____.

✂ -

I am a dinosaur.

1. _____

2. _____

3. _____

4. _____

5. _____

6. _____

7. _____

8. _____

9. _____

10. _____

I am a _____.

The End of the Dinosaurs

What could have killed all the dinosaurs? Scientists are not really sure. They have many different **theories**, or explanations, for why the dinosaurs died out.

Several theories are listed below. Each theory has a **cause** and an **effect**. A cause is a change that happened on Earth and an effect is what resulted from the change on Earth.

Directions: Draw a line from each cause to its effect.

Cause

- A huge meteor hit the Earth, starting fires and making a thick cloud of dust and smoke that covered the Earth.

- Small, fast mammals that liked to eat eggs quickly spread around the world.

- New kinds of flowering plants started to grow on the earth. These plants had poison in them that the dinosaurs could not taste.

- When dinosaurs were living, the earth was warm all year long. Suddenly the earth became cooler with cold winter months.

Effect

- Dinosaurs were cold-blooded. They couldn't find places to hibernate. They had no fur or feathers to keep themselves warm. They froze to death.

- The sunlight was blocked and plants couldn't grow. The dinosaurs starved to death.

- Fewer and fewer baby dinosaurs were born.

- The dinosaurs ate poison without even knowing it and they died.

Name _____

Lumps, Bumps and Scars

It's exciting when a **paleontologist** (a scientist who studies fossils) finds a dinosaur fossil. The fossil might be from a dinosaur no one has ever discovered before.

It might take years for paleontologists to put together most of a dinosaur's bones. The lumps, bumps and scars on the bones give them clues as to what the dinosaur might have looked like. These marks on the bones show where muscles were attached. By looking at the whole skeleton and the lumps, bumps and scars on each bone, paleontologists can guess the shape of the dinosaur's body.

Directions: The two skeletons below are make-believe dinosaurs that nobody has ever found. Study the skeletons. Use colored pencils, crayons or markers to draw right over the skeleton to show what these dinosaurs might have looked like. Then, name your dinosaurs.

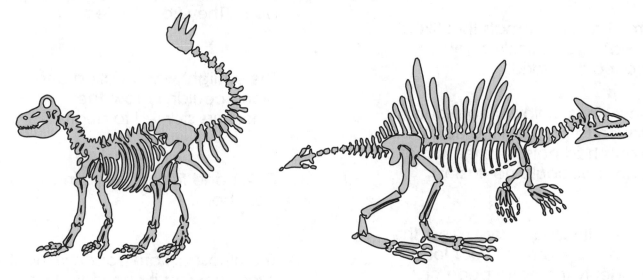

_____   _____

Fantastic Fact
Not all dinosaurs were huge giants. The **Compsognathus** (komp-SAHG-nay-thus) was the smallest dinosaur. It was about the same size as a crow, and it could run very fast.

Mold Fossils

You will need: leaves, clay, petroleum jelly, a small ink roller, plaster of Paris, a rolling pin, table knife

Directions:

1. Using the rolling pin, roll the clay until it is about ½" thick. Cut around the edges to make an oval or rectangle. Remove the excess clay.

cut

2. Roll out more clay. Cut it into strips. Put the strips around the oval and pinch them securely into place.

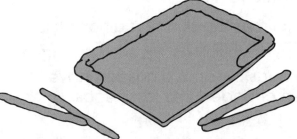

3. Rub petroleum jelly over the rectangle or oval and the inside of the strips.

PETROLEUM JELLY

4. Press a leaf into the bottom of the clay tray. Use the ink roller to roll over the leaf and make an impression. Remove the leaf.

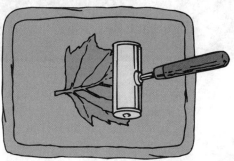

5. Pour plaster of Paris into the clay tray and let it set. When set, separate the clay and plaster.

Extension:

This may be done with bones, too! Those of a small fish work well.

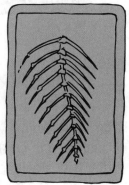

Name _____

Fossils

Besides bone fossils, scientists have found other kinds of fossils. Below are the pictures of some of these other kinds of fossils.

Directions: Draw a line from the description of the kind of fossil to its picture.

- A dinosaur makes footprints in the soft mud. The mud hardens and turns into rock.

- Sometimes the skin of a dinosaur is changed into a fossil.

- The eggs of some dinosaurs have been changed into fossil eggs.

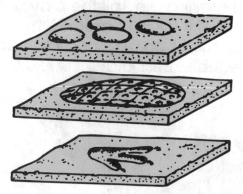

Directions: Carefully study these dinosaur footprints. Draw a line from the dinosaur to its footprints.

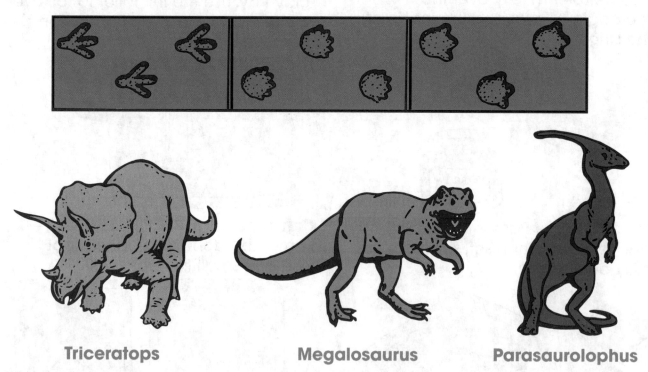

Triceratops   **Megalosaurus**   **Parasaurolophus**

Fantastic Fact
Fossil eggs of the **Protoceratops** (pro-toe-SAIR-uh-tops) have been found with the skeletons of tiny baby Protoceratops inside!

Petroglyphs

A petroglyph is a carving or line-drawing on rock.

You will need:
large pieces of cardboard
dirt
water
a bucket
soft stones
charcoal
a black pen
newspapers

Directions:

Select one of three mediums—stone, charcoal or mud—with which to create a message. If you select mud, you must use your hands to mix dirt with water in a bucket until it is the consistency of paint. You will also use your hands when you work with it on a piece of cardboard. Put newspaper over the surface on which you work.

You will make pictures that tell a story or that form a message on cardboard. No letters may be used. You should write your story or message on the back first using a pen. When you have finished your message, share it with someone else.

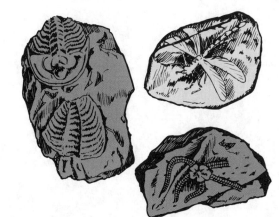

Fossil Find

Go on a walk in the neighborhood or in a park. Look for rocks with fossils in them. Take photographs and make rubbings of them, but do not remove them from the site.

.This page intentionally left blank.

Dinosaur Mobile

Directions:

1. Color the dinosaurs.

2. Cut out the dinosaurs and glue them on tagboard.

3. Match the dinosaurs with the descriptions below. Write the dinosaur's name on the back of its picture.

4. Assemble the dinosaurs with string and a hanger to make a mobile.

Triceratops: large dinosaur; three horns, one over each eye and one over its nose; large shield of bone protected its neck.

Parasaurolophus: large dinosaur; big crest curved backward from its head to beyond its shoulders.

Tyrannosaurus: giant meat-eater; large head; jaws filled with sharp teeth.

Brontosaurus: giant dinosaur; weighed almost 40 tons; massive body and tail; its front legs were shorter than its hind legs.

Ankylosaurus: body covered with armored plates; large bony club on the end of its tail.

This page intentionally left blank.

Section 2
Animals, Birds, Insects

Name _____

Living Things

Look at the many living things above. A scientist calls these, and any other living things, **organisms**. Many organisms are alike in some way. They can be put into groups according to the ways they are alike. Putting organisms into groups is called **classifying**.

Directions:

1. Sort the organisms pictured above into two groups. Color all of the organisms in one group. Leave the other group plain. How are all of the organisms in the colored group alike?

_____

How are all of the organisms in the uncolored group alike?

_____

2. Find the ten organisms hidden in the word search. Unscramble the group names and list the organisms under the correct group heading.

```
C A R R O T U B
O F A F E A D T
R O B I N S O J
N A B E D U G M
O F I H R O C O
H E T R E E L U
U R I G R A S S
I N S E C T H E
```

tlanp _____   limaan _____

1. _____   1. _____
2. _____   2. _____
3. _____   3. _____
4. _____   4. _____
5. _____   5. _____

Fantastic Fact

There are more than 700,000 kinds, or **species**, of insects in the world. This is more than all the other species of animals grouped together.

Scales, Feathers, Hair

Directions:

Before this activity, collect pictures of animals. Examine the exterior, or the outside, of your animals. Write down two or more observations regarding the outside of your animals (for example, the birds are colorful, the puppies are furry, the snakes don't look that slimy, etc.). Share your observations.

Directions:

Categorize your pictures into three groups by looking at what is on the exterior of your animals. How did you decide which animals would be grouped together? On paper, create three columns. Title one **"Fish,"** one **"Birds"** and one **"Mammals"** and glue pictures under the specific category listed.

Glue each animal under the proper category. When the supply of pictures has been exhausted, make generalizations about the coverings of animals (for example, if an animal has feathers, it is a bird). You **CAN** judge an animal by its cover!

Name _____

Backbone or No Backbone?

Which part of your body helps you stand tall or sit up straight? It is your backbone. You are a member of a large group of animals that all have backbones. Animals with backbones are called vertebrates. Birds, fish, reptiles, amphibians and mammals are all vertebrates.

Some animals do not have backbones. These animals are called invertebrates. Worms, centipedes and insects are all invertebrates.

Directions:

Find the names of five vertebrates and five invertebrates hidden in the word search. Then, write them in the correct group.

Invertebrates

1. _____
2. _____
3. _____
4. _____
5. _____

```
B R A B B I T B U D
E A G I R A F F E L
E W O F H E P R U W
T O G K L C M O T H
L R N F R Y S G I A
E M L I O N O J E L
R S P I D E R M R E
```

Vertebrates

1. _____
2. _____
3. _____
4. _____
5. _____

Your neighborhood has many animals in or near it. Add their names to the lists.

Invertebrates

6. _____
7. _____
8. _____
9. _____
10. _____

Vertebrates

6. _____
7. _____
8. _____
9. _____
10. _____

Investigate

There are many more invertebrates than vertebrates. Nine out of ten animals are invertebrates. Which group has the largest animals? Which group has the smallest animals?

Name _____

One Happy Community

Most animals are more comfortable living with certain other animals and plants. This special group is called a **community**.

There are many kinds of communities. Some animals live in a forest community or a pond community. Others live in a desert, seashore or grassland community.

Directions: Look at the communities below and list five animals in each.

Pond Community   **Forest Community**

_____   _____

_____   _____

_____   _____

_____   _____

_____   _____

1. Why do you think these animals live together in the pond community?

_____

2. Why do you think these animals live together in the forest community?

_____

3. Some animals may live in more than one kind of a community. Name some

   animals that live in both a pond and forest community. _____

_____

Investigate
Your backyard can be an animal community. Make a list of the animals that visit or live in your backyard. Don't forget those tiny ones you can't easily see.

Name _____

Self-Defense

Have you ever tried to see a fawn standing silently in a forest? You have to look very closely. Its coloring makes it hard to see. This is called camouflage.

Some animals use camouflage to protect themselves from their enemies. Other animals use their strength or speed for protection. How do the animals pictured below protect themselves?

Skunk

Armadillo

Walking Stick

Many animals have other ways of protecting themselves. Match each animal in the word search with the animal's means of protection.

Speed	Strength	Skin Covering
_____	_____	_____
_____	_____	_____
_____	_____	_____

```
A  P  O  R  C  U  P  I  N  E
R  C  T  R  B  D  Z  B  K  L
M  R  A  N  T  E  L  O  P  E
A  S  T  P  N  X  A  Z  O  P
D  E  E  R  L  F  O  R  P  H
I  L  R  N  D  Z  P  K  L  A
L  I  T  U  R  T  L  E  S  N
L  O  X  K  R  A  B  B  I  T
O  N  P  R  N  M  K  L  S  B
```

Fantastic Fact
Smoke Screen—The octopus and the squid have a special defense weapon. They squirt out a special inky chemical when threatened. This chemical acts like a smoke screen and also dulls the senses of their enemies.

Name _____

The Mighty Bear

Bears are large and powerful animals. Depending on the type of bear, they can weigh from 60 to 2,000 pounds.

Directions:

Listed below are four kinds of bears. The lengths of these bears are 3 feet, 5 feet, 8 feet and 9 feet. Use the clues to match each bear to its length. Write the answers in the blanks.

Clues:

Alaskan brown bear + American black bear = 14 feet

Polar bear + Alaskan brown bear = 17 feet

American black bear + sun bear = 8 feet

The Alaskan brown bear is ____ feet in length.

The American black bear is ____ feet in length.

The polar bear is ____ feet in length.

The sun bear is ____ feet in length.

The Life Cycle of a Frog

The frog goes through many changes during its life. Read about the frog's life cycle below. Then, complete the word puzzle using what you have learned.

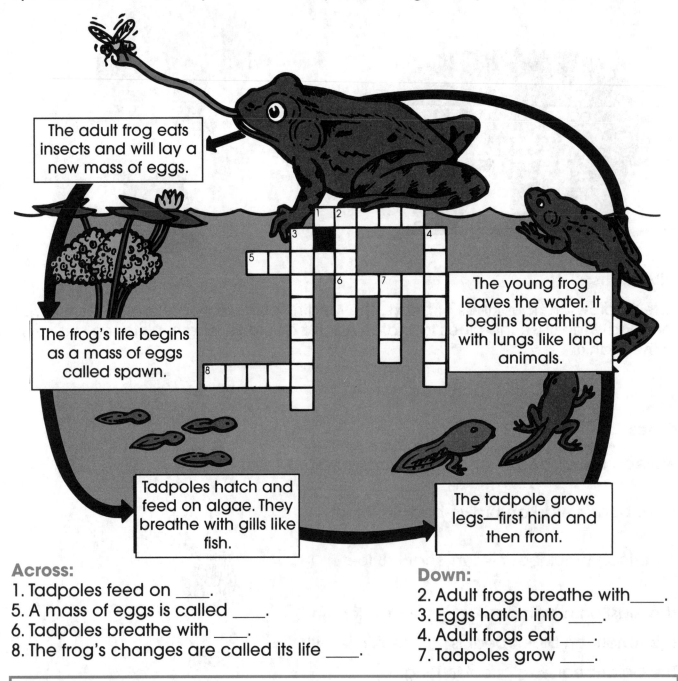

The adult frog eats insects and will lay a new mass of eggs.

The frog's life begins as a mass of eggs called spawn.

The young frog leaves the water. It begins breathing with lungs like land animals.

Tadpoles hatch and feed on algae. They breathe with gills like fish.

The tadpole grows legs—first hind and then front.

Across:
1. Tadpoles feed on ____.
5. A mass of eggs is called ____.
6. Tadpoles breathe with ____.
8. The frog's changes are called its life ____.

Down:
2. Adult frogs breathe with____.
3. Eggs hatch into ____.
4. Adult frogs eat ____.
7. Tadpoles grow ____.

Investigate
In many areas, ponds and streams freeze in the winter. What happens to the frogs that live in the pond?

Name _____

From Egg to Tadpole to Frog

The poem below tells about the changes that occur in a frog's life cycle. In every line, there is one word that doesn't make sense. Find the correct word in the Word Bank below and write it in the puzzle. **Hint:** The correct word rhymes with it.

The Life Cycle of a Frog

There is jelly on the legs (13)
    To protect the entire match. (11)
It takes tree to twenty-five days (7 down)
    Until they're ready to catch. (5)

Out comes a pollihog (18)
    When the time is just bright. (8)
It breathes using hills (14)
    And its size is very light. (4)

It loses its long scale (9)
    After pegs begin to grow. (1)
Digestion and breathing strange (12)
    In a process fast and glow. (2)

What helps a frog to seethe (3)
    Is its thin and moist chin. (6 down)
It also uses rungs (15)
    To let the hair in. (10)

Some frogs can skim like a duck. (6 across)
    And some can mop like a rabbit. (16)
Others climb bees like a squirrel (7 across)
    Which may seem a bunny habit. (17)

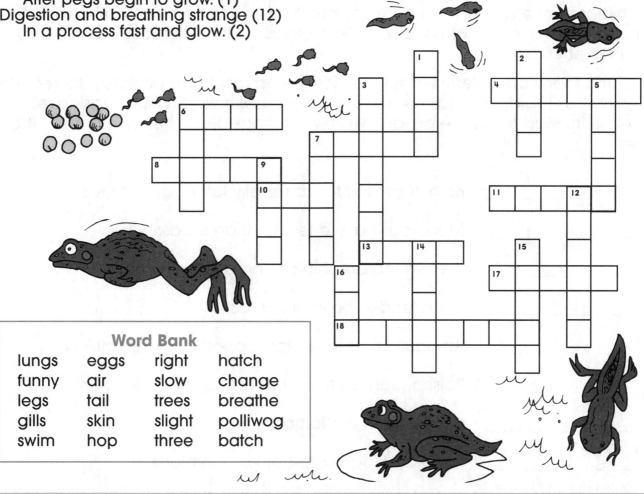

Word Bank

lungs	eggs	right	hatch
funny	air	slow	change
legs	tail	trees	breathe
gills	skin	slight	polliwog
swim	hop	three	batch

Name _____

Toadly Froggin' Around

Directions:

Read the information about frogs and toads.
Then, write **true** or **false** in front of each statement at the bottom.

Frogs and Toads

Both frogs and toads are amphibians. Amphibians spend part of their lives as water animals and part as land animals. In the early stages of their lives, amphibians breathe through gills, while as adults they develop lungs. Most amphibians lay eggs near water. Newly hatched frogs and toads both have tails that they later lose. Both often have poison glands in their skin to protect them from their enemies.

Frogs and toads are different in several ways. Most toads are broader, darker and flatter. Their skin is drier. Toads are usually covered with warts while frogs have smooth skin. Most toads live on land while most frogs prefer being in or near the water.

_____1. Both frogs and toads usually lay eggs near water.

_____2. Most frogs have drier skin than toads.

_____3. Very young amphibians breathe with lungs.

_____4. Frogs tend to be lighter in color.

_____5. An adult frog's tail helps support him while sitting.

_____6. Poison glands often protect frogs from an enemy.

_____7. A toad's skin is often bumpy.

_____8. Frogs and toads are both amphibians.

A Re-Appearing Act

The starfish is a very interesting sea animal. Most starfish have five "arms" on their bodies. When a starfish is in danger, it can drop off its arms to escape. It then grows new arms to replace the missing ones. Also, if a starfish is cut in two, each of the pieces can grow into a new starfish.

Directions:

Use the information above to solve these puzzles.

Puzzle #1 - This starfish originally had five arms. If two of these arms were broken off and grew back twice and the other three were dropped off and grew back five times each, how many arms did this starfish have during its lifetime? _____

Puzzle #2 - At first, this starfish had ten arms. It was then cut in half. Each of the halves grew new arms again so that they had the same number as the original starfish. Eventually, the same thing happened again to both new starfish. How many arms were involved in all? _____

Puzzle #3 - This starfish had 24 arms when it was born. If half of these arms broke off and grew back 4 times and one quarter of the original arms dropped off and grew back 3 times, how many arms did this starfish have during its lifetime? _____

Name _____

A Shark's Fringe Benefit

The largest carnivorous (flesh-eating) fish that can be dangerous to man is the great white **shark**. Although it doesn't have a very large brain, it has excellent senses.

Great white sharks have several rows of jagged-edged teeth. New teeth from the back move forward to replace worn or broken teeth.

Imagine this. A shark had three rows containing two dozen teeth each on the bottom jaw and the top jaw.

First, the shark broke off 8 top teeth and wore down 10 bottom teeth, and these were replaced by new teeth.

Next, it wore down 6 top teeth and 4 bottom teeth and these were replaced by new teeth.

Finally, the shark broke off 9 top teeth and 9 bottom teeth and these were replaced.

How many total teeth did the shark have in its mouth at one time or another?

_____

Pretend the "Tooth Fairy" put 25¢ under the shark's pillow for each tooth that was broken off. How much money would she leave?

$ _____

Name _____

A Sampling of Snakes

The Snake House is a very popular place to visit at the zoo. There are many different types and sizes of snakes. Some snakes are poisonous while others are not. Some snakes are harmless to most creatures, and some are very dangerous.

Directions:

The five snakes described here are held in the cages below. Decide which snake belongs in each cage by using the clues given here and beneath the boxes. Then, write each name in the correct cage.

The King Cobra is the longest poisonous snake in the world. One measured almost 19 feet long. It lives in southeast Asia, Indonesia and the Philippines.

The Gaboon Viper, a very poisonous snake, has the longest fangs of all snakes (nearly 2 inches). It lives in tropical Africa.

The Reticulated Python is the longest snake of all. One specimen measured 32 feet, $9\frac{1}{2}$ inches. It crushes its prey to death. It lives in southeast Asia, Indonesia and the Philippines.

The Black Mamba, the fastest-moving land snake, can move at speeds of 10-12 miles per hour. It lives in the eastern part of tropical Africa.

The Anaconda is almost twice as heavy as a reticulated python of the same length. One anaconda that was almost 28 feet long weighed nearly 500 pounds. It lives in tropical South America.

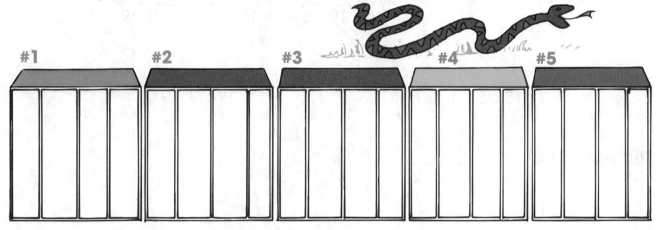

#1   #2   #3   #4   #5

Clues:

• The snake in cage #5 moves the fastest on land.
• The longest snake of all is between the snake that comes from tropical Africa and the longest poisonous snake.
• The very heavy snake is to the left of the longest poisonous snake.

33

Secret Code for Worm Lovers

Directions:

To decode the secret words, use the code below.

A	B	C	D	E	F	G	H	I	J	K	L	M
1	2	3	4	5	6	7	8	9	10	11	12	13

N	O	P	Q	R	S	T	U	V	W	X	Y	Z
14	15	16	17	18	19	20	21	22	23	24	25	26

1. Earthworms can also be called __ __ __ __ __   __ __ __ __ __ __ __ __.
   14 9 7 8 20   3 18 1 23 12 5 18 19

2. Earthworms have no __ __ __ __ or __ __ __ __.
   5 1 18 19   5 25 5 19

3. Sections of an earthworm are called __ __ __ __ __ __ __ __.
   19 5 7 13 5 14 20 19

4. Earthworms __ __ __ __ __ __ __ through their __ __ __ __.
   2 18 5 1 20 8 5   19 11 9 14

5. Earthworms eat __ __ __ __.
   19 15 9 12

6. As they __ __ __ __ __ __ through the soil, they give plants the __ __ __
   2 21 18 18 15 23   1 9 18
   that they need.

Name _____

Hibernation

Have you ever wondered why some animals hibernate? Some animals sleep all winter. This sleep is called hibernation.

Animals get their warmth and energy from food. Some animals cannot find enough food in the winter. They must eat large amounts of food in the autumn. Their bodies store this food as fat. Then, in winter, they hibernate. Their bodies live on the stored fat. Since their bodies need much less food during hibernation, they can stay alive without eating anymore food during the winter.

Some animals that hibernate are bats, chipmunks, bears, snakes and turtles.

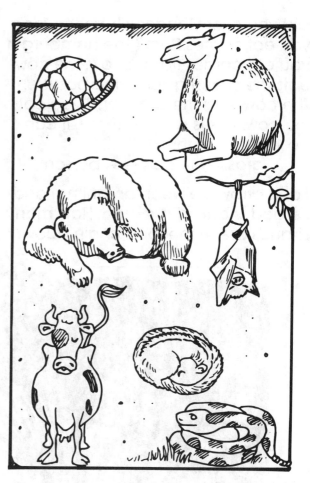

Directions:

Match:

Animals that hibernate . . .

    eat and store food   in the winter.

    go to sleep   in the autumn.

Underline:

Hibernation . . .   is a sleep that some animals go into for the winter.

                  is the time of year to gather food for the winter.

Circle Yes or No:

Animals get their warmth and energy from food.	Yes	No
Some animals cannot find enough food in the winter.	Yes	No
Animals hibernate because they are lazy.	Yes	No
Animals need less food while they are hibernating.	Yes	No

Color the animals that hibernate.

Food Chains

Did you ever wonder where the food you eat comes from? The hamburger you eat comes from a cow. The cow eats the green grass in the pasture. The cow eats the grass and you eat the cow. This is a food chain. It can be written like this:

grass ⟶ cow ⟶ person

Each arrow between an animal and its food is called a strand. How many strands are in the food chain above?

_____

Directions: Look carefully at the picture above. Write four food chains that you found in the picture. Use arrows to show the strands.

_____

_____

Fantastic Fact
All animals need food and water. But the desert jack rabbit doesn't drink water. It gets all the water it needs from eating the giant saguaro cactus. The saguaro is almost 90 percent water!

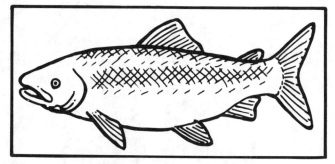

Food Chain Mobile

There are many kinds of animals on this page. Arrange them in the order of a food chain. You may be able to make two food chain mobiles.

Directions:

1. Color the pictures.
2. Cut out the pictures and glue them to tagboard.
3. Assemble them with string and a hanger in the order of the food chain.

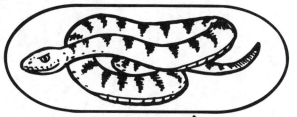

This page intentionally left blank.

Food Chains in the Sea

All living things in the seas also depend on each other for food. The food chain begins with sea plants called phytoplankton. A huge variety of tiny animals called zooplankton feed on the phytoplankton. These animals include shrimp, copepods and jellyfish. Some of the most common fish—herring, anchovies and sprats—feed on zooplankton. These fish are eaten by others, such as tuna and mackerel, which in turn are eaten by the superpredators, such as sharks and dolphins. This pattern of eating is called a food chain.

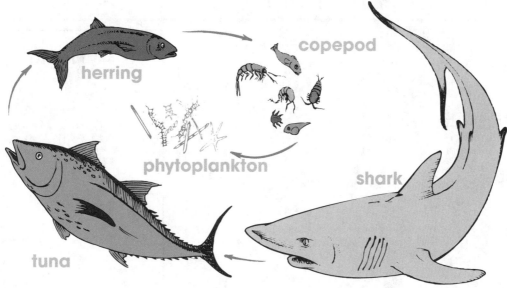

herring

copepod

phytoplankton

shark

tuna

Directions:

Use the diagram to answer the following questions on another piece of paper.

1. Describe the food chain above.

2. If there was a decrease in the copepod population, what would happen to the herring population? Why?

3. What would happen to the phytoplankton population? Why?

4. If the tuna population became endangered, what would the result be?

5. What does it mean to say, "The death of one species in the food chain upsets the rest of the chain?"

6. An example of a land food chain might be fly-spider-bird-cat. Give another example of a land food chain.

7. Draw another sea food chain. Explain and give an example for each step.

Name

Adopt an Animal

The seas of the world are filled with an amazing variety of life. Starfish, crabs, flying fish, angelfish, worms, turtles, sharks and whales all make their home underwater. The shape, color and size of most sea animals depend on their lifestyle and where they live in the seas. Select a sea animal and become an expert on it. Research your animal and complete the profile below.

Common Name _____

Scientific Name _____

Description:

weight:

length:

body shape:

tail shape:

color:

unusual characteristics:

Picture

Behaviors:

Description of Habitat _____

_____

Food and Feeding Habits _____

_____

_____

Migration (if applicable) _____

_____

_____

Animal Comparisons

Directions: Use the Venn diagram below to compare these animals of the seas. Fill in the circle below the dolphin with characteristics common only to the dolphin. Fill in the circle below the shark with characteristics common only to the shark. Where the circles overlap, fill in characteristics both animals share. Write a story about your findings on another piece of paper.

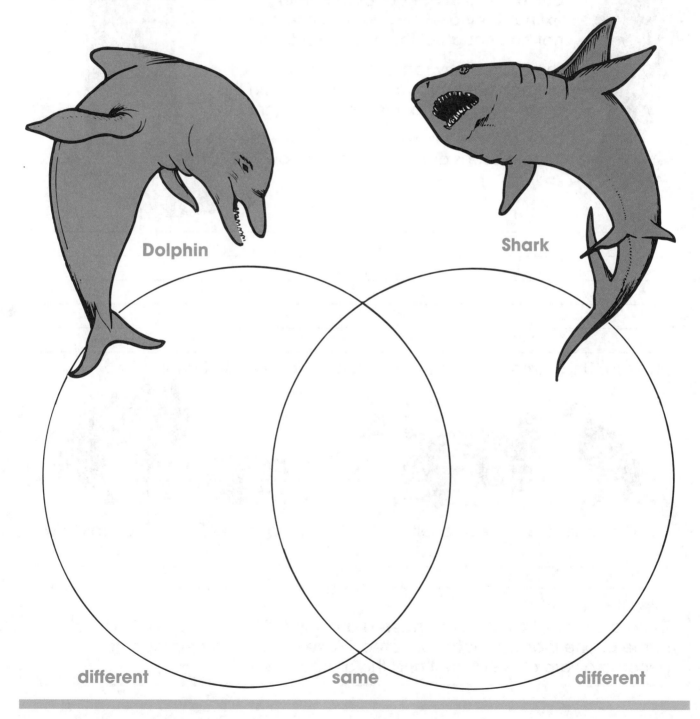

Dolphin

Shark

different   same   different

Name _____

Endangered Animals

You will never see a dodo bird or a saber-tooth tiger. These animals are gone forever. They are **extinct**.

The animals on this page are not extinct, but they are in danger of becoming extinct. They are **endangered**. There may not be enough of them to reproduce.

There are many reasons why some animals are endangered. The signs on this page give clues to three main reasons.

Look at the signs. What do you think the three reasons are? Write them below.

1. _____

_____

2. _____

_____

3. _____

_____

Directions: Unscramble the names of these endangered animals.

dalb gleae   nereg teltur   lueb laweh   bremit lofw

_____ _____ _____ _____

Investigate
There are more than 100 endangered animals in North America. Find the name of one that lives near your area. Make a poster to help people become aware of this animal and the danger it is in.

Name _____

Endangered Animal Acrostic

Directions: Using the animal names in the Word Bank and the clues below, fill in the blanks in the spaces provided. The circled letters are used as clues for your answers.

WORD BANK	blue whale	jaguar	pronghorn
	cheetah	okapi	polar bear
	vicuna	yak	giant panda

1. _ Ⓞ _ _ _   _ _ _ _ _

2. _ Ⓡ _ _ _ _ _ _ _

3. _ _ Ⓐ _ _

4. _ _ _ Ⓝ _ _ _ _ _ _

5. _ _ Ⓖ _ _ _

6. _ _ _ Ⓤ _ _ _ _ _

7. _ _ _ _ Ⓣ _ _

8. _ Ⓐ _

9. _ _ _ _ Ⓝ _

Clues:

1. large animal with white coat

2. upright horns and sheeplike feet

3. only living relative of the giraffe

4. lives in bamboo forests in southwestern China

5. largest wild cat in the Western Hemisphere

6. largest animal on Earth

7. cat that can run over 60 miles per hour

8. species of wild cattle in Tibet

9. member of the camel family in South America

Name _____

Endangered Animals

Many of the earth's animals are endangered or extinct. Use the names of the animals to build a puzzle. Only use the **bold-faced** words.

Word Bank

brown **hyena**	Darwin's **rhea**	red **wolf**	black-footed **ferret**
Spanish **lynx**	Philippine **eagle**	**gavial**	ring-tailed **lemur**
giant **panda**	blue **whale**	**numbat**	resplendent **quetzal**
Arabian **oryx**	Grevy's **zebra**	**dugong**	Galapagos **penguin**
Indian **python**	wild **yak**	**kakapo**	

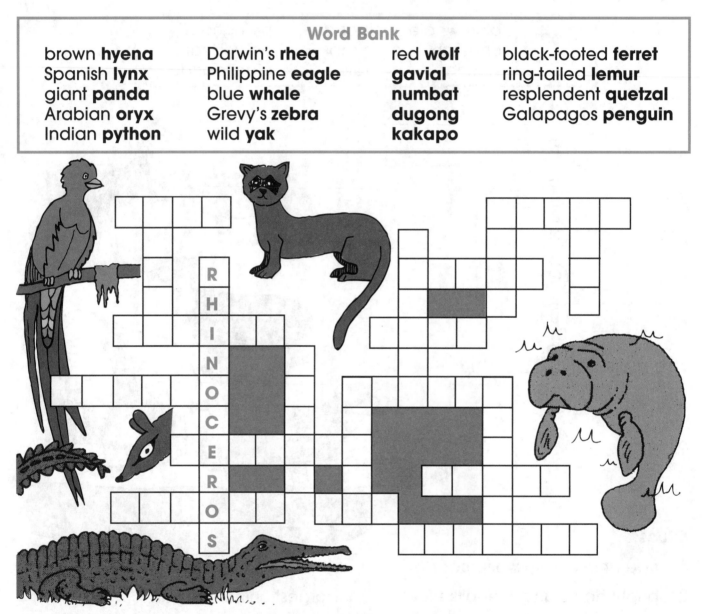

Directions: Use an encyclopedia to answer each question.

1. Which animal above is related to the manatee? _____

2. Which is the largest animal on earth? _____

3. Which is related to the ostrich? _____

Name _____

Animal Magic Challenge

Directions: Read **Column A**. Choose an answer from **Column B** that matches. Write the number of the answer in the Magic Square. The first one has been done for you. You may need to research some of these animals on your own!

Column A	Column B
A. grizzly bear	1. large bear of the American grasslands
B. koala	2. lives on dry grasslands of South Africa
C. peregrine falcon	3. the most valuable reptile in the world
D. California condor	4. largest soaring bird of North America
E. black-footed ferret	5. the tallest American bird
F. cheetah	6. the fastest animal on land
G. orangutan	7. the only great ape outside Africa
H. giant panda	8. large aquatic seal-like animal
I. Florida manatee	9. large black and white mammal of China
J. kit fox	10. small, fast mammal; nocturnal predator
K. blue whale	11. largest animal in the world
L. whooping crane	12. member of the weasel family
M. red wolf	13. has interbred with coyotes in some areas
N. green sea turtle	14. also called a duck hawk; size of a crow
O. brown hyena	15. eats leaves of the eucalyptus tree
P. jaguar	16. known as *el tigre* in Spanish

A 1	B ___	C ___	D ___
E ___	F ___	G ___	H ___
I ___	J ___	K ___	L ___
M ___	N ___	O ___	P ___

Add the numbers across, down and diagonally. What answer do you get? _____
Why do you think this is called a magic square?

Bald Eagle Puzzler

Directions: Research the bald eagle. Read each statement about the **bald eagle**. If the statement is false, darken the letter in the circle to the left of that statement. The letters not darkened spell out the name of the chemical that affected the bald eagle's food supply.

(P) Because of federal protection, the bald eagle population is increasing.

(R) It is legal to shoot this bird today.

(E) This bird has keen eyesight and strong wings.

(N) The wingspan of this bird is about 3 feet.

(A) The nest of a bald eagle is made of mud and rocks.

(S) This bird eats mainly fish.

(T) This bird likes to eat only berries and seeds.

(T) The bald eagle is found only in North America.

(B) Only four bald eagles exist today in the United States.

(M) An injured bald eagle may be kept as a pet.

(I) Chemical poisons in the bald eagle's food caused its eggs to crack before incubation could be completed.

(C) The nest of a bald eagle is built high on a cliff or in a tree.

(I) This bird is the national symbol of the United States.

(L) The bald eagle is noted for its bright orange head.

(D) The bald eagle has a hooked beak.

(E) The nest of a bald eagle is called an aerie.

What is the type of chemical? ___ ___ ___ ___ ___ ___ ___ ___

Bird Watching Is Fun!

Bird-watching can be an interesting hobby. Read some books about birds or bird-watching before you actually try bird-watching (*The Bird Book* by Neil and Karen Dawes is a good one). Study the markings and habits of specific birds.

You will probably be able to observe many kinds of birds in your yard. You may want to create several simple feeders to attract some feathery friends (see page 51).

Take a pencil and notepad to jot down the names or descriptions of birds you observe. Binoculars will also be very helpful if you have them.

Birds are very alert and often move before you have time to get a good, long look at them. Try to remember key features to look for when trying to identify a new bird. A copy (or several copies) of the Bird Identification Chart on page 49 would be helpful to take with you as well.

Bird Watching Is Fun!

Size—Compare the bird's size with another familiar object or animal.

Shape—Is the bird's tail long or short? What is the shape of its bill? Is it fat or thin? Is its head smooth or crested?

Color—Look at the bird's feathers, feet, eyes and bill.

Habits—Does the bird walk or fly? Is it in the trees or on the ground?

Flight—Watch the path in which the bird flies. Is it a wavy path or does it fly in a straight line?

Voice—Each species of birds has a unique song. Try to remember the songs of the different birds.

Bird Identification Chart

Sketch of bird/name of bird.	Size: compared to a familiar object.	Shape: tail, bill, body (fat or thin), head (smooth or crested).	Color: feathers, bill, eyes, feet.	Habits: walks, hops, in trees, on ground.	Flight path: wavy or straight.	Voice

This page intentionally left blank.

Feathered Friend Feeders

You will need: grapefruit halves, cereal, peanuts, birdseed, string or yarn, stale bread, peanut butter, plastic knives, cookie cutter shapes

Directions:

1. Grazing Grapefruits

Start with half of an empty grapefruit skin. (Clean this beforehand and share the fruit if you like.) Poke three holes in the skin and thread three pieces of string through the holes. Tie them together so the grapefruit will be balanced when it hangs. Fill the grapefruit skin with nuts, cereal or birdseed. Hang the bird feeders on a tree branch.

2. Cookie Cutter Café

Cut a shape out of a slice of stale bread using a cookie cutter. Then, spread one side of the bread with peanut butter and sprinkle nuts or seeds onto the peanut butter until the bread is well coated. Next, carefully poke a small hole through the center of the bread and thread a piece of yarn through it. Hang the bird feeder in a tree to create a yummy café for your feathered friends.

Note: Birds may become dependent on the feeder for their food supply. You should continue feeding the birds during the winter months when food may be scarce.

House for Rent

Here is another simple way to attract birds to your yard for observation. You will need a ½ gallon cardboard milk carton, scissors, bendable wire, wire cutters, ruler, nails, waterproof tape, dried grass, paper

Directions:

1. Rinse the carton well and completely open the top so that it is square.

2. Cut about a 1½" round hole on one side a couple inches below the top fold.

3. On the side opposite the hole, make two holes side-by-side using a nail. The holes should be about the same level as the other hole.

4. Cut a piece of wire about a foot long. Put it in through one of the holes, then out the other.

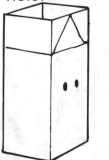

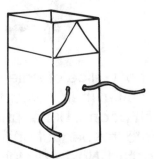

5. Put some dried grass in the carton.
6. Close the carton. Tape it shut.

7. Take it outside. Twist the wire ends to form a loop around a limb. Attach so the back of the house rests against the trunk for stability.

Circling Whirly Birds

Bring the beauty of the birds indoors by creating these "whirly bird" mobiles.

You will need:
construction paper
scissors
markers
glue
drinking straws
yarn

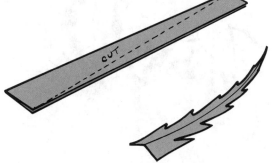

3. Cut angles in the last two strips to form the wings. Use markers to add details to the birds.

5. Tie a piece of yarn through each bird head loop. Thread one piece of yarn through the straw. Then, tie it to the other piece. Suspend the mobile from the ceiling by tying one more piece of string in the center of the straw. Open a window and let a gentle breeze whirl these birds to life!

1. Cut eight strips of construction paper (about ½" wide by about 8" long) to create two birds. Bring the ends of four of the strips together and glue them to create four loops.

2. Fold the fifth and sixth strips in half lengthwise and cut from the bottom corner of one side to the top corner of the opposite side. This triangle shape will be the tail. Make cuts in them to give the "tail" a feathery look.

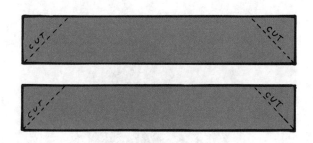

4. To assemble each bird, glue the wings to the top of one of the loops. Then, glue the wide end of the tail on top of the wings. Finally, glue the last loop to the body. Draw a beak and an eye.

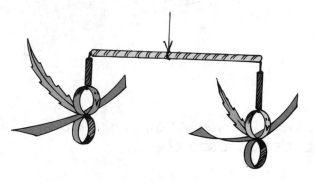

Bird Card

Use the Bird Card Pattern on the next page to complete this project. First, select a bird to research. Use non-fiction books to discover what the bird looks like, where it lives (its habitat), what it eats and an interesting fact about it. Record this information on the Bird Card Pattern. Glue the page to the right side of a large piece of construction paper.

Using the information you gathered about your bird, sketch the bird on a piece of drawing paper. Remember to include important identification markings and color. Glue your drawing to the left side of the construction paper.

Extension: Do another Bird Card. Compare the characteristics of the birds you researched!

Name _____

Bird Card Pattern

_____

name of bird

Characteristics: _____
_____
_____
_____
_____
_____
_____
_____
_____

Habitat: _____
_____
_____
_____
_____
_____

Food: _____
_____
_____
_____
_____

Bird Bills

Different kinds of birds like different kinds of foods. A bird's beak sometimes gives a hint about what it likes to eat. You will be able to find out for yourself how useful different "beaks" are for different "foods."

You will need:
sunflower seeds
tweezers
salad tongs
birdseed
pliers
fish-tank net
gummy fish
eyedropper
string
small paper cups
food coloring
small square of indoor/outdoor carpet
shallow pan of water

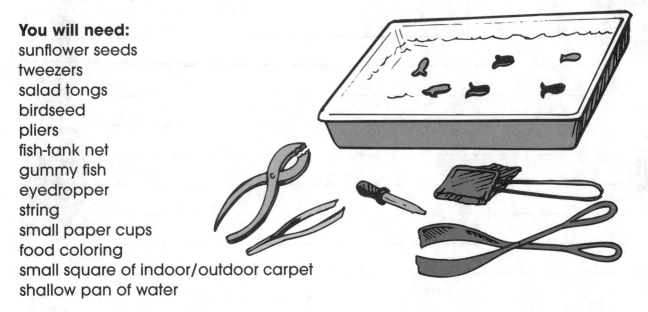

Directions:

1. Float several gummy fish in a shallow pan of water.

2. Place some water in a small paper cup. Add a drop of food coloring to it. This represents nectar or sap from plants.

3. Sprinkle some birdseed onto a table.

4. Lay a piece of string on a small square of indoor/outdoor carpet to represent worms.

5. Line the bottom of a small paper cup with shelled sunflower seeds to represent insects in trees.

6. Imagine that the tools are the beaks of different birds. Experiment with the various tools to determine which tool is best for gathering each kind of "food."

Bird Bills

You have already begun to research different species of birds. Describe the beaks of some birds and their diets. Here are some examples:

Seed-eating: short thick bill for crunching seeds—grosbeak, finch	**Insect-eating:** slender, pointed beak for picking up insects—warbler, swallow	**Probing:** long slender bill for probing for food in mud or flowers—hummingbird, flamingo
Preying: strong, sharp hooked beak for tearing flesh of prey—owl, hawk	**Straining:** broad, flat bill for straining food from mud—duck, goose	**Fish-eating:** long, sharp bill for spearing or with a pouch—heron, pelican

Investigate: Various species of birds have also developed adaptations of their feet, wings and tails. Read and research these other wonderful examples of nature's amazing ingenuity in solving the problems of survival.

Name _____

Going Places

Looking at a bird's feet can tell you a lot about how they are used. Look at the birds' feet below. Unscramble each bird's name. Write the bird's name by the sentence that best describes it.

kawh

noreh

ckud
_____

reckwoodep
_____

_____ "My webbed feet are great for swimming."

_____ "My feet are great for walking up trees."

_____ "I use my feet with long toes to wade in the water and mud."

_____ "I use my strong, powerful feet to catch small animals."

Can the shape of a bird's bill tell you anything about what it eats? Look closely at the bills below. Unscramble each bird's name. Write the bird's name by the sentence that best describes it.

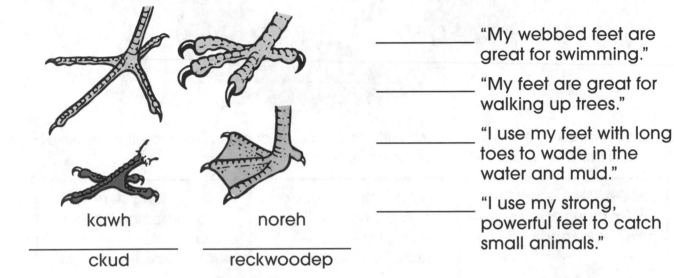

noreh
_____

reckwoodep

bumminghird
_____

kawh

panicel
_____

dinalcar

_____ "I pound holes in wood to find insects."

_____ "I use my long bill to get nectar from flowers."

_____ "I use my strong bill to crack open seeds."

_____ "I use my sharp bill to tear the flesh of animals."

_____ "I stab at small fish with my sharp bill."

_____ "I scoop up large mouthfuls of water and fish."

State Birds of North America

Each of the 50 states has a state bird. Take a closer look at one of these birds to learn about its living habits.

✂

State	Picture of Bird	Description: color, size, etc.	Interesting Fact
Habitat: temperature, geography, etc.	Nests	Eggs: size, number, etc.	Food

Fill in the information in the appropriate categories on the chart. Sketch and color a picture of the bird. Be sure to have a map of North America handy for quick geographical references.

This page intentionally left blank.

Feathered Friend

Make your own feathered friend. Color, cut out and glue this bird together on another sheet of paper. Write a short paragraph that tells where your new bird lives, what it eats and what its living habits are.

legs

tails

wings

bills

This page intentionally left blank.

Name _____

Insects in Winter

In the summertime, insects can be seen buzzing and fluttering around us. But as winter's cold weather begins, suddenly the insects seem to disappear. Do you know where they go?

Many insects, such as flies and mosquitoes, find a warm place to spend the winter. They live in cellars, barns, attics, caves and tree holes.

Beetles and ants try to dig deep into the ground. Some beetles stack up in piles under rocks or dead leaves.

In the fall, female grasshoppers and crickets lay their eggs and die. The eggs hatch in the spring.

Bees also try to protect themselves from the winter cold. Honeybees gather in a ball in the middle of their hive. The bees stay in this tight ball trying to stay warm.

Winter is very hard for insects, but each spring the survivors come out and the buzzing and fluttering begins again.

Directions: Circle Yes or No.

In the winter, insects look for a warm place to live.	Yes	No
Noise, such as buzzing, can be heard all winter long.	Yes	No
Some beetles and ants dig deep into the ground.	Yes	No
Every insect finds a warm home for the winter.	Yes	No
Crickets and grasshoppers lay their eggs and die.	Yes	No
The honeybees gather in a ball in their hive.	Yes	No
Survivors of the cold weather come out each spring.	Yes	No

Name _____

Six-Legged Friends

The largest group of animals belongs to the group called invertebrates—or animals without backbones. This large group is the **insect** group.

Insects are easy to tell apart from other animals. Adult insects have three body parts and six legs. The first body part is the **head**. On the head are the mouth, eyes and antennae. The second body part is the **thorax**. On it are the legs and wings. The third part is the **abdomen**. On it are small openings for breathing.

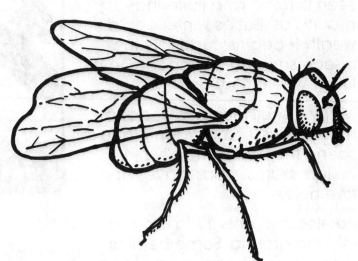

Directions: Color the body parts of the insect above: head-red, thorax-yellow, abdomen-blue.

Draw an insect below. Make your insect one-of-a-kind. Be sure it has the correct number of body parts, legs, wings and antennae. Fill in the information.

Insect's name_____   Warning _____

Length _____   _____

Where found _____   _____

Food _____   _____

Investigate
Many people think that spiders are insects. Spiders and insects are alike in many ways, but spiders are not insects. Find out how the two are different.

A Model of Metamorphosis—
The Monarch Butterfly

Insects pass through many changes in their life cycle. This is called metamorphosis. Watching a caterpillar experience metamorphosis as it changes into an adult butterfly is exciting. "The Butterfly Garden" is a live butterfly-raising kit which gives you the opportunity to watch metamorphosis firsthand. These kits are available from Insect Lore, P.O. Box 1535, Shafter, CA 93263.

If you work with the kit, keep an observation diary. Entries should be kept daily noting changes that occur as the larva changes into the chrysalis and then into the adult butterfly.

Record the color, shape, size, texture and anything else you notice in each stage. Write down any questions you have about the process. Notice the symmetry of the wing design on the emergent adult butterfly. Notice the slender body, jointed legs and two antennae on its head.

Research any answers you have not been able to answer from the Research Form. Use this page to write a report about metamorphosis. Make sure to use complete sentences and paragraph form and to illustrate your report.

Research Form

1. What kind of animal is a butterfly? _____

2. Describe the larva. _____

   _____

   _____

3. How was the chrysalis formed?_____

   _____

   _____

4. How long did it take for the butterfly to emerge? _____

   _____

5. What did the butterfly look like? _____

   _____

   _____

6. Did the butterfly make any sounds? _____

7. What do a butterfly's wings look like when it lands? _____

   _____

   _____

8. How is a moth different from a butterfly? _____

   _____

   _____

9. How is a moth the same as a butterfly? _____

   _____

   _____

10. What other animals change in appearance as they grow into the adult stage? _____

    _____

Let's Make a Butterfly!

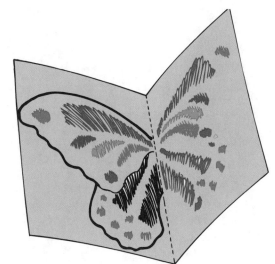

You will need:

construction paper
glue
watercolor paints
1 pipe cleaner
pattern on this page

Directions:

Fold the piece of construction paper in half so that it measures 9" x 6". With the straight end on the fold, trace around the butterfly pattern and cut it out. Use the paint to paint the design and coloration on the wing pattern only. Then, fold the construction paper over onto the painted pattern while the paint is still wet so that the other wing is also painted. Glue a pipe cleaner to the head for the antennae. You can also design your own flowers to make a more colorful welcome for your monarch butterfly!

This page intentionally left blank.

Name _____

Butterflies and Moths

People sometimes confuse butterflies with moths, but there are some important differences.

Butterflies . . .

- fly by day.
- have antennae with "knobs."
- have thin, hairless bodies.
- rest with their wings held upright.

Moths . . .

- fly at night.
- have antennae without "knobs."
- have plump, furry bodies.
- rest with their wings spread out flat.

Suppose you decided to start a butterfly and/or moth collection. Each mounting page would be divided into 16 sections. Large butterflies or moths would require two sections for mounting. Small butterflies or moths would require only one.

If you had three large butterflies for this page and the rest were small, how many small butterflies could you mount?_____

Draw and color these butterflies on the page.

If you had four large moths and you didn't want them to be next to each other, how would you mount them with smaller moths so that all of the sections would be used?

Draw and color them on this page.

Ant Antics

Read *Ant Cities* by Arthur Dorros. On a piece of paper, write some fantastic facts about ants described in the book.

You will need:

large glass jar
dark construction paper
cotton
cheesecloth
tape

Now you are ready to observe ants firsthand. To begin, fill a large glass jar about half-full with dirt. Tape dark construction paper around the jar. (This will encourage the ants to go underground.) Then, take a nature walk to find an ant hill. Take time to observe the ants coming and going to the hill with food.

Carefully dig up the ant hill, including the surrounding dirt, and place it all in the jar. Place a wet cotton ball on the dirt and keep it damp to provide moisture for the ants. The ants may also be fed by adding crumbs of cookies or bread to the jar twice weekly. Finally, poke tiny holes in the lid. Put cheese-cloth over the top of the jar to keep the ants from escaping and secure the lid.

To observe the ants, remove the dark paper. You will be able to see tunnels that are close to the sides of the jar. Enjoy watching your own ant city, but be sure to keep it only for about a month. Then, return your friends to their natural environment.

Ants in Your Pants!

Ants are busy insects, always moving, always working hard. They live together in colonies, and every ant has a job to do to help the others. When someone cannot sit still and is wiggly and eager to get going, people sometimes ask, "Are there ants in your pants?"

You will need:

ink pad
construction paper
pen
crayons

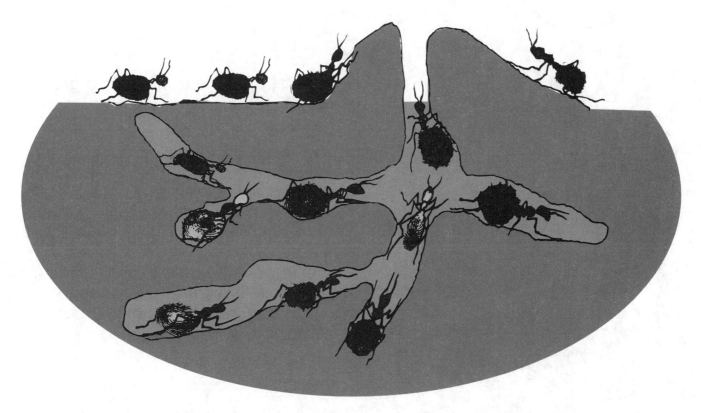

Directions: Create a drawing of an ant city. Begin by drawing a series of underground tunnels on a piece of construction paper. To create ants in their tunnels, press your fingertips onto an ink pad and then press your inky prints onto the paper. When the ink dries, you can use a pen to draw legs and antennae on the ants.

As an added touch, create a story about your busy ant community.

Getting the Message Across—Bee Style

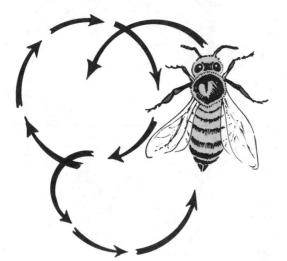

Bees in a hive have many jobs to do. The work is divided into several kinds, and bees specialize by doing one particular job. One of the most important jobs is finding food. When one of the bees finds food, it communicates the location to other bees by using special body movement.

Directions:

Play this bee dance game with a group of friends.

Provide the group with an object to represent a food source. Instruct one member of the group to hide the food. Then, using only body language, the "hider" must communicate to the other group members where the "food" is located. They then try to find the food source. Repeat the activity until all the "food finders" have had a chance to hide and communicate the information to the group.

Extension: Have the group try to develop some standard body movements which would indicate something to the group (i.e., one foot in front of the other—indicates straight path; tip one's head—indicates a direction, etc.).

The Hive Is the Place to Be!

A beehive is divided into efficient hexagonal (six-sided) storage shapes called cells. These cells are massed together to form a honeycomb. This activity will help you explore the reasons bees use hexagon cells.

Directions:

Trace a circular shape onto a piece of paper. Mark the circle with an **X**. This is now the center circle. Predict how many circles of the same size will fit around the center circle. Then, draw the circles to test your prediction.

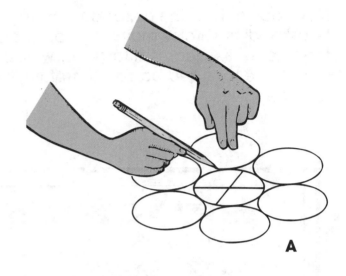

A

Would the number of circles you could make change if all of the circles were larger or smaller?

Continue to make circles as instructed above. Then, put a dot in the center of the triangle-shaped spaces (see diagram **B**) that are formed between the circles. Connect these dots with lines, and you have created the hexagonal clusters of a real honeycomb!

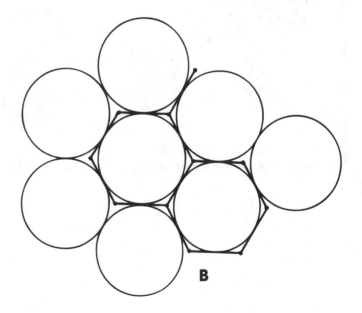

B

The Hive Is the Place to Be!

Now, look at how the hexagonal shapes of the cells relate to the shapes of the bees' bodies. Circles may be good shapes for bees' bodies, but they do not fit together well. Squares fit together well, but the space would be wasted since bees have rounded bodies. Therefore, the hexagon is the perfect shape for a beehive.

Extension: Create a honeycomb of bee facts for an attractive display board. On hexagon shapes, record new and interesting facts about bees. Post these on the display board with the title "Honeycomb of Bee Facts."

Name _____

Guess What?

Directions: Use the following hints and the Word Bank to decide what insect each riddle describes.

1. I have stout, spiny forelegs.
   I eat insects, including some of my own kind.
   I camouflage well in my surroundings.
   My forelegs make me appear to be praying.

   What am I?_____

2. I have clear wings.
   My body is quite round.
   The males of my species make long, shrill sounds in summer.
   Some of us take 17 years to develop.

   What am I?_____

3. I have two pair of long, thin wings.
   I eat mosquitoes and other small insects.
   I live near lakes, ponds, streams and rivers.
   My abdomen is very long . . . as long as a darning needle.

   What am I?_____

4. I am a type of beetle.
   My young are often called glowworms.
   My abdomen produces light.

   What am I?_____

5. I like warm, damp and dark places and come out at night.
   Humans hate me.
   I am a destructive household pest.
   I am closely related to grasshoppers and crickets.

   What am I?_____

Word Bank			
lightning bug			termite
mosquito	cicada	dragonfly	praying mantis
bumblebee	ladybug	cockroach	aphid

Challenge: Research an insect. Draw a detailed picture and write a report about it.

Section 3
Human Body

Name _____

Body Building Blocks

Just like some houses are built with bricks, your body is built with cells. Every part of your body is made of cells.

Cells differ in size and shape, but they all have a few things in common. All cells have a nucleus. The nucleus is the center of the cell. It controls the cell's activities.

Cells can divide and become two cells exactly like the original cell.

Your body has many kinds of cells. Each kind has a special job. Muscle cells help you move. Nerve cells carry messages between your brain and other parts of your body. Blood cells carry oxygen to other cells in your body.

muscle cell

Directions:

Complete each sentence using the words in bold from above.

The __ __ __ __ __ __ controls the cell's activities.
   3

Cells differ in __ __ __ __ and __ __ __ __ __.
                 2   1

One cell can __ __ __ __ __ __ into two cells.
                        6

__ __ __ __ __ __ cells help you move.
        5

Blood cells carry __ __ __ __ __ __ to other cells in your body.
                          4

Unscramble the numbered letters above to discover this amazing fact.

You began life as a __ __ __ __ __ __ cell!
                     1 2 3 4 5 6

nucleus

nerve cell

blood cells

Fantastic Fact
People and most animals are made of billions or even trillions of cells. But some animals are made of only one cell. To find out more about these animals, look up protozoans in your library.

Name _____

"Oh my, how you have grown!"

"My swimsuit doesn't fit. It fit me fine last summer." Surprise! You're growing! What makes your body grow? Your body is made up of about 50 trillion cells. One of the most important jobs of a cell is to make you grow. One cell divides and forms two cells. Two cells divide and form four cells and so on.

Not all of your cells keep dividing. Some cells die. But don't worry. Other cells are dividing and replacing those that died. There are even a few left over to help you grow.

Amanda kept a record of her growth. You can take your own measurements, too. Then, fill in the chart and compare your growth with Amanda's growth. You may need a friend to help you.

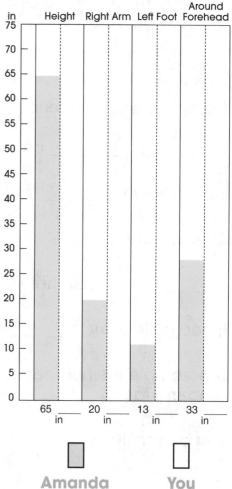

1. Who is taller, Amanda or you?_____

   By how many inches?_____

2. Measure your arms from your shoulder to your wrist.

   Who has longer arms?_____

3. What makes your body grow?_____

   _____

Personal History
Ask your parents what your height and weight were when you were born. How much have you grown?

_____

Fantastic Fact
Your fastest growing stage happened before you were born. During the first week, when you were first inside your mother, you grew from one cell into billions of cells!

Name _____

Blood Work

If you could look at a drop of your blood under a microscope, you would see some odd-shaped cells floating around in a liquid called **plasma**. These are the **white blood cells**. White blood cells are "soldiers" that fight germs which cause disease.

You would also see many smaller, saucer-shaped cells called **red blood cells**. Red blood cells give your blood its red color. They also have the important job of carrying **oxygen** to all of the cells in your body.

Blood **platelets** go to work when you have a cut. They form a plug, called a clot, that stops the bleeding.

Blood travels throughout your whole body. It goes to the **lungs** to pick up oxygen and to the intestines to pick up digested food. It carries the oxygen and food nutrients to all part of your body. It also takes away carbon dioxide and other waste products.

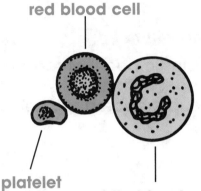

red blood cell

platelet

white blood cell

Directions: Fill in the spaces with words from the Word Bank.

1. Red blood cells carry __ __ __ __ __ __.

2. The blood gets oxygen from your __ __ __ __ __.
   ₅

3. Blood carries __ __ __ __ nutrients from the intestines.
   ₄

4. __ __ __ __ __ blood cells fight germs.

5. Blood travels to all parts of your __ __ __ __.
   ₂

6. The liquid part of the blood is called __ __ __ __ __ __.
   ₆

7. __ __ __ blood cells give blood its color.
   ₇

8. __ __ __ __ __ __ __ __ __ form blood clots.
   ₃

9. Adults donate blood at a blood __ __ __ __.
   ₁

Word Bank

oxygen
platelets
red
white
bank
lungs
plasma
food
body

Challenge
Use the numbered letters to finish the sentence. "Dirty" blood is cleansed by two large bean-shaped organs. These organs are called __ __ __ __ __ __ __.

Name _____

Build a Blood Cell!

Each blood cell has its own parts. Look at the picture below and study the parts of the red blood cells. Remember, this is much bigger than a real cell.

You will need:

1 plastic bag that seals
1 dark button
½ cup prepared red gelatin

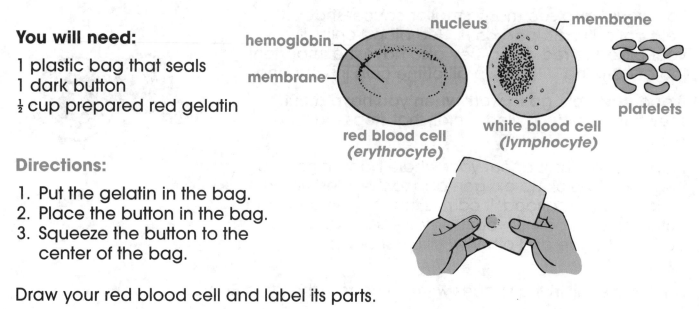

hemoglobin
nucleus
membrane
membrane
red blood cell (erythrocyte)
white blood cell (lymphocyte)
platelets

Directions:

1. Put the gelatin in the bag.
2. Place the button in the bag.
3. Squeeze the button to the center of the bag.

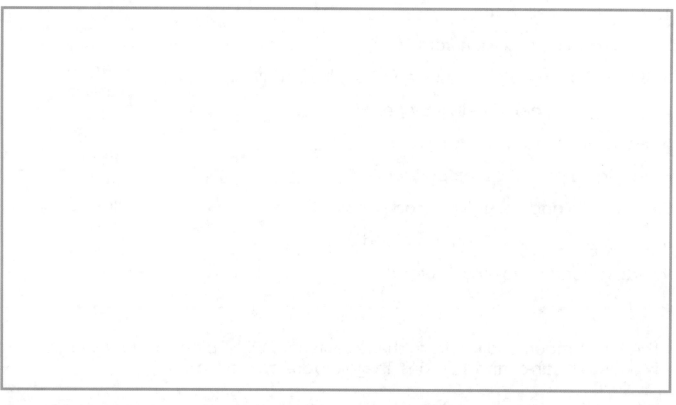

Draw your red blood cell and label its parts.

Name _____

Blood Types

Everyone has a blood type. These types are based on the presence or absence of certain **antigens**, or germ fighters, of the red blood cells. Scientists have labeled these antigens with the letters A, B, and O. Blood types can be combinations of these antigens, like AB. Blood types can also be positive or negative, like A+ or B-.

Find out what blood type you have. Check with other family members to see what their blood types are, too. Compile the data and fill in a bar graph. Use a different colored marker for each blood type. You can then draw conclusions about the most common and least common blood types and what value it is to know one's blood type.

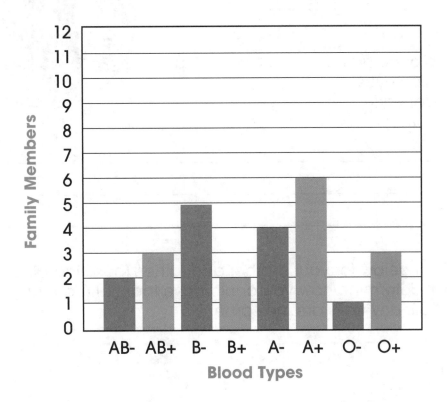

Investigate
Check the public library or call the Red Cross for more information on blood types, heredity, and blood transfusions.

Name _____

Ingenious Genes

Your body is made up of cells. Each cell holds threadlike structures called **chromosomes** that contain genes. Genes are inherited from your parents and determine how you will look. This is why we often look like our parents. Some genes are stronger, or **dominant**, and some are carried down through generations. Below is a table listing the characteristics of a mother and a father. See if you can find all of the possible combinations for their children and write them in the space provided. There are 16 possibilities!

	hair	eyes	skin color	height
Mom	blonde	green	dark	short
Dad	red	blue	fair	tall

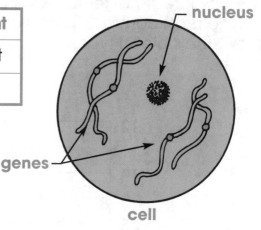

nucleus

genes

cell

Examples:

blonde hair   blonde hair
green eyes   blue eyes
dark skin   dark skin
short   tall

_____

_____

_____

Complete the chart below for your mother and father. Then, find all of the combinations that determine how you could have looked! (You may have fewer than 16 if any traits are the same.)

	hair	eyes	skin color	height
Mom				
Dad				

_____

_____

_____

Name _____

Framework

What gives you your **shape**? Like a house's frame, your body also has a frame. It is called your **skeleton**. Your skeleton is made of more than two hundred bones.

Your skeleton helps your body move. It does this by giving your **muscles** a place to attach. Your skeleton also **protects** the soft organs inside your body from injury.

Bones have a hard, outer layer made of **calcium**. Inside each bone is a soft, **spongy** layer that looks like a honeycomb. The hollow spaces in the honeycomb are filled with **marrow**. Every minute, millions of **blood** cells die. But you don't need to worry. The bone marrow works like a little factory, making new blood cells for you.

Directions:

Use the highlighted words above to finish the sentences below.

1. Your skeleton __ __ __ __ __ __ __ __ your soft organs.
                          5

2. Bone __ __ __ __ __ __ makes new blood cells.
          2

3. Inside the bone is a soft, __ __ __ __ __ __ layer.
                                      3

4. Millions of __ __ __ __ __ cells die every minute.
              4

5. The hard, outer layer of bone is made from __ __ __ __ __ __ __.
                                                      1

6. More than two hundred bones are in your __ __ __ __ __ __ __ __.
                                                                  6

7. Your skeleton is a place for __ __ __ __ __ __ __ to attach.
                                          7

8. Your skeleton gives your body its __ __ __ __ __.
                                      8

Challenge
What do you call a skeleton that won't get out of bed? Use the numbered letters above to find out.
__ __ __z __   __ __ __ __ __
1 2 3   4 5 6 7 8

Name _____

Bone Up on Your Bones!

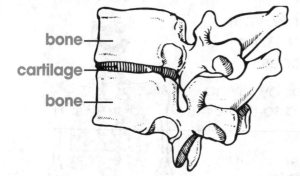

bone
cartilage
bone

When you were born, your skeleton was made of soft bones called cartilage. As you grew, most of that cartilage turned into bone. However, all people still have some cartilage in their bodies. Our noses and our ears are cartilage, and there are pads of cartilage between sections of our backbone that act as cushions.

Besides supporting the body, the bones also serve other important purposes. They are storage houses for important minerals like calcium and phosphorous. The center of the bone, called bone marrow, produces new blood cells for our bodies.

You will need:

soup bones from a butcher sawed in half (shin bones are ideal)

Directions:

1. Look at the end of the whole bone. Find the parts labeled on the diagram to the right.

2. Now, separate the bone. Look inside the cavity which is filled with marrow. Write 5 adjectives to describe the marrow.

_____

_____

3. Pull away the skin covering the bone. What is the name for this outer skin?

_____

   If the bone is fresh, you will see small red dots where blood vessels enter the bone.

4. Carefully scoop out the bone marrow. Ask your parents to boil the bone to get it really clean. What do you see now? Write three facts about bones.

_____

_____

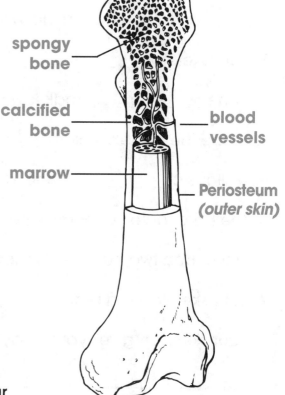

spongy bone

calcified bone

marrow

blood vessels

Periosteum
(outer skin)

Strong Bones

The skeleton is a framework of 206 bones with three main jobs: to hold up your body, to protect your inner organs and to produce new blood cells. That means our bones must be healthy. The outer part of our bones contains calcium to keep our bones strong. What would happen if our bones lacked calcium? Try the experiment below to find out.

You will need:
a chicken bone
a glass jar with a lid
1 cup vinegar

Directions:

1. Clean the chicken bone.
2. Place the bone in the jar and cover it with vinegar.
3. Cover tightly.
4. Let it sit for two weeks.

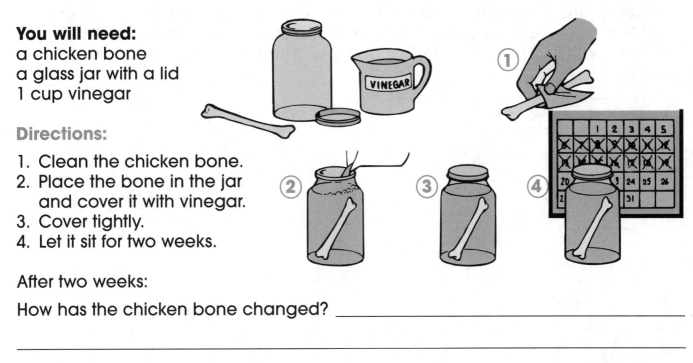

After two weeks:

How has the chicken bone changed? _____

_____

What would happen to your body without calcium? _____

_____

Rickets is a disease caused by too little calcium in your body. Calcium is found in many of the foods we eat. Check the labels of several foods. List at least ten that contain calcium.

1. _____   6. _____

2. _____   7. _____

3. _____   8. _____

4. _____   9. _____

5. _____   10. _____

Name _____

Your Pizza's Path

The organs of the digestive system work together to gain fuel from the foods we eat. Food is broken down into simple substances the body can use. These substances are absorbed into the bloodstream and any leftover waste matter is eliminated.

When you eat pizza (or any food), each bite you take goes through a path in the human body called the **alimentary canal**, or the digestive tract. This canal consists of the mouth, esophagus, stomach and small and large intestines. It is in this path that foods are broken down, vitamins are saved and poisons are discarded.

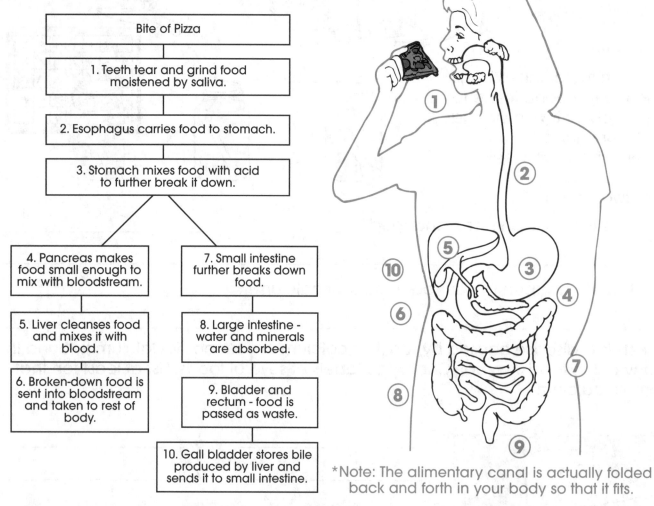

Bite of Pizza

1. Teeth tear and grind food moistened by saliva.

2. Esophagus carries food to stomach.

3. Stomach mixes food with acid to further break it down.

4. Pancreas makes food small enough to mix with bloodstream.

7. Small intestine further breaks down food.

5. Liver cleanses food and mixes it with blood.

8. Large intestine - water and minerals are absorbed.

6. Broken-down food is sent into bloodstream and taken to rest of body.

9. Bladder and rectum - food is passed as waste.

10. Gall bladder stores bile produced by liver and sends it to small intestine.

*Note: The alimentary canal is actually folded back and forth in your body so that it fits.

1. Name 3 parts of the pizza that are healthy. _____
2. Use a black crayon to trace the path of the healthy parts of the pizza.
3. Name 3 parts of the pizza that are unhealthy. _____
4. Use a blue crayon to trace the path of the unhealthy parts of the pizza.

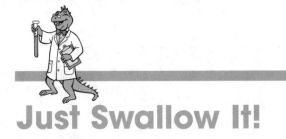

Name _____

Just Swallow It!

Directions: Use this diagram to help you number the sentences below in the correct order to show what happens when you swallow a bite of food.

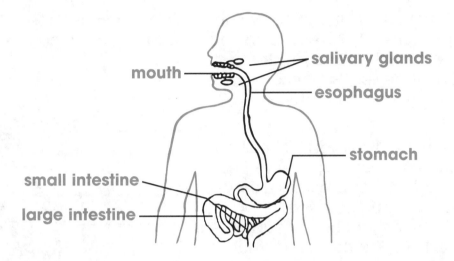

____ While your teeth are breaking the food into tiny pieces, saliva is making the food softer.

____ Whatever the body cannot use goes into the large intestine.

____ While the food is in your stomach, more juices help to dissolve it.

____ When the food in your mouth is soft enough, you swallow it.

____ When the food has dissolved in your stomach, it goes to your small intestine.

____ As you swallow your food, it moves down the esophagus to your stomach.

____ Use your teeth to take a bite of the sandwich.

____ While the food is in your small intestine, the body absorbs whatever it needs.

What happens when you try to swallow too big of a bite?_____

_____

Write a sentence about a kind of food that is good for your body._____

_____

_____

Name _____

Breathing Tree

Did you know that you have a tree inside your chest? This tree has a special job. It takes air from your windpipe and spreads it all through your lungs. This tree is called your **bronchial tree**.

Air enters through your **nose**. It passes over the hairs inside your nose. This warms and cleanses the air. Then, it travels down your **windpipe** until it comes to your bronchial tree. The bronchial tree divides into two tubes. One tube sends air into your right **lung**. The other tube sends air into your left lung.

Inside the lungs, the air fills almost 300 million tiny, spongy **air sacs**. These air sacs give fresh **oxygen** to the blood. At the same time, they take away **carbon dioxide** from the blood. Carbon dioxide is the air that has already been used. When you exhale, the carbon dioxide flows up the bronchial tree and out of your mouth and nose. The nose, windpipe, bronchial tree, lungs and air sacs work as a team. The team is called the **respiratory system**.

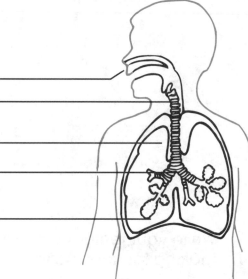

Label the parts of the respiratory system.

Who am I?

Inhale these scrambled words. Exhale the answers to the riddles.

1. I warm and clean the air you breathe. SNOE _____

2. There are 300 million of me in your lungs. RAI SCAS _____

3. You breathe me out. RONBAC DOXEIDI _____

4. I am your special tree. CHONRBALI REET _____

5. I am a long tube connecting your mouth to your lungs. DINWIPPE _____

6. I go through the air sacs and into the blood. YXONEG _____

Investigate
Smoking is harmful to your lungs. How can smoking affect breathing?

Your Body's Pipeline

Blood travels through three kinds of tubes. **Arteries** carry oxygen-rich blood from your heart to other parts of your body. Blood vessels, called **veins**, carry carbon dioxide-rich blood back to your heart. **Capillaries** are tiny vessels that connect arteries and veins. Capillaries take carbon dioxide from the cells and give the cells oxygen. Capillaries are fifty times thinner than a hair. They are so small that the blood cells must line up one at a time to travel through them.

Your heart, blood, arteries, veins and capillaries work as a team. This team is called your **circulatory system**.

Directions:

Name three kinds of blood vessels.

1. _____

2. _____

3. _____

The picture shows your circulatory system.

1. Color the veins **blue**.
2. Color the arteries **red**.
3. Color the heart **brown**.

veins

arteries

Fantastic Fact
With every beat of your heart, blood starts a fantastic journey. Your blood travels through 60,000 miles of blood vessels to all the cells in your body.

Name _____

Going Around in Circles!

The circulatory system is responsible for moving blood throughout your body. This system also carries disease-fighting substances that help prevent you from getting sick.

The main components of your body's circulatory system are the heart, blood vessels, blood and the lymphatic system. Your heart controls this system.

The heart's constant pumping is responsible for sending oxygen-rich blood to the rest of your body through blood vessels called arteries. Blood vessels called veins return blood to your heart. Back toward the heart, the blood gathers more oxygen as it passes through your lungs and becomes red. Blood with oxygen is bright red. Blood without oxygen is dark red. This cycle occurs about once every minute.

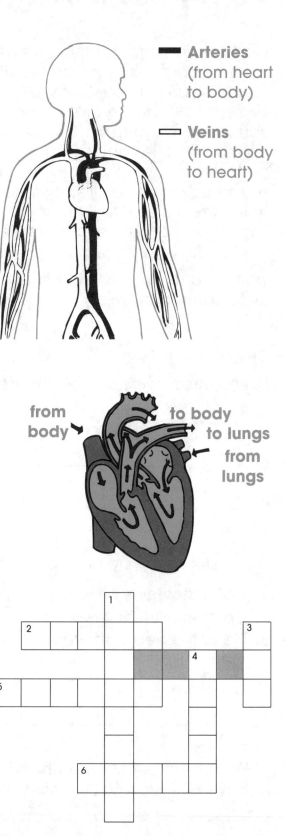

■ **Arteries** (from heart to body)

▭ **Veins** (from body to heart)

from body → to body
to lungs
from lungs

Directions:

Use the information above to solve the puzzle.

Across:

2. The _____ controls the circulatory system.
5. Arteries carry blood mixed with _____ from the heart to the rest of your body.
6. _____ carry blood to the heart.

Down:

1. _____ carry blood away from the heart.
3. Blood is _____ when it contains oxygen.
4. Blood gets oxygen from your _____.

Name _____

I Can Feel My Heartbeat

Each time your heart pumps the blood through veins and arteries, you can feel it! It's called a **pulse**. You can feel your pulse in two places where the arteries are close to the surface of your skin. Gently, place two fingers on the inside of your wrist or on your neck next to your windpipe. Silently count the pulses and complete the chart below.

*An adult should time and direct each part. Time for 6 seconds, then multiply by 10.

Pulse Rate	Sitting	Walking around room for 1 minute	Wait 2 minutes, then standing	After 25 jumping jacks	Wait 1 minute, then lying down	After jogging in place for 2 minutes	After resting for 5 minutes
In 6 seconds							
In 1 minute							

You should have found that your heart beats faster when you are active. That's because your body uses more oxygen when it exercises, and the blood must circulate faster to get more oxygen to your muscles! With your family, compare pulse rates and find the average for your family (using the 1-minute rate).

Pulse Rate	Sitting	After walking	After standing	After jumping	After lying down	After jogging	After resting
You							
Person #2							
Person #3							
Person #4							
Total							
÷ 4 to find average							

Heartbeats

Read the poems "What is Red?" by Mary O'Neill in
The Random House Book of Poetry for Children; "Much Love," "Bohemian Folk
Song" or "The Light-Hearted Fairy," by Josephine Barton found in
Favorite Poems for the Children's Hour.

Then, write a poem about the heart. It can be a love poem, a poem about the
function of the heart, a poem about how your heart skipped a beat, etc. Next,
fold a 9" x 12" sheet of drawing paper in half. Trace the picture of the heart on
one side. Copy the poem neatly on the other side. Color the heart.

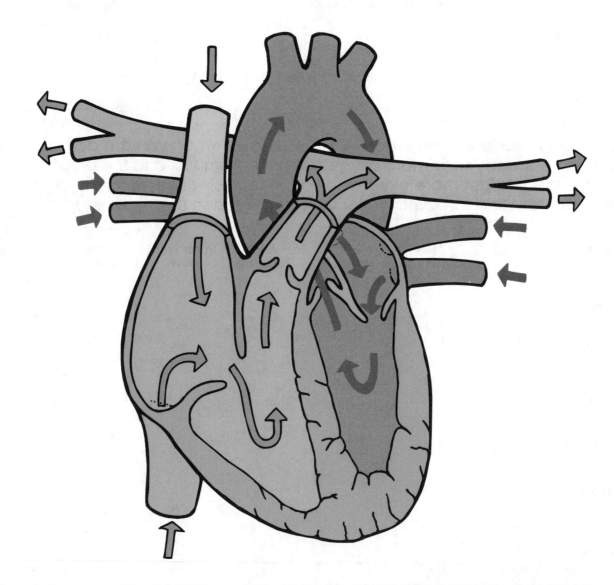

Name _____

Lub-Dub, Lub-Dub

Place your hand on the left side of your chest. *Lub-dub, lub-dub*. Did you feel it? This is your heart pumping oxygen-rich blood to all parts of your body.

Your heart is really two pumps. It is divided down the middle. Each half of the heart is divided into two chambers. The **right half** pumps blood filled with a waste called carbon dioxide gas into the lungs. The **left half** of the heart takes oxygen-rich blood from the lungs. It sends the oxygen-rich blood to the cells in your body.

What about lub-dub? These are the sounds made by the little "trap doors" called **valves**. The valves open and close to let the blood flow in and out of the heart.

to the lungs

from the lungs

to the body

to the lungs

from the lungs

The arrows show the direction of blood flowing through the heart.

Directions:

Answer the questions below, using the information from above.

1. How many pumps does your heart have? _____

2. Where does the right half pump its blood? _____

3. Where does the left half pump its blood? _____

4. Which part of the heart makes the lub-dub sound? _____

Respiration Connected to Circulation

Research a condition or problem of the circulatory or respiratory system. Read current periodicals and/or encyclopedias to find out about the chosen topic. Write a short report on that topic. Some suggestions for topics are:

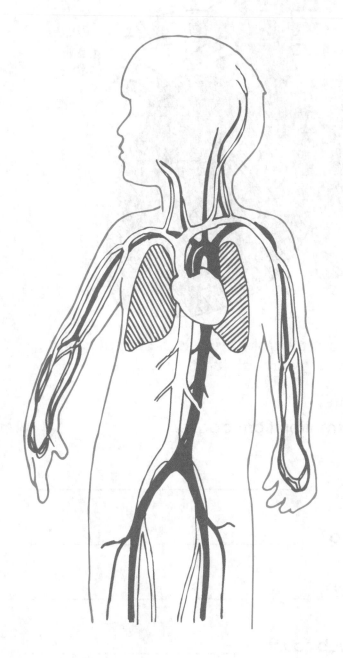

anemia

arteriosclerosis

artificial hearts

blood pressure

blood vessels

cardiovascular disease

diaphragm

emphysema

hypertension

hyperventilation

leukemia

lung cancer

nose, trachea, larynx, mouth

plasma

red cells

route blood takes through body

transfusions

white cells

Name _____

Think Tank

Your brain has a very important job. It must keep your body working smoothly all day and night.

Your brain has three parts. The **cerebrum** is the largest part. It controls your body movement, such as running, walking, jumping, throwing a ball, holding a fork and other actions. It controls your five senses: hearing, smelling, tasting, seeing and touching. The cerebrum also controls your thinking and speaking.

The cerebrum is divided into two halves. The right half controls movements in the left side of your body. The left half controls movements in the right side of your body.

The part below the cerebrum is the **cerebellum**. The cerebellum makes sure that all of your muscles work together the way they should. It also helps you keep your balance.

The third and smallest part of the brain is the **brain stem**. The brain stem's job is extremely important. It controls breathing and the beating of your heart.

Directions: Label the three major parts of the brain.

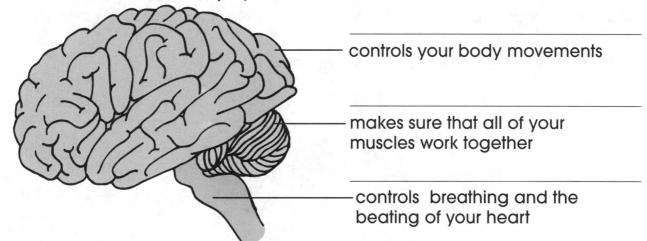

_____
controls your body movements

_____
makes sure that all of your muscles work together

_____
controls breathing and the beating of your heart

1. Which part of the skeleton protects the brain from injury?

2. Give the common name and the scientific name.

   common name:_____ scientific name:_____

Fantastic Fact

In order to function properly, the brain must have a constant supply of blood. The blood provides oxygen and other vitamins and nutrients needed by the brain to stay healthy.

Think Tank

Your body's **central nervous system** includes your brain, spinal cord and nerves that transmit information. It receives information from your senses, analyzes this information and decides how your body should respond. Once it has decided, it sends instructions triggering the required actions.

The central nervous system makes some simple decisions about your body's actions within the spinal cord. These **spinal reflexes** include actions like pulling your hand away from a hot object. However, the brain still makes the majority of the decisions.

Your brain weighs about three pounds and is made up of three major parts: the cerebrum, the cerebellum and the brain stem. The **cerebrum** is divided into two hemispheres which are responsible for all thought and learning processes. The **cerebellum** is also divided into two parts, which control all voluntary muscle movement. The **brain stem**, which is about the size of your thumb, takes care of all involuntary functions.

Directions:

Fill in the jobs of each part of the brain. Then, answer the questions below.

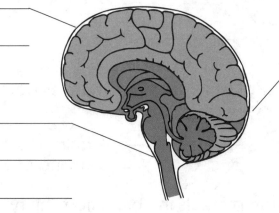

1. Name someone in your family who is using his/her cerebellum. _____

2. What is he/she doing? _____

3. Name someone who is using his/her brain stem. _____

4. What is he/she doing? _____

5. Name someone in your home who is using his/her cerebrum. _____

6. What is he/she doing? _____

Name _____

Find Your Brain Dominance

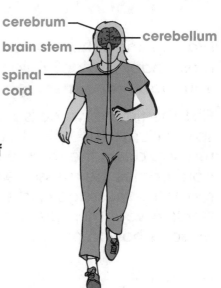

cerebrum

cerebellum

brain stem

spinal cord

The two sides of the cerebellum work to control all voluntary movements. These include walking, running, writing and all other movements that we consciously want to do. One side of the cerebellum is usually dominant, or depended upon more heavily. The side that is dominant depends on the person. The left side of the brain controls the right side of your body and vice versa. That means that if a person writes with his/her right hand, he/she is probably left-brain dominant.

Directions: Answer these questions to find your dominance.

Try This	Right	Left
Clasp your hands together. Which hand is on top?		
Pick up a pencil to write. Which hand do you use?		
Take 3 steps. Which foot did you start with?		
Try to do the splits. Which leg is in front?		
Hold your arms. Which arm is on top?		
Wink your eye. Which one did you wink?		
Pick up a fork. Which hand do you eat with?		
Hop 5 times on one foot. Which foot did you use?		
Look through a camera, telescope or microscope. Which eye did you use?		

How many times did you use your right? _____

How many times did you use your left? _____

Which side of your brain is probably more dominant? _____
(Be careful . . . they're opposite!)

Extension: Make a family graph showing dominant sides.

Name _____

Your Body's Messenger Service

Did you know that your nervous system has its own messenger service? Billions of tiny nerve cells throughout your body send messages to your brain.

First, the tiny nerve cells send their message to the spinal cord. (The spinal cord is a thick bundle of nerves running down the middle of your back.) Next, the spinal cord carries the message to your brain. Your brain reads the message and sends a new message back to your muscles. The new message tells your muscles how to move.

Think Fast!

How fast do you react to brain messages? Place your hand flat on a table. Have a friend hold an eraser about 1 ft. above your hand. Try to pull your hand away before your friend can drop the eraser on it.

Try five times and record each result.

Put a (✓) in either the "hit" or "miss" box.

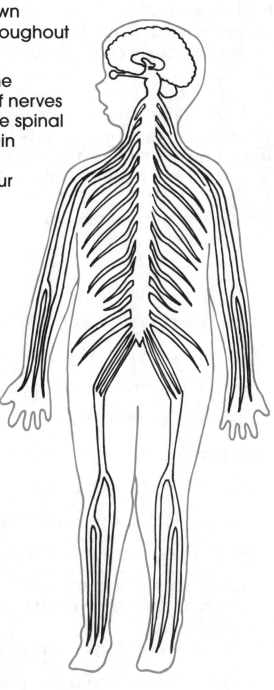

	#1	#2	#3	#4	#5
Hit					
Miss					

Color the parts of the nervous system.

brain - **gray**
spinal cord - **blue**
nerves - **red**

Investigate
What are some occupations that require a quick reaction time?

Name _____

Round Windows

"Oh, what beautiful brown eyes you have!" Whether you know it or not, those eyes are not totally brown. Only the iris is colored brown.

Your eye is shaped like a ball. It has a clear, round window in front called the cornea. The colored iris controls the amount of light that enters the eye. Light enters through an opening called the pupil. In bright light, your pupil is a small dot. In dim light, it is much larger. Behind the pupil is the lens. It focuses the light onto the back wall of your eye. This back wall is called the retina. The retina changes the light into nerve messages. These messages are sent to the brain along the optic nerve. Close your eyes. Gently touch them. They are firm because they are filled with a clear jelly called vitreous humor.

Directions:

Label the parts of the eye using the words in bold from above.

What am I?

I focus the light. __ __ __ __
                    2   4

I become smaller in bright light. __ __ __ __ __
                                  11   1

I am the clear window. __ __ __ __ __ __
                       3   6

I am the colored part of the eye. __ __ __ __
                                  10

I send pictures to the brain. __ __ __ __   __ __ __ __ __
                              12 5   7

I am the clear jelly. __ __ __ __ __ __ __   __ __ __ __
                      9   13   8

What did the teacher say when his glass eye went down the drain?
Use the numbered letters to find out.

__ __ __ __ __   __ __ __ __ __ __ __   __ __ __ __ __ !
1 2 3 4 5   6 7 3 5 8 9 10   11 13 12 1 2

Name _____

Oh, Yes, I See Now!

One of the most sensitive nerves in your body is the optic nerve. It connects your eyes to your brain. The optic nerve receives messages from other nerves that surround your eyes in the retina. As light is caught in the pupils of your eyes, it is sent to the retina, then to the optic nerve and at last to the brain. Try this experiment to watch your pupils change!

1. Close your eyes and cover them with your hands. Count to 100, open your eyes, and immediately observe them in a mirror. Draw how your eyes look.

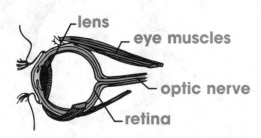

2. Now look at a light in your room. Count to 100 and then draw your eyes again.

3. How did your pupils change from one experiment to another?_____

_____

4. Why do you think they changed? _____

_____

5. Why do people wear sunglasses? _____

_____

Name _____

Sound Collectors

A large jet plane rumbles as it takes off down the runway. You can feel the ground vibrate. The plane is also filling the air with vibrations. When the vibrations reach your ear, you hear them as sound.

Your **outer ear** collects the vibrations just like a funnel. The vibrations strike your **eardrum**, making it vibrate, too. These vibrations are passed through a series of three small bones. The last bone vibrates against a snail-shaped tube. This tube is called the **cochlea**. It is filled with liquid. Small hair-like sensors in the cochlea pick up the vibrations and send them to the **auditory nerve**. The auditory nerve sends the sound message to your brain.

Directions: Label the parts of the ear using the highlighted words above.

Sounds Around Us

1. What is the loudest sound you have ever heard? _____

2. What is the softest sound you have ever heard? _____

3. What sound wakes you up in the morning? _____

4. What sound relaxes you? _____

5. What sound frightens you? _____

Extensions:

Try some of these sound experiments with a friend. Keep your eyes closed for all of the experiments!

1. Cover one ear and listen for the sounds around you. Then, uncover your ear and listen again. What is the difference?

2. Choose a friend to make several sounds with objects found in the room. Can you identify the sounds?

3. We usually hear the loudest sounds around us. Listen for the soft, "far away" sounds. List the sounds. Try this experiment outside.

Name _____

Yum-Yum

Without the sense of taste, many things in life would not be as pleasant. What would it be like if all of your favorite foods had no taste at all?

Your sense of taste is found mainly in the tiny **taste buds** on your tongue. To taste food, it must be chewed and mixed with **saliva**. The taste message is sent to the brain by nerves.

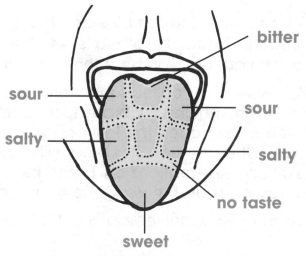

Each of the four tastes has a special center on the tongue. In each center, one of the main tastes is tasted more strongly.

1. Look at the map of the tongue. List the four main tastes. Next to each taste, write a food which is tasted in that taste center.

   Taste _____   Food _____

   _____   _____

   _____   _____

   _____   _____

2. Which taste center tastes an ice cream cone? _____

3. Why is it more enjoyable to lick an ice cream cone with the tip of your tongue? _____

Extension:

Where will each of these foods be tasted most strongly? Draw a line from the symbol for each food to its taste center on the tongue.

candy

vinegar

saltine cracker

lemon

Name _____

Mouth Full of Teeth

The boy in the picture has two sets of teeth. You do, too!

Your first set are baby teeth that come in your first two years. When you are young, your jaw is small. It has just enough room for twenty baby teeth. As you grow older, your jaw becomes larger. The thirty-two permanent teeth push out the baby teeth.

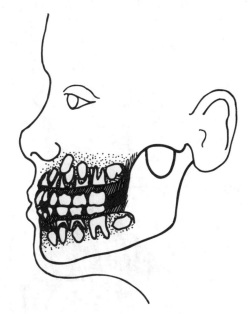

Taking good care of your teeth will help them last a lifetime. Sticky, chewy food sticks to your teeth. Germs in your mouth change these foods—especially sugar—into acid. The acid can eat holes, or cavities, in your teeth. Brushing and flossing your teeth removes the food and acid, helping to prevent cavities.

1. What are at least two things you can do to prevent cavities?

   _____

2. It is easy to brush at home. What can you do after eating your lunch away from home to keep your teeth clean? _____

Sweet, sticky foods are tooth destroyers. But some foods keep your teeth clean and slick. Check a health book or an encyclopedia for foods that are good for your teeth. List tooth destroyers and tooth savers on the lines below.

Tooth Destroyers	Tooth Savers
_____	_____
_____	_____
_____	_____

Investigate

Lyle says, "Why should I brush my baby teeth? They will just fall out anyway. I will take care of my permanent teeth when they come in." Is this a good idea? Why or why not?

Name _____

Tooth Talk

Directions: Study the drawing of the tooth to help you fill in the blanks.

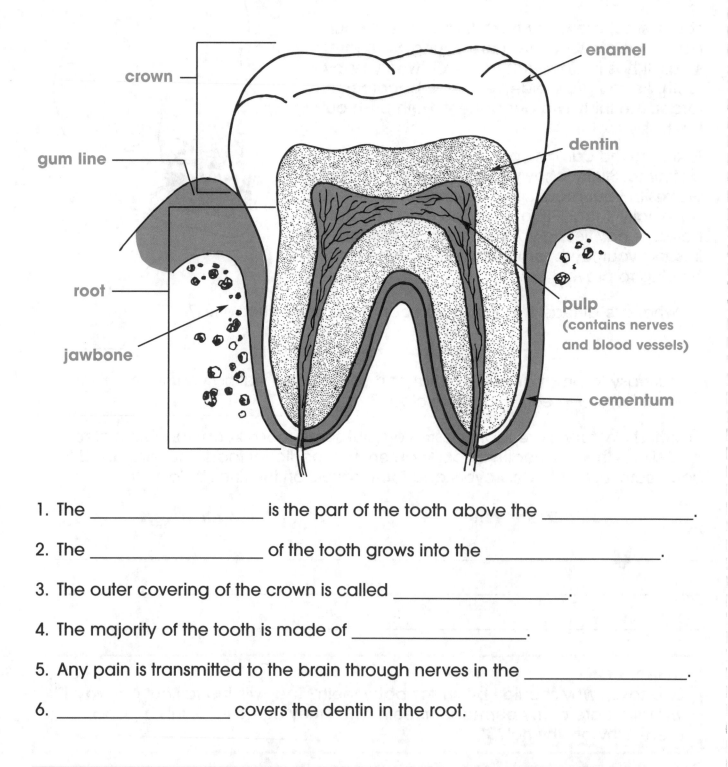

1. The _____ is the part of the tooth above the _____.

2. The _____ of the tooth grows into the _____.

3. The outer covering of the crown is called _____.

4. The majority of the tooth is made of _____.

5. Any pain is transmitted to the brain through nerves in the _____.

6. _____ covers the dentin in the root.

Section 4
Health

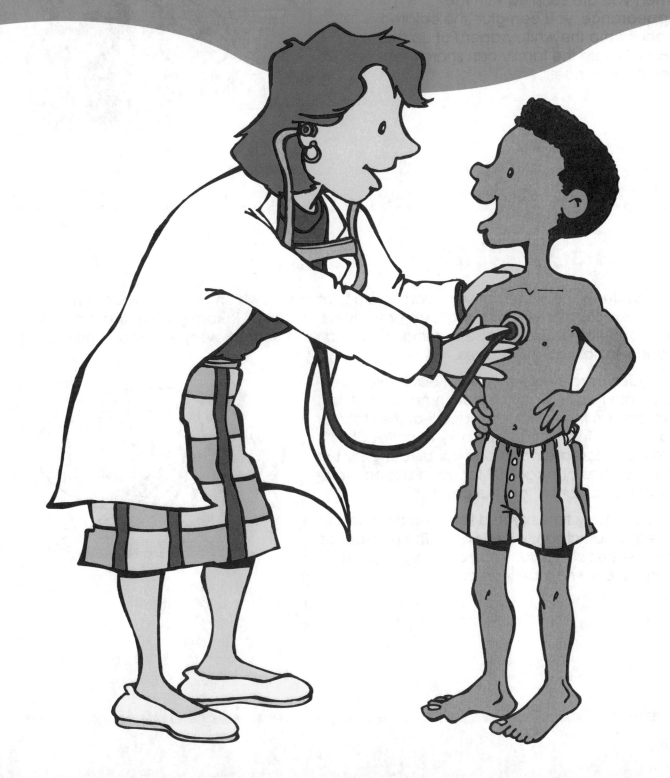

Stay Well

Design health posters on Nutrition, Exercise, Smoking, Preventions, etc. Cut out lettering and figures from colored paper and lay them on a large piece of white paper. When you are satisfied with the appearance, you can glue the colored pieces onto the white paper. Put up the poster where the family can share them as healthy reminders.

Exercise for Life

Designate areas of the house or yard to be "stations" in which you and your family members will have room to perform prescribed exercises. Before you do them on your own, practice each exercise together, one at a time, so that everyone knows how to do it and will not hurt themselves.

On index cards, write a copy of each exercise you want to do. Write the station number of the exercise on the card and place it at the station. Have participants start with only ten of each exercise. Increase each additional round by ten. Make copies of page 109 for each station. Have each participant fill out the chart.

After so many times (you decide on the number), give the participant a certificate. The number of exercises each person should do on the next round should now be increased.

*Before starting, it would also be beneficial to read over the information on page 110, Counting Beats.

Name _____

Exercise for Life

Station #1—Push-Ups

Lie facedown on the floor. Put your hands on the ground at about shoulder level and about shoulder-width apart. Keep your knees on the ground. Keep your back straight and your stomach pressed against your spine. Raise and lower your upper body ____ times.

Station #2—Sit-Ups

Lie on your back with your knees bent and your feet flat on the floor. Fold your arms across your chest with hands grasping opposite shoulders. Raise your head, shoulders and waist until you touch your upper legs. Lower yourself to the floor, slowly letting one vertebra at a time touch the ground. Repeat this ____ times.

Station #3—Knee Bends and Heel Raises

Stand with feet shoulder-width apart and hands on hips. Squat until your thighs are parallel to the ground. Then, return to standing position. Do this ____ times. Assume the same position with your hands. Put your feet under your hips. Raise up on your toes as high as you can and then lower your heels to the floor. Do this ____ times.

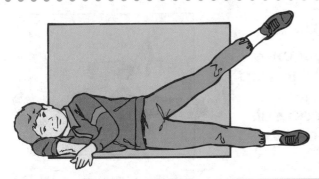

Station #4—Side Leg Lifts

Lie on your right side with your head resting on your right arm and your left arm on the floor. Make sure your body is straight. Lift and lower your left leg, keeping your knee facing forward. Do this ____ times. Repeat on the other side.

Name _____

Exercise for Life

Station #5—Hip Raisers

Sit on the floor with your hands flat, fingertips forward, next to your hips and your legs extended straight out. Keep your elbows straight. Raise your hips off the floor until your body is slanting at a 45° angle. Only your hands and feet will be on the floor. Repeat this exercise _____ times.

Station #6—Hamstring Stretch

You will need a chair about 18" high. Stand facing the chair. Put one foot on it. Form a right angle with the standing leg. Bend your upper body forward, toward your raised leg. Hold this position for a few seconds. Repeat on the opposite side. Do this _____ times.

Station #7—Calf Stretch

Stand about 12" from a wall. Put your hands on the wall, fingertips up. Lean forward. Keep your right leg where it is. Extend your left leg back and bend your right one. Keep both heels on the floor. Hold this position for a few seconds. Repeat on the other side. Do this _____ times on each side.

Station #8—Lower Back Stretch

Lie on your back. Bend your right knee to your chest. Clasp your hands under your right knee. Pull it toward your chest. At the same time, flatten your back toward the floor. Let your left leg relax, stretched out. Hold the position for a few seconds. Repeat on the other side. Do this _____ times.

Name _____

Exercise for Life

Station Name: _____ Number to be done each time _____

Number of times to do this station to earn a certificate: _____

Name	Date	Date	Date	Date	Date	Date	Date	Date	Date	Date

_____ has completed

_____ rounds of

_____ (station) of

_____ each round

What a star!

_____ is a WIZARD

_____ (station)

Name _____

Counting Beats

While working on your Exercises for Life, it would be an excellent idea to chart your pulse rate. Remember to use your index or pointer finger and your middle finger to take your pulse. Everyone in your family who is exercising should also fill out a chart.

Directions:

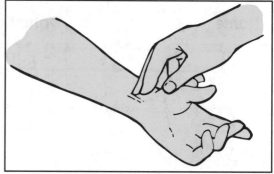

1. Give each person a copy of the pulse rate chart.

2. When you are ready to begin, have one person sit still. Find his/her pulse and start counting the beat for one minute. The timer watches the second hand of a clock or watch and says "Stop" after 60 seconds. Record the rate on the chart after the date and under the column marked Before Exercise. Do the same for everyone else.

3. Next, exercise. After exercise, take pulses as you did in Step 2. Mark charts.

4. Cool down by walking around slowly for one minute. Then, Step 2 is repeated and the pulse rate is recorded under Recovery on the same line.

5. Repeat three more times on three other dates.

6. Everyone should also have someone take his/her pulse rate while he/she is sleeping. This can be recorded under the column marked Resting.

Name		Timer		
Date	Resting	Before exercise	After exercise	Recovery

My Body Homework

To keep your body working and looking its best, you should start good habits now and maintain them as you grow older. Use this checklist to keep yourself on track for the next week. Keep it on your bathroom mirror or next to your bed where it will remind you to do your "homework!"

	Sun.	Mon.	Tues.	Wed.	Thurs	Fri.	Sat.
I slept at least 8 hours.							
I ate a healthful breakfast.							
I brushed my teeth this morning.							
I ate a healthful lunch.							
I washed my hands after using the bathroom.							
I exercised at least 30 minutes today.							
I drank at least 6 glasses of water.							
I stood and sat up straight.							
I ate a healthful dinner.							
I bathed.							
I brushed my teeth this evening.							

This page intentionally left blank.

Counting Beats

Name					
	Timer				
Date	Resting	Before exercise	After exercise	Recovery	

Name					
	Timer				
Date	Resting	Before exercise	After exercise	Recovery	

Name					
	Timer				
Date	Resting	Before exercise	After exercise	Recovery	

Name					
	Timer				
Date	Resting	Before exercise	After exercise	Recovery	

This page intentionally left blank.

Section 5

Nutrition

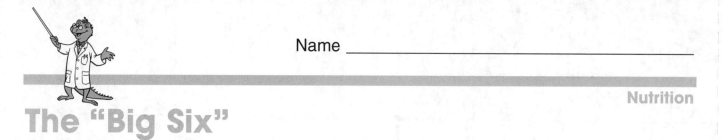

The "Big Six"

Your body will get the nutrients it needs if you follow the rules of the food group pyramid. Be sure to make fruits, vegetables and grains the basic foods of your diet. Eat plenty of nutritious foods from the bottom of the pyramid every day.

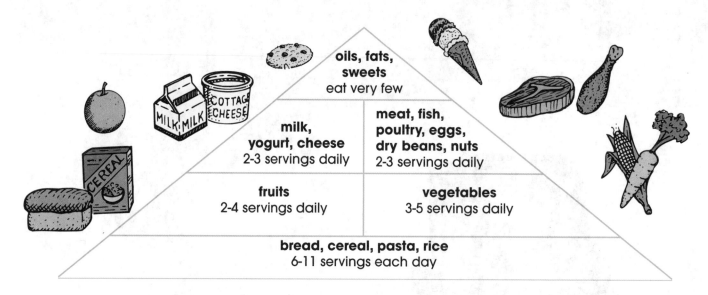

What foods do you eat each day? Choose a day and fill in the chart below. Record the kind of food and the number of servings you eat.

Group	Breakfast	Lunch	Dinner	Snack
Bread, cereal, pasta, rice				
Vegetables				
Fruits				
Meat, fish, poultry, eggs, dry beans, nuts				
Milk, cheese, yogurt				
Fats, oils, sweets				

How did you do? Compare your servings with what is indicated on the food pyramid.

Name _____

Peanut Butter and Sardine Sandwich

Your idea of a good meal may not be a peanut butter and sardine sandwich. But you do have a favorite food—everyone does. Eating would be boring if we didn't have some favorites.

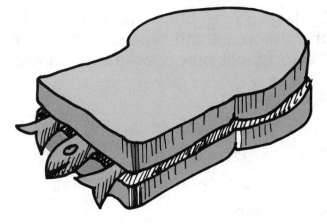

Directions:

List your seven favorite foods. Then, complete the chart by placing a check (✓) in the correct column(s).

Favorite foods	Top three favorites	Snack food	Prepare by myself	Eat in a restaurant	Ethnic food
1.					
2.					
3.					
4.					
5.					
6.					
7.					

Extension:

Royal Feast
You are the ruler for the day and may eat anything you want. Write a menu for today's royal feast.

Royal Menu

_____

_____

_____

_____

_____

_____

_____

Go Power

Carbohydrates are the main source of quick energy. Foods with lots of sugar and starch are rich in carbohydrates. You get carbohydrates from many foods like spaghetti, bread, cake and candy.

Directions:

Complete the sentences using words from the Word Bank.

Carbohydrates are the _____ foods to be digested.

_____ are changed to sugars.

Sugar gives us _____.

Leftover sugar is stored as _____.

Word Bank
fat
first
starches
energy

Fill in the plate with carbohydrate-rich foods. Find pictures of these foods in magazines, cut them out and glue them on the plate.

Investigate: Sweet Test
1. Chew a soda cracker well. Keep it in your mouth for five minutes.
2. What is the new taste in your mouth?
3. What happened to the starch in the cracker?

Name _____

Energy Savers

Fats give you twice as much energy as proteins or carbohydrates. Your body uses fats to save energy for future use. The fats we eat come from animals in the form of meat, eggs, milk and much more. We also get fats from some plants like beans, peanuts and corn. But not all plants give us fats in our diet.

Directions:

Circle the foods which are rich in fat.
Then, list them on the chart.

Fat Food Sources	
Animal	**Plant**

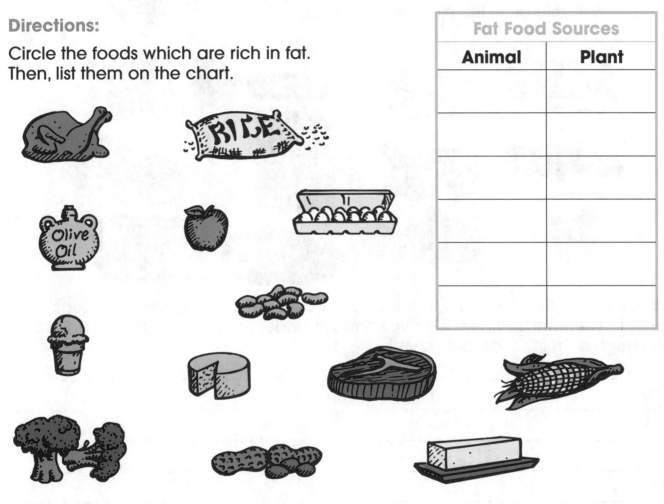

Extension:

Here is a simple test to tell if a food has fat.

1. Cut a brown paper bag into several four-inch squares.
2. Rub a piece of food on a square until it looks wet.
3. Label the paper.
4. Let the paper dry overnight.
5. Hold the paper up to the window the next day. If there is a grease spot, the food contains fat.

Name _____

Protein: The Body Builder

Protein is the nutrient that repairs and builds new body tissue. Most of the foods we eat contain some protein. We call these "high protein foods."

Directions: Circle all of the high protein foods.

Did you notice that most of the foods you circled belong to two food groups? Name these groups and list the circled foods under the correct group. Add two more high protein foods to each list.

Group: _____   Group: _____

1. _____   1. _____

2. _____   2. _____

3. _____   3. _____

4. _____   4. _____

5. _____   5. _____

6. _____   6. _____

Investigate:

Legumes (dry peas and beans) are an important protein source in many countries around the world. List as many kinds of legumes as you can think of. (Hint: A trip to your favorite grocery store will help you answer this.)

Name _____

Amazing "Vita-Men"

Vitamins do many important jobs. They help us grow and stay healthy. We can get all of the vitamins we need by eating a well-balanced diet.

Directions: Guide the Vita-Men through the mazes to find out the jobs they do.

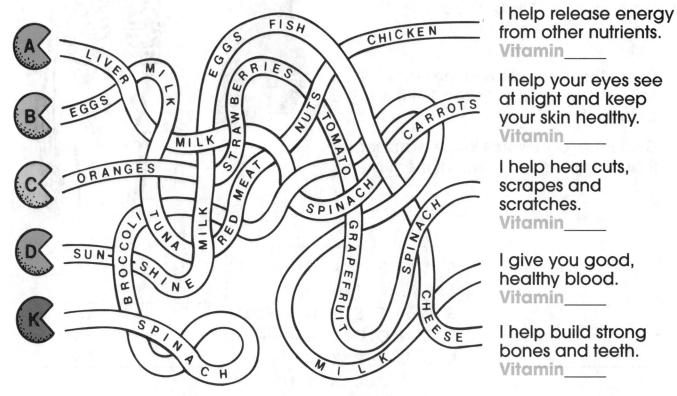

I help release energy from other nutrients. **Vitamin_____**

I help your eyes see at night and keep your skin healthy. **Vitamin_____**

I help heal cuts, scrapes and scratches. **Vitamin_____**

I give you good, healthy blood. **Vitamin_____**

I help build strong bones and teeth. **Vitamin_____**

List the food sources for each vitamin. (Hint: Use the maze.)

Vitamin A	Vitamin B	Vitamin C	Vitamin D	Vitamin K

Investigate:
Sailors who were at sea for a long time often became sick with a disease called "scurvy." What is scurvy? Which one of the Vita-Men could have helped the sailors? Why were British sailors called "limies"?

Name _____

Minerals

Minerals like calcium and iron are very important nutrients. Calcium helps build strong bones and teeth. Iron helps build rich, healthy blood. Calcium and iron are found in many different kinds of food.

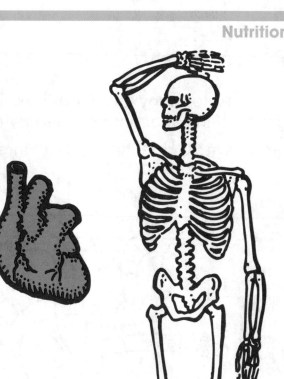

Directions:

1. Circle the food words in the word search that are rich in iron. List them below.

2. Circle the food words in the word search that are rich in calcium. List them below.

Iron-Rich Foods

_____

_____

_____

_____

_____

Calcium-Rich Foods

_____

_____

_____

_____

_____

B	A	P	B	E	A	N	S	Y	S
L	B	E	F	T	M	O	K	Y	P
S	R	A	I	S	I	N	S	O	C
G	O	N	O	Q	L	A	P	G	H
R	C	U	B	F	K	Y	I	U	E
U	C	T	P	E	A	S	N	R	E
N	O	S	N	U	T	S	A	T	S
S	L	M	E	A	T	S	C	C	E
L	I	V	E	R	A	H	H	Z	B

What calcium-rich or iron-rich foods have you eaten today? _____

_____

Investigate:
Mystery Mineral: I am found in the toothpaste that you brush with each day. I am also added to water in some cities. I help fight tooth decay. What am I?

You Are What You Eat!

You are not made out of pickles and carrots. The food you eat must be digested before your body can use it. Digested food is changed into nutrients which help your body grow and give you energy.

Unscramble the names of the six nutrient groups. Use the Word Bank.

netroips _____

ralmenis _____

afts _____

ratew _____

timnivas _____

droracbaytesh _____

Word Bank
proteins
vitamins
minerals
carbohydrates
water
fats

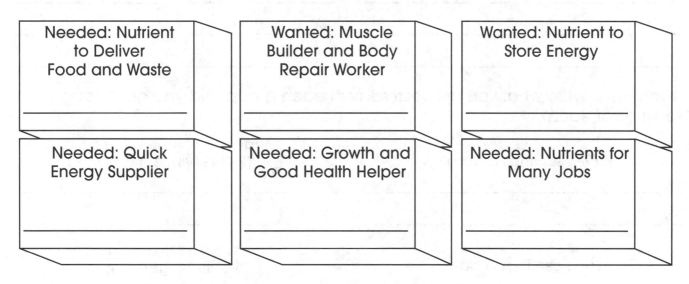

Nutrient Job Board

Match each nutrient from above with the job that it does for your body.
(**Hint:** Look back at pages 120-122 for help.)

Needed: Nutrient to Deliver Food and Waste	Wanted: Muscle Builder and Body Repair Worker	Wanted: Nutrient to Store Energy
_____	_____	_____
Needed: Quick Energy Supplier	**Needed: Growth and Good Health Helper**	**Needed: Nutrients for Many Jobs**
_____	_____	_____

Investigate:
How much of your body is water?

You Are What You Eat!

A nutritious diet helps your body fight diseases. Write the foods from the Word Bank in their correct category(s). Use references if necessary.

Word Bank

tomatoes	bread	eggs	milk	potatoes
oranges	sugar	fish	cereal	green beans
chicken	margarine	cheese	noodles	rice
	apples	red meat	butter	

Carbohydrates

_____   _____

_____   _____

_____   _____

_____   _____

_____   _____

Proteins

_____   _____

_____   _____

_____   _____

_____   _____

_____   _____

Fats

_____   _____

_____   _____

_____   _____

Minerals

_____   _____

_____   _____

_____   _____

Directions: Write what you ate yesterday in each group. Did you get enough servings of each?

Milk Group
(2–3 servings a day)

_____

_____

Meat-Egg-Nut-Bean Group
(2–3 servings a day)

_____

_____

Grain Group
(6-11 servings a day)

_____

_____

Fruit & Vegetable Groups
(5-9 servings a day)

_____

_____

Name _____

Munch, Munch - Nibble - Crunch!

Do you have a bad case of the munchies, crunchies or nibbles? Some snack foods can be healthy for you, while others are not. Foods that are lower on the food pyramid are usually much better for you because they contain smaller amounts of fat.

Take a **Snacker's Survey**.

Snacker's Survey

Write the food group to which each snack belongs. Then, using a scale of 1–10, with 1 being the lowest, give each snack a taste score and a nutrition score.

Snack	Food group	Taste score	Nutrition score
Apple			
Cheese			
Cookie			
Potato Chips			
Orange			
Carrot			
Cake			
Candy Bar			
Bagel			
Beef Jerky			
Popcorn			
Pretzels			

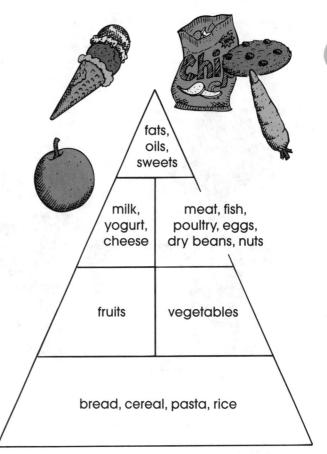

fats, oils, sweets

milk, yogurt, cheese

meat, fish, poultry, eggs, dry beans, nuts

fruits

vegetables

bread, cereal, pasta, rice

Fantastic Fact
Labels might not use the name sugar when it lists a sweetener. Watch for these other names for sugar.

Dextrose   Lactose
Corn Syrup   Fructose
Molasses   Sucrose

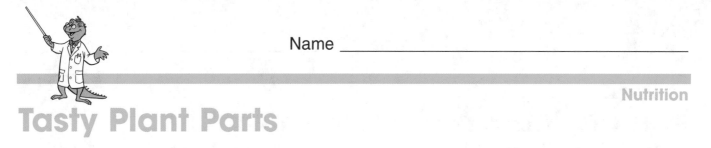

Tasty Plant Parts

All of the fruits and vegetables you eat come from plant parts. Some parts are much tastier than others. Carrot roots probably taste better than walnut tree roots.

Directions: Unscramble the names of the plant parts and label the pictures.

ealf_____   truif_____   frowel_____

smet_____   toors_____   eseds_____

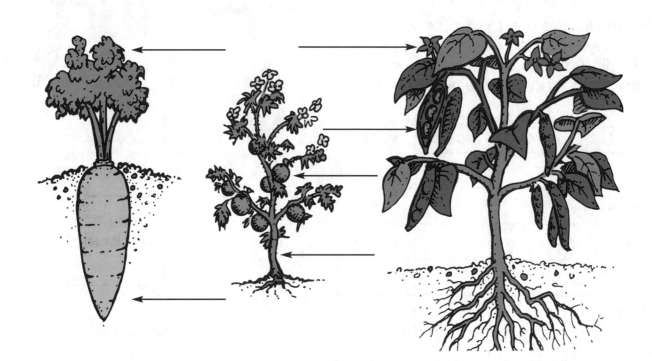

Extension:

Garbage Gardening

1. Collect and wash the seeds from some fresh fruits and vegetables such as pumpkins, apples or beans.

2. Soak the seeds overnight.

3. Plant the seeds ½ inch deep in a container of potting soil.

4. Keep the soil moist and in a warm place.

5. Watch for the seedlings!

Name _____

Vegetable Stand

Help Leon sort all of his produce. List the letter of each of the fruits and vegetables under the correct plant part.

Leon's Fresh Produce

A. celery · B. spinach · C. peanuts · D. asparagus · E. onion

F. carrots · G. broccoli · H. orange · I. radish · J. garlic

K. cabbage · L. apple · M. lettuce · N. peas · O. tomato

Stem	Leaf	Flower	Fruit	Seed	Root	Bulb
A						

Fruity Vegetables

Circle the vegetables that are the fruits (parts that contain seeds) of the plant.

pea pod	cabbage	carrot	string bean
cucumber	avocado	broccoli	green pepper
spinach	zucchini	potato	turnip

Extension:

How many kinds of vegetables can you name? Write a list of as many vegetables as you can name. Circle the ones you like. Draw an **X** in front of the ones you dislike. Draw a **?** in front of the ones you have never tasted.

Labels

Name _____

Labels give us all kinds of information about the foods we eat. The ingredients of a food are listed in a special order. The ingredient with the largest amount is listed first, the one with the next largest amount is listed second and so on.

Directions:

Complete the "Breakfast Table Label Survey" using the information from the label on this page.

Breakfast Table Label Survey

1. What does R.D.A. mean? _____

_____

2. Calories per serving with milk _____

3. Calories per serving without milk _____

4. Calories per $\frac{1}{2}$ cup serving of milk _____

5. Protein per serving with milk _____

6. Protein per serving without milk _____

7. Protein in $\frac{1}{2}$ cup serving of milk _____

8. Percentage U.S. R.D.A. of Vitamin C _____

9. First ingredient _____

10. Is sugar a listed ingredient? _____

    If yes, in what place is it listed? _____

11. Were any vitamins added? _____

12. What preservative was added? _____

Investigate
What food product has this ingredient label? Carbonated water, sugar, corn sweetener, natural flavorings, caramel color, phosphoric acid, caffeine.

Nutrition Information Per Serving

Serving Size: 1 OZ. (About 1 1/3 Cups) (28.35 g)

Servings Per Package: 14

	1 OZ. (28.35 g) Cereal	with 1/2 Cup (118 ml.) Vitamin D Fortified Whole Milk
Calories	110	190
Protein	1 g	5 g
Carbohydrate	25 g	31 g
Fat	1 g	5 g
Sodium	195 mg	255 mg

Percentages of U.S. Recommended Daily Allowances (U.S. RDA)

Protein	2%	8%
Vitamin A	25%	30%
Vitamin C	•	•
Thiamine	25%	30%
Riboflavin	25%	35%
Niacin	25%	25%
Calcium	•	15%
Iron	10%	10%
Vitamin D	10%	25%
Vitamin B6	25%	30%
Folic Acid	25%	25%
Vitamin B12	25%	30%
Phosphorus	2%	10%
Magnesium	2%	6%
Zinc	10%	15%
Copper	2%	4%

•Contains less than 2% of the U.S. RDA for these nutrients.

Ingredients: Corn Flour, Sugar, Oat Flour, Salt, Hydrogenated Coconut and/or Palm Kernel Oil, Corn Syrup, Honey and fortified with the following nutrients: Vitamin A Palmitate, Niacinamide, Iron, Zinc Oxide (Source of Zinc), Vitamin B6, Riboflavin (Vitamin B2), Thiamine Mononitrate (Vitamin B1), Vitamin B12, Folic Acid and Vitamin D2. BHA added to packaging material to preserve freshness.

Carbohydrate Information

	1 OZ. (28.35 g) Cereal	with 1/2 Cup (118 ml.) Whole Milk
Starch and Related Carbohydrates	14 g	14 g
Sucrose and Other Sugars	11 g	17 g
Total Carbohydrates	25 g	31 g

Name _____

Pizza Party

Nutritious food is not dull, boring food. Angelo's pizza is very nutritious. It has food from all six food groups.

Directions:

Match each ingredient with its food group.

Angelo's Pizza Supreme

1 loaf frozen bread dough, thawed
Mozzarella cheese (shredded)
hamburger (cooked)
pepperoni (sliced)
anchovies
sausage (cooked)
vegetable oil
pizza sauce (6 oz. can)
tomatoes (chopped)
onion (chopped)
green pepper (chopped)
mushrooms (sliced)
olives (sliced)

Bread and Cereal

Dairy

Meat and Protein

Fats

Fruit and Vegetable

Press thawed bread dough onto a greased pizza tin. Prick with a fork and brush with oil. Bake at 400° until light brown (about 10 minutes). Cover crust with tomato sauce, cheese and other ingredients. Bake at 400° until cheese is melted.

See the next page for more recipes for nutritious foods.

Challenge
Have fun creating your own nutritious pizza recipe. You can use food from any of the six food groups. Share your recipe with your family. Which recipe sounds yummy? Which recipe sounds nutritious? Which ingredient do you absolutely want to avoid?

Recipes

Barbeque Sauce (Makes one quart.)

Ingredients: 1-12 oz. can tomato paste
⅓ cup water
1½ cups stock
1 tablespoon vinegar
2 teaspoons lemon juice
½ cup chopped onion
½ cup chopped bell pepper
1 tablespoon Worcestershire sauce

1 tablespoon sugar
1 tablespoon honey
1 teaspoon garlic powder
1 tablespoon chili powder
1 tablespoon dry mustard
2 teaspoons dry basil
¼ teaspoon celery seed
¼ teaspoon salt (optional)

Directions: Combine all ingredients except basil and celery seed (and salt if using) in saucepan. Bring to low boil. Then, reduce heat and simmer for 20 minutes. Add basil, celery seed and salt and simmer for another five minutes.

Barbecued Chicken

Ingredients: 3½ pounds skinless chicken pieces, 1 cup barbecue sauce

Directions: Place chicken "skin" side down in baking pan. Baste with barbecue sauce. Bake at 350° for 20 minutes. Turn chicken over, baste and bake 25 minutes or until tender. Baste occasionally during cooking.

Oatmeal Crisps

Ingredients: vegetable oil spray
½ cup firmly packed brown sugar
½ cup vegetable oil
1 tablespoon honey
1 teaspoon vanilla extract
2 cups quick-cooking oats
½ teaspoon baking powder
1 teaspoon ground cinnamon

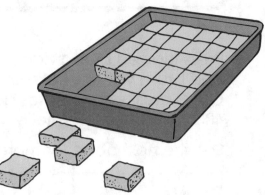

Directions: Preheat oven to 325°. Spray 9" square pan with vegetable oil spray. Combine oil, sugar, honey and vanilla in bowl. Add oats, baking powder and cinnamon. Mix until blended. Press mixture evenly into pan. Bake 20-25 minutes or until edges are golden brown. Cut into 36 squares while hot. Allow to cool in pan. Store in container with a loose-fitting lid.

Section 6

Plants

Name _____

Plant Parts

Green, flowering plants grow all around you. Beautiful red roses, tall cornstalks or prickly thistle weeds are all green, flowering plants. Green, flowering plants have six parts: **stem**, **root**, **leaf**, **flower**, **fruit** and **seeds**.

Directions: Complete the word puzzle. Then, use the words from the puzzle to label the plant.

Across:

1. I often have bright colors, but my real job is to make seeds.
3. I carry water from the roots to the leaves and food back to the roots.
4. I collect energy from the sun to make food for the plant.

Down:

1. I often taste delicious, but my job is to hold and protect the seeds.
2. I hold the plant tight like an anchor, but also collect water and minerals from the soil.
3. Someday a new plant will grow from me.

Fantastic Facts

The American Indians used every part of the sunflowers they grew. They ate the root and fed the stem and leaves to their animals. They ground the seeds for meal flour and used the yellow petals for dye. They even used the oil from the seeds for their hair.

Name _____

Garden Fresh Produce

Plants give us all the fruits, vegetables, grains, spices and herbs we eat. Amy has just planted her garden. List all of the fruits and vegetables in Amy's garden under the correct plant part that can be eaten.

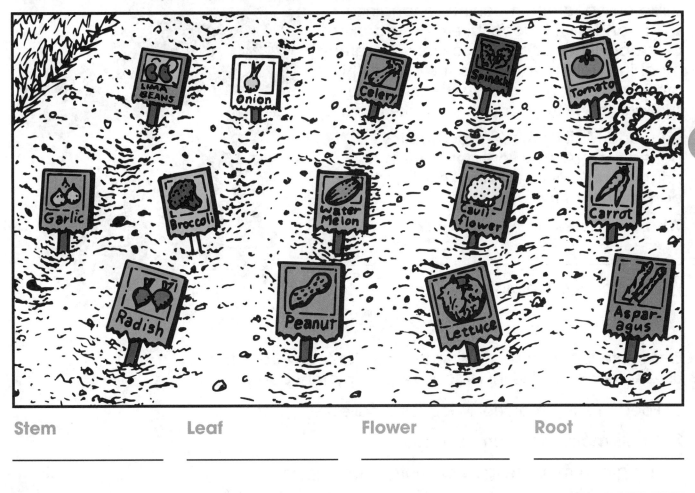

Stem _____

Leaf _____

Flower _____

Root _____

Fruit _____

Seed _____

Bulb _____

Make a chart like the one below. Complete the chart with as many kinds of fruits and vegetables as you can name.

Vegetable or Fruit	Root	Stem	Leaf	Flower	Bulb	Fruit	Seed
kiwi						✓	

Name _____

Light Work

Leaves work like little factories making food for the plant, using a green material called chlorophyll. In each leaf, chlorophyll is like a little "green machine," changing water and air into food. Like most machines, chlorophyll needs energy to work. The green machine gets its energy from sunlight. This process is called photosynthesis. Without sunlight, the leaves could not make food.

Amy and Matt both received healthy, potted flowers. Amy kept her plant in a bright, sunny window. Matt kept his in a dark corner of his room.

What happened to Amy's plant?

_____

What happened to Matt's plant?

_____

Amy's plant   **Matt's plant**

Complete the sentences using the highlighted words above. Use the numbered letters to answer the mystery question.

1. Food-making material in leaves is called __ __ __ __ __ __ __ __ __ __ .
                                              3   1 2 7

2. Plants make food from air and __ __ __ __ __ .
                                      4

3. The green machine gets its energy from __ __ __ __ __ __ __ __ .
                                              8 9

4. Food is made in the plant's __ __ __ __ __ __ .
                                  6

5. The color of chlorophyll is __ __ __ __ __ .
                                  5

Mystery Question

What is the scientific name for the process of making food with the help of light?

__ __ __ __ __ __ __ __ __ __ __ __ __ __
1 2 3 4 3 6 7 8 4 2 5 6 9 6

Investigate
What do we call the food that is made by the leaves?

Name _____

Flower Power

Flowers are beautiful to look at and pleasant to smell, but they also have a very important job. Most plants make seeds inside the flower.

Directions: Color and label each flower part. Use the chart below to help you.

Flower part	Description	Color
pistil	A large center stalk, often shaped like a water bottle.	yellow
stamen	A tall, thin stalk with a knobbed tip. It holds grains of pollen.	brown
petal	Brightly colored and sweet-smelling leaves.	red
sepal	Small leaf-like part at the base of the flower.	green
ovary	Ball-shaped part at the base of the pistil. This is where the seeds develop.	blue

Name _____

Jogging Geraniums

You will probably never see a flower running down the sidewalk, but you might see one climbing a fence. Most plants are rooted in one place, but they still move.

Roots, stems, leaves and even flowers move in different ways. The leaves grow toward the light. Roots will grow toward water. Even gravity will make a plant grow straight up in the air, away from the center of the earth.

Directions: Look at the three plants below.
Tell what made the plants "move" or grow the way they did.

_____   _____   _____

_____   _____   _____

_____   _____   _____

Scientists give special names to the three kinds of plant movements above. The names come from combining two words. Write the new word. Label the pictures above with the correct new word.

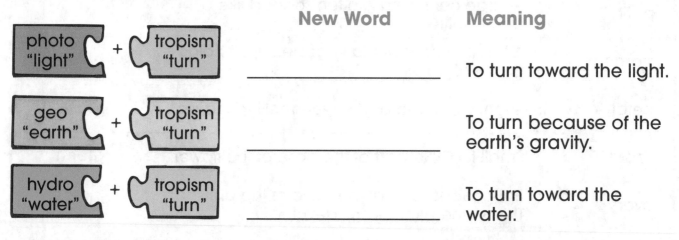

	New Word	Meaning
photo "light" + tropism "turn"	_____	To turn toward the light.
geo "earth" + tropism "turn"	_____	To turn because of the earth's gravity.
hydro "water" + tropism "turn"	_____	To turn toward the water.

Name _____

Dirty Work

Soil does more than just make your hands dirty. It is important for making plants grow.

Soil is made of rock, humus, air, and water. The rock is often in the form of sand or clay. Sand is easy to dig, but it doesn't hold water. Clay holds water, but is packed too tightly to let plants grow. Humus is matter that was once alive, but now it is decayed or rotted. Humus gives nutrients to the soil. Plants need nutrients to grow.

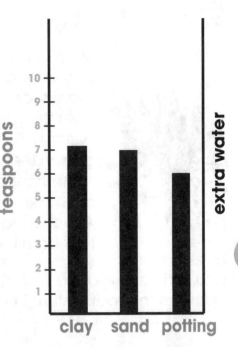

Matt's Experiment

Matt wanted to find out how much water three kinds of soil would hold. He tested clay, sand, and potting soil. (Potting soil is a mixture of clay, sand, and humus.) Matt took three baby food jars and filled each one half-way with one of the soils. Then, he poured 10 teaspoons full of water into each one. After mixing each jar of soil and water, he poured off the extra water. Matt measured the extra water.

Directions: Look at the graph to see his results.

1. Which soil had the most extra water? _____

2. Which soil had the least extra water? _____

3. To find how much water each soil held, you must subtract the extra water from 10 teaspoons. Look at the example and then find out how much water each of the other two soils held.

   Clay: 10 teaspoons – 7 teaspoons = 3 teaspoons of water held.
   Sand: 10 teaspoons –____ = ____ teaspoons of water held.
   Potting: 10 teaspoons –____ = ____ teaspoons of water held.

4. Draw your results of the "water held" for each soil on Matt's chart. Use a red crayon or marker.

5. Which soil had the most nutrients?_____

6. Which soil would you use for planting? _____
   Why?_____

Challenge
Try Matt's experiment on your own. Compare your results.

Name _____

Slurp, Slurp

Slurp, slurp! On a hot summer day, a cherry soda is cool and refreshing. Plants like to drink, too. The plant's root system slurps water and minerals from the ground. There are two kinds of root systems. Some plants have one main root that grows deep into the ground. This is called a tap root. Other plants have shallow roots with many branches. These roots are called fibrous roots. Attached to both root systems are tiny root hairs that do all the work of absorbing water.

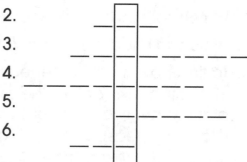

Directions:
Color the tap root orange. Color the fibrous roots brown. Write the name of the root system in the blank space. Label the root hairs.

Use the highlighted words to complete the word puzzle.
Then, find the mystery word in the puzzle.

1. The _____ root grows deep into the ground.

2. Roots "slurp" water and _____ .

3. Fibrous roots have many _____ .

4. Tiny root _____ absorb water.

5. There are _____ types of root systems.

6. _____ roots grow shallow.

Use the mystery word in the puzzle to solve the riddle.

A ship's is made of iron,
To hold it fast at berth.
A plant's roots work like one,
To hold it firm in the earth.

What is it? _____

Fantastic Fact
The American Indians boiled the balsam root to make tea. They drank the tea when they had a sore throat, cough, pneumonia or hay fever.

Plants Need . . .

Plants need light, air, water, soil and proper temperature in order to grow.

You will need:

six growing plants (identical if possible), two clear plastic bags, large jar, water, rubber band, a science notebook

Directions:

Choose six healthy plants. (Try to find six that are identical—this will make it easier to make observations and draw conclusions.) Take time to examine the plants, perhaps measuring their height, number of leaves, color, etc.

Then, vary the conditions as follows:

Plant 1—Put in an unlighted area. Water regularly.

Plant 2—Do not water. Set in sunlight.

Plant 3—Remove plant from the pot. Put a plastic bag around the roots and soil. Secure the bag with a rubber band. Then, submerge the entire plant in a large jar filled with water so that no parts come in contact with air.

Plants Need . . .

Plant 4—Place the plant in an area of extreme temperature (i.e., on the heater, outside the window).

Plant 5—Take the plant out of the pot. Wash the soil away from the roots. Place the roots in a container of water.

Plant 6—Control Plant—Give this plant normal care with regular watering, exposure to light, etc.

Observe each plant for one week and record any changes that occur in your notebook. After one week, identify what was deprived from each plant. You will generally find that:

Plant 1 will turn yellow.

Plant 2 will shrivel and die.

Plant 3 will rot.

Plant 4 will wilt or have stunted growth.

Plant 5 will eventually die due to lack of nutrients.

Plant 6 will thrive and show growth.

You should conclude that plants need light, air, water, soil and the proper temperature in order to thrive.

Tree-mendous Plant

What is the largest plant growing near your home? It is probably a tree. It may be a maple, oak, pine or palm. All trees have many of the same parts as the plants that grow in your garden— only much larger.

The riddles below tell about the jobs of the tree parts. Use the tree parts listed in the Word Bank to solve each riddle. Then, label the parts of the tree.

Word Bank
seed
trunk
leaves
roots
bark

• *Green and flat*
  Or needle-like,
  We make food by day
  And rest at night.

  _____

• *From roots to branches,*
  Short or long,
  My tough wood
  Keeps me tall and strong.

  _____

• *Scattered by wind*
  When breezes blow,
  I'll make a new tree
  When I sprout and grow.

  _____

• *Thin-like hair,*
  Or thick and round,
  We hold the tree
  Firmly in the ground.

  _____

• *Rough or smooth,*
  A very tough cover,
  I keep out insects,
  Fire and weather.

  _____

Investigate
Very few trees have smooth bark. Find out why most bark is rough and has scales or cracks.

Name _____

Leaves or Needles

Everyone has seen trees, but how do you tell one kind of tree from another? Trees have different leaves, seeds, bark and flowers. There are two main kinds of trees. The conifers are trees with needle-like leaves. Their seeds are found in cones. Conifers stay green all year long. The broad-leaved trees have leaves of different sizes and shapes. Broad-leaved trees often lose their leaves in the fall. In warm regions, some broad-leaved trees keep their leaves all year long.

Find the hidden names of conifer trees in the conifer tree. Find the hidden names of broad-leaved trees in the broad-leaved tree. Use the Word Bank to help you.

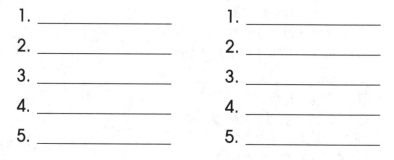

Word Bank	
oak	ash
pine	elm
beech	spruce
redwood	cedar
fir	maple

1. _____ 1. _____

2. _____ 2. _____

3. _____ 3. _____

4. _____ 4. _____

5. _____ 5. _____

Directions: Solve the word puzzle.

Across:

2. Conifers stay _____ all year long.
3. Broad-leaved trees lose their leaves in the _____.
4. Conifer seeds are in _____.

Down:

1. Conifer leaves are shaped like _____.

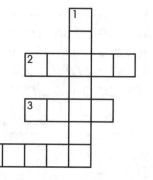

Name _____

"Color-fall" Leaves

Directions: Fill in the blanks with words from the Word Bank.

Some broad-leaved trees like the maple are very colorful in the _____.
The beautiful reds, oranges and yellows were always in the leaves. But their colors
were hidden by the _____ during the spring and _____.

The green is _____. Chlorophyll is the matter in the _____
that makes food for the tree. When fall comes, the tree stops making food, and
the green chlorophyll dies. As the green disappears, the beautiful colors of fall
appear.

Complete the word puzzle using words from the Word Bank.
Find the hidden word in the puzzle. Use it to answer the riddle at the bottom.

1. Food is made in the _____.   1. _ _ _ _ _ ⬜

2. Trees make food in the spring and _____.   2. _ ⬜ _ _ _ _

3. Fall colors are hidden by the _____.   3. _ ⬜ _ _

4. Leaves stop making food in the _____.   4. _ ⬜ _ _

5. The green matter that makes food is _____. 5. _ _ _ ⬜ _ _ _ _ _ _

Word Bank

fall	green
leaves	summer
chlorophyll	

Kids really like me,
I'm food for the trees.
My taste is really sweet,
And I'm made by the leaves.

What am I? _____

Name _____

Living History Books

You can learn a lot about a tree by reading its special calendar of rings. Every year a tree grows a new layer of wood. This makes the tree trunk get fatter and fatter. The new layer makes a ring.

You can see the rings on a freshly cut tree stump. When the growing season is wet, the tree grows a lot and the rings are wide. When the season is dry, the tree grows very little. Then, the rings are narrow.

Directions: This tree was planted in 1976. Use the picture clues to color the rings of the tree stump. Where will the very first ring be?

1976
The tree was planted. Color the ring **green**.

1991
The tree was cut down. Color the ring **yellow**.

1985
A very wet growing season. Color the ring **blue**.

1990
A very dry growing season. Color the ring **brown**.

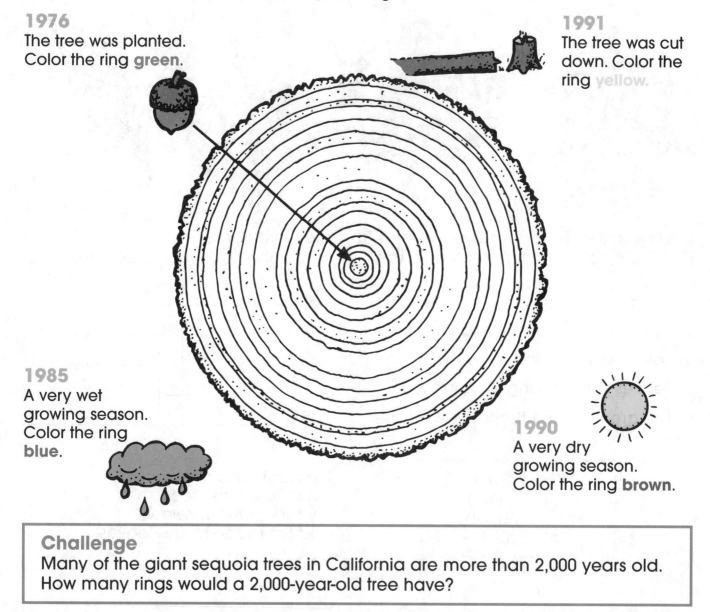

Challenge
Many of the giant sequoia trees in California are more than 2,000 years old. How many rings would a 2,000-year-old tree have?

144

How Does Your Garden Grow?

Experience planting, caring for, harvesting
and packaging vegetables by planting a small garden
of radishes.

You will need:

paper cups
radish seeds
potting soil

Directions:

1. Fill the paper cups three-fourths full with soil.

2. Plant radish seeds according to the package
   directions. (Radishes are great for this activity as they are fast-growing
   vegetables, and you will be able to harvest them within 20-30 days.)

3. When they are ready to harvest, or pull, wash them and package
   them in sandwich bags. Enjoy!

Extension:

Throughout the care and growth of vegetable production, discuss the various ways in
which vegetables are packaged. Have samples of fresh, frozen, canned and dried
vegetables available to examine. Discuss where each should be stored.

Name That Vegetable

This is a great project for the spring when a larger variety of vegetables is available. Visit your local produce department and purchase several types of common vegetables as well as some that you might not have ever tried. Arrange your purchases on a table to examine. Name all the vegetables that you already know.

Using nonfiction books, research background information about the vegetables you have, such as where they grow, how they are grown, which is the edible (eatable) part of the plant and how to prepare it to eat.

Copy the garden markers on the following pages. Summarize your facts about the vegetables on the marker. Draw and color a picture of that vegetable. Finally, place all the markers by the actual vegetable on the table.

Extension:

The leading vegetable-producing states are California, Idaho, Washington, Wisconsin and Oregon. Locate these states on a map. Which vegetables on the display table might have come from these states? What other areas do the produce come from? Which produce, if any, came from your state?

Name That Vegetable

Use this page to make your garden markers.

This page intentionally left blank.

Name That Vegetable

Use this page to make your garden markers.

This page intentionally left blank.

Dissecting a Seed

Directions:

One day prior to beginning the experiment, soak several dried beans in water. They will swell as they absorb some of the water.

When you are ready to begin, get a paper towel and a lima bean. First, identify the seed coat of the bean. (This is the outer protective skin or coating of the seed.) Carefully rub the seed between your forefinger and thumb. The seed coat should be soft enough to crack and peel open. The large oval part of the seed is the cotyledon. This is the part of the seed that contains stored food used by the embryo for its initial growth (before it breaks out of the seed coat and can obtain nutrients from soil and water).

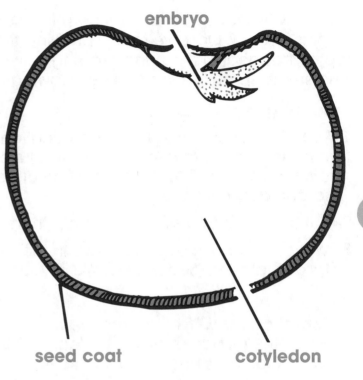

embryo

seed coat   cotyledon

You should also be able to see the rudimentary plant contained in the seed. This is the embryo, or baby plant. Observe and explore these seed parts using a magnifying glass.

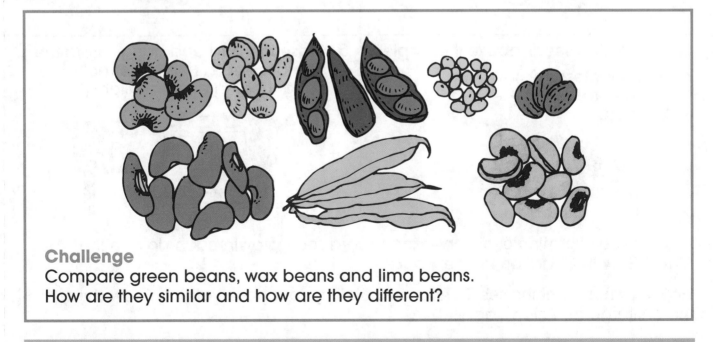

Challenge
Compare green beans, wax beans and lima beans.
How are they similar and how are they different?

Sprouting Seeds Without Soil

This activity shows how a seed germinates and begins to grow. Observe roots, sprouting from the top of the seed, turning and growing downward, and stems, sprouting from below, growing upward.

Preparing the Seeds:

1. To help prevent mold in the germination bags, dip the bean and pea seeds in a solution of diluted bleach (1 tablespoon of chlorine bleach to one quart of water).

2. Put the seeds in a strainer and dip them in the solution for 15 seconds.

3. Without rinsing, place the seeds in the germination bags—plastic sandwich bags that seal. (See below.) Wash your hands after handling the seeds.

Assembling the Germination Bags:

1. Place the paper towel in the clear bag, folding as necessary so that it will lay flat.

2. Staple across approximately 1 in. from the bottom of the bag.

3. Position the seeds above the staples.

4. Add 3 tablespoons of water to the bag.

5. Close the bag and hang it from the side of a table. (It is better not to hang these in direct sunlight.)

As the seeds germinate, observe and record seed growth each day on the "Seed Growth Chart" on the next page.

Note: Do not plant the seeds. After completing your observations, throw away the entire germination bag.

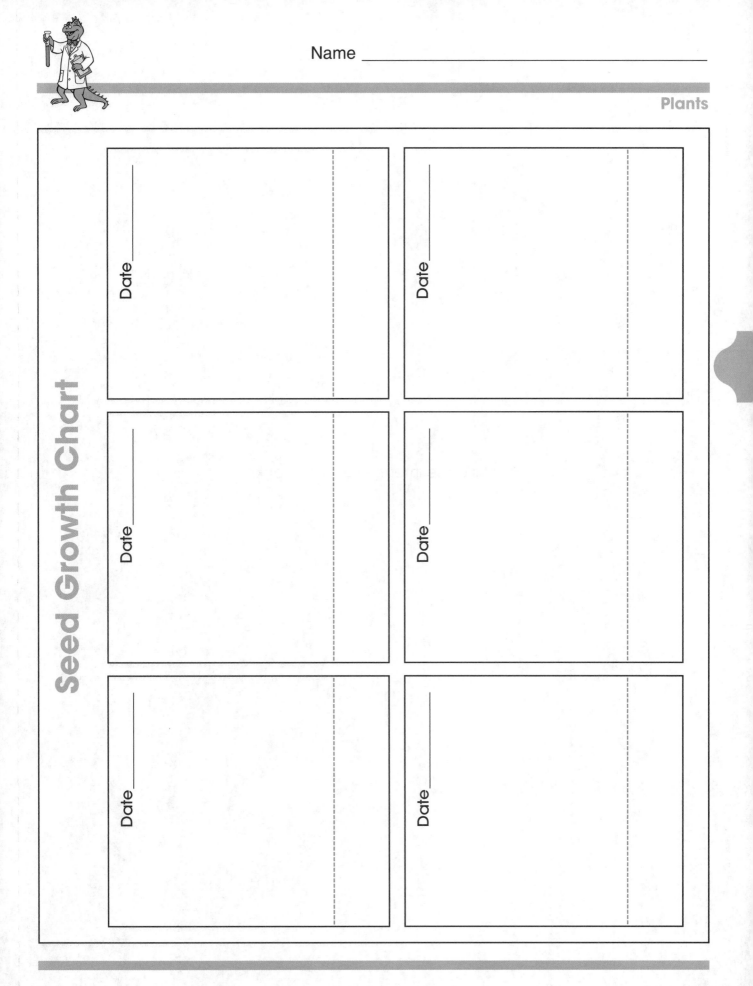

Seed Growth Chart

Date _____

Date _____

Date _____

Date _____

Date _____

Date _____

This page intentionally left blank.

Name _____

Cruising Coconuts

"Look at this coconut!" Amy called to Matt as they walked along the beach. Safe inside its thick husk, the coconut had floated across the water. Once it washed up on shore, the green leaves sprouted from this large seed.

Seeds travel in many ways. Below are five ways that seeds travel. Tell how each seed travels.

Fantastic Fact
Blast Off—The seed pod of the "touch-me-not" swells as it gets ripe. Finally, the seed pod bursts and launches seeds in all directions.

155

Corny Medicine

Directions:

Use the words from the Word Bank to complete the puzzle. Cross out each word as you use it. The remaining words will help you answer the "Corny Medicine" riddle.

Across:

4. Deep-growing type of root
6. Beautiful, seed-making part of plant
7. Brightly colored "leafy" parts of the flower
9. Large part of seed that supplies food
10. Sweet food made by the leaves

Down:

1. Making food with the help of light
2. Green food-making material in a leaf
3. Plant's "food factory"
5. Plant's anchor
8. Plants get their energy from the _____.

Corny Medicine

Why did the cornstalk go to the doctor's office?

_____

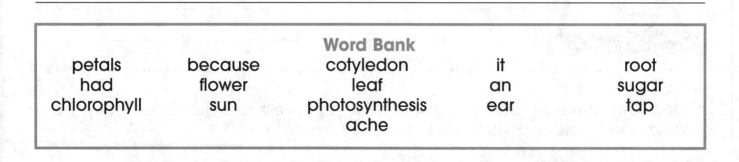

Word Bank

petals	because	cotyledon	it	root
had	flower	leaf	an	sugar
chlorophyll	sun	photosynthesis	ear	tap
		ache		

156

Section 7

Solar System

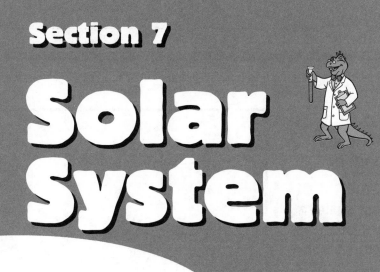

Name _____

The Solar System

Our **solar system** is made up of the sun and all the objects that go around, or **orbit**, the sun.

The sun is the only star in our solar system. It gives heat and light to the eight planets in the solar system. The planets and their moons all orbit the sun.

The time it takes for each planet to orbit the sun is called a **year**. A year on Earth is 365 days. Planets closer to the sun have shorter years. Their orbit is shorter. Planets farther from the sun take longer to orbit, so their years are longer.

Asteroids, comets and meteors are also part of our solar system.

Draw the eight planets around the sun.

Underline:

The solar system is: the sun without the nine planets.

the sun and all the objects that orbit it.

Check:

☐ is the center of our solar system.

☐ is the only star in our solar system.

☐ is a planet in our solar system.

☐ gives heat and light to our solar system.

Write:

A _____ is the time it takes for a planet to orbit the sun.
         month   year

Match:

Planets closer to the sun . . .   have a longer year.
Planets farther from the sun . . .   have a shorter year.

Name _____

Sun-sational Puzzle

If we could travel from the sun's core, or center, to the surface we would be at the photosphere, which is the surface part of the sun seen from Earth. Flashes of light seen by scientists on the surface of the sun are called flares, and dark patches are called sunspots. Sometimes eruptions of gas, called prominences, can also be seen during a solar eclipse. Just above the sun's surface is a layer of bright gases called the chromosphere. The corona, the region beyond the chromosphere, consists of white concentric circles of light that radiate from the sun.

Directions:

Use words from the Word Box to complete the crossword puzzle.

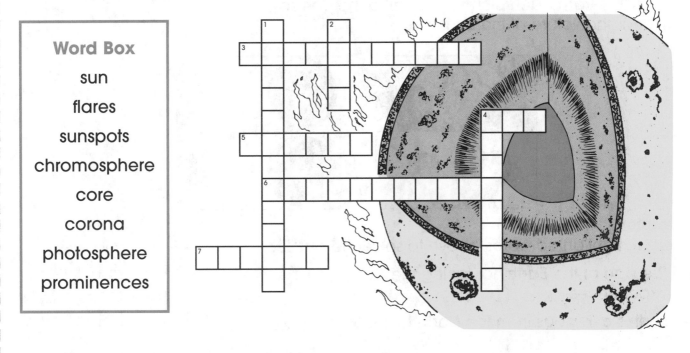

Word Box

sun

flares

sunspots

chromosphere

core

corona

photosphere

prominences

Across:

3. the part of the sun you can see

4. huge glowing ball of gases at the center of our solar system

5. the region of the sun's atmosphere above the chromosphere

6. big, bright eruptions of gas

7. flashes of light on the sun's surface

Down:

1. the middle part of the sun's atmosphere

2. the center of the sun

4. dark patches that sometimes appear on the sun

Name _____

Spinning Top

Whir-r-r-ling! Matt's top is spinning very fast. Just like Matt's top, the Earth is also spinning.

The Earth spins about an imaginary line that is drawn from the North **Pole** to the South Pole through the center of the Earth. This line is called Earth's **axis**. Instead of using the word "spin," though, we say that the Earth **rotates** on its axis.

The Earth rotates **one** time every 24 hours. The part of the Earth facing the sun experiences day. The side that is away from the sun's light experiences **night**.

Draw a line from each picture of Matt to the correct day or night picture of the Earth.

Directions:
Use the highlighted words above to solve the puzzle.

1. The part of the Earth not facing the sun experiences _____.

2. Earth's axis goes from the North to the South _____.

3. The Earth spins, or _____.

4. Number of times the Earth rotates in 24 hours.

5. Imaginary line on which the Earth rotates.

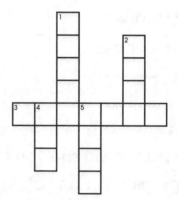

Fantastic Fact
At the Equator, the Earth is spinning at a speed of almost 1,000 miles per hour. At a point halfway between the poles and the Equator, the speed is about 800 miles per hour. Spin a globe and you will see how this happens.

Periodic Table of the Elements

Z	Symbol	Name	Atomic Mass	Electron Configuration
1	H	Hydrogen	1.00794	1
88	Ra	Radium	(226)	2, 8, 18, 32, 18, 8, 2
41	Nb	Niobium	92.90638	2, 8, 18, 12, 1
77	Ir	Iridium	192.217	2, 8, 18, 32, 15, 2
114	Uuq		(289)	
66	Dy	Dysprosium	162.50	2, 8, 18, 28, 8, 2
96	Cm	Curium	(247)	2, 8, 18, 32, 25, 9, 2
48	Cd	Cadmium	112.411	2, 8, 18, 18, 2
8	O	Oxygen	15.9994	2, 6
2	He	Helium	4.002602	2
3	Li	Lithium	6.941	2, 1
21	Sc	Scandium	44.95591	2, 8, 9, 2
42	Mo	Molybdenum	95.94	2, 8, 18, 13, 1
78	Pt	Platinum	195.078	2, 8, 18, 32, 17, 1
116	Uuh		(289)	
67	Ho	Holmium	164.93032	2, 8, 18, 29, 8, 2
97	Bk	Berkelium	(247)	2, 8, 18, 32, 27, 8, 2
49	In	Indium	114.818	2, 8, 18, 18, 3
9	F	Fluorine	18.9984032	2, 7
10	Ne	Neon	20.1797	2, 8
11	Na	Sodium	22.989768	2, 8, 1
22	Ti	Titanium	47.867	2, 8, 10, 2
43	Tc	Technetium	(98)	2, 8, 18, 13, 2
79	Au	Gold	196.96654	2, 8, 18, 32, 18, 1
57	La	Lanthanum	138.9055	2, 8, 18, 18, 9, 2
68	Er	Erbium	167.26	2, 8, 18, 30, 8, 2
98	Cf	Californium	(251)	2, 8, 18, 32, 28, 8, 2
50	Sn	Tin	118.710	2, 8, 18, 18, 4
14	Si	Silicon	28.0855	2, 8, 4
18	Ar	Argon	39.948	2, 8, 8
19	K	Potassium	39.0983	2, 8, 8, 1
23	V	Vanadium	50.9415	2, 8, 11, 2
44	Ru	Ruthenium	101.07	2, 8, 18, 15, 1
104	Rf	Rutherfordium	(261)	2, 8, 18, 32, 10, 2
89	Ac	Actinium	(227)	2, 8, 18, 32, 18, 9, 2
69	Tm	Thulium	168.93421	2, 8, 18, 31, 8, 2
99	Es	Einsteinium	(252)	2, 8, 18, 32, 29, 8, 2
51	Sb	Antimony	121.76	2, 8, 18, 18, 5
15	P	Phosphorus	30.973762	2, 8, 5
36	Kr	Krypton	83.80	2, 8, 18, 8
37	Rb	Rubidium	85.4678	2, 8, 18, 8, 1
24	Cr	Chromium	51.9961	2, 8, 13, 1
45	Rh	Rhodium	102.9055	2, 8, 18, 16, 1
105	Db	Dubnium	(262)	2, 8, 18, 32, 11, 2
58	Ce	Cerium	140.116	2, 8, 18, 20, 8, 2
70	Yb	Ytterbium	173.04	2, 8, 18, 32, 8, 2
100	Fm	Fermium	(257)	2, 8, 18, 32, 30, 8, 2
80	Hg	Mercury	200.59	2, 8, 18, 32, 18, 2
16	S	Sulfur	32.066	2, 8, 6
54	Xe	Xenon	131.29	2, 8, 18, 18, 8
55	Cs	Cesium	132.90543	2, 8, 18, 18, 8, 1
25	Mn	Manganese	54.93805	2, 8, 13, 2
46	Pd	Palladium	106.42	2, 8, 18, 18, 0
106	Sg	Seaborgium	(266)	2, 8, 18, 32, 12, 2
59	Pr	Praseodymium	140.90765	2, 8, 18, 21, 8, 2
71	Lu	Lutetium	174.967	2, 8, 18, 32, 9, 2
101	Md	Mendelevium	(258)	2, 8, 18, 32, 31, 8, 2
81	Tl	Thallium	204.3833	2, 8, 18, 32, 18, 3
17	Cl	Chlorine	35.4527	2, 8, 7
86	Rn	Radon	(222)	2, 8, 18, 32, 18, 8
87	Fr	Francium	(223)	2, 8, 18, 32, 18, 8, 1
26	Fe	Iron	55.845	2, 8, 14, 2
47	Ag	Silver	107.8682	2, 8, 18, 18, 1
107	Bh	Bohrium	(262)	2, 8, 18, 32, 13, 2
60	Nd	Neodymium	144.24	2, 8, 18, 22, 8, 2
90	Th	Thorium	232.0381	2, 8, 18, 32, 18, 10, 2
102	No	Nobelium	(259)	2, 8, 18, 32, 32, 8, 2
82	Pb	Lead	207.2	2, 8, 18, 32, 18, 4
33	As	Arsenic	74.92159	2, 8, 18, 5
113	Uut			
4	Be	Beryllium	9.012182	2, 2
27	Co	Cobalt	58.9332	2, 8, 15, 2
72	Hf	Hafnium	178.49	2, 8, 18, 32, 10, 2
108	Hs	Hassium	(263)	2, 8, 18, 32, 14, 2
61	Pm	Promethium	(145)	2, 8, 18, 23, 8, 2
91	Pa	Protactinium	231.03588	2, 8, 18, 32, 20, 9, 2
103	Lr	Lawrencium	(262)	2, 8, 18, 32, 32, 9, 2
83	Bi	Bismuth	208.98037	2, 8, 18, 32, 18, 5
34	Se	Selenium	78.96	2, 8, 18, 6
115	Uup			
12	Mg	Magnesium	24.305	2, 8, 2
28	Ni	Nickel	58.6934	2, 8, 16, 2
73	Ta	Tantalum	180.9479	2, 8, 18, 32, 11, 2
109	Mt	Meitnerium	(268)	2, 8, 18, 32, 15, 2
62	Sm	Samarium	150.36	2, 8, 18, 24, 8, 2
92	U	Uranium	238.0289	2, 8, 18, 32, 21, 9, 2
13	Al	Aluminum	26.981539	2, 8, 3
84	Po	Polonium	(209)	2, 8, 18, 32, 18, 6
35	Br	Bromine	79.904	2, 8, 18, 7
117	Uus			
20	Ca	Calcium	40.078	2, 8, 8, 2
29	Cu	Copper	63.546	2, 8, 18, 1
74	W	Tungsten	183.84	2, 8, 18, 32, 12, 2
110	Ds	Darmstadtium	(271)	2, 8, 18, 32, 17, 1
63	Eu	Europium	151.964	2, 8, 18, 25, 8, 2
93	Np	Neptunium	(237)	2, 8, 18, 32, 22, 9, 2
30	Zn	Zinc	65.39	2, 8, 18, 2
5	B	Boron	10.811	2, 3
52	Te	Tellurium	127.60	2, 8, 18, 18, 6
38	Sr	Strontium	87.62	2, 8, 18, 8, 2
39	Y	Yttrium	88.90585	2, 8, 18, 9, 2
75	Re	Rhenium	186.207	2, 8, 18, 32, 13, 2
111	Rg	Roentgenium	(272)	2, 8, 18, 32, 18, 1
64	Gd	Gadolinium	157.25	2, 8, 18, 25, 9, 2
94	Pu	Plutonium	(244)	2, 8, 18, 32, 24, 8, 2
31	Ga	Gallium	69.723	2, 8, 18, 3
6	C	Carbon	12.0107	2, 4
53	I	Iodine	126.90447	2, 8, 18, 18, 7
56	Ba	Barium	137.327	2, 8, 18, 18, 8, 2
40	Zr	Zirconium	91.224	2, 8, 18, 10, 2
76	Os	Osmium	190.23	2, 8, 18, 32, 14, 2
112	Uub	Ununbium	(277)	2, 8, 18, 32, 18, 2
65	Tb	Terbium	158.92534	2, 8, 18, 27, 8, 2
95	Am	Americium	(243)	2, 8, 18, 32, 25, 8, 2
32	Ge	Germanium	72.61	2, 8, 18, 4
7	N	Nitrogen	14.00674	2, 5
85	At	Astatine	(210)	2, 8, 18, 32, 18, 7

Name _____

Lo-o-o-ng Trip

What is the longest trip you have ever taken? Was it 100 miles? 500 miles? Maybe it was more than 1,000 miles. You probably didn't know it, but last year you traveled 620 million miles.

The Earth travels in a path around the sun called its **orbit**. Earth's orbit is almost 620 million miles. It takes 1 year, or 365 days, for the Earth to orbit or **revolve** around the sun.

Earth's orbit is not a perfect circle. It is a special shape called an **ellipse**.

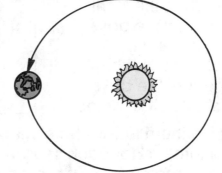

1. How long does it take for the Earth to revolve around the sun? _____

2. How many times has the Earth revolved around the sun since you were born?

_____

3. How many miles has the Earth traveled in orbit since you were born?

_____

4. Draw an **X** on Earth's orbit to show where it will be in six months.

Experiment:

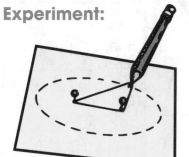

You can draw an ellipse. Place two straight pins about 3 inches apart in a piece of cardboard. Tie the ends of a 10 inch piece of string to the pins. Place your pencil inside the string. Keeping the string tight, draw an ellipse.

Make four different ellipses by changing the length of the string and the distance between the pins. How do the ellipses change?

Fantastic Fact
Hold on tight. The Earth travels at a speed of 62,000 miles per hour in its orbital path around the sun.

Name _____

Leaning Into Summer

Why isn't it summer all year long? The seasons change because the Earth is tilted like the Leaning Tower of Pisa. As the Earth orbits the sun, it stays tilting in the same direction in space.

Let's look at the seasons in the Northern Hemisphere. When the North Pole is tilting toward the sun, the days become warmer and longer. It is summer. Six months later, the North Pole tilts away from the sun. The days become cooler and shorter. It is winter.

Directions: Label the Northern Hemisphere's seasons on the chart below. Write a make-believe weather forecast for each season. Each forecast should show what the weather is like in your region for that season.

Today's Weather

High_____ Low_____

Sunrise_____

Sunset _____

Forecast

_____

_____

_____

_____

Today's Weather

High_____ Low_____

Sunrise_____

Sunset _____

Forecast

_____

_____

_____

_____

Today's Weather

High_____ Low_____

Sunrise_____

Sunset _____

Forecast

_____

_____

_____

_____

Today's Weather

High_____ Low_____

Sunrise_____

Sunset _____

Forecast

_____

_____

_____

_____

Investigate
Where is the "land of the midnight sun"? Why does it have that name?

Name _____

Just Imagine . . .

Earth is a very special planet because it is the only planet known to have life. Only Earth has the necessities to support life—water, air, moderate temperatures and suitable air pressure. Earth is about 92,960,000 miles from the sun and is 7,926 miles in diameter. Its highest recorded temperature was 136°F in Libya and the lowest was -127°F in Antarctica.

Venus is known as Earth's "twin" because the two planets are so similar in size. At about 67,230,000 miles from the sun, Venus is 7,521 miles in diameter. Venus is the brightest planet in the sky, as seen from Earth, and is brighter even than the stars. The temperature on the surface of this planet is about 850°F.

Mercury is the planet closest to the sun. It is about 35,980,000 miles from the sun and is 3,031 miles in diameter. The temperature on this planet ranges from -315°F to 648°F.

Pretend you were going to Venus or Mercury for spring break. Make a list of the things you would bring (you may have to invent them in order to survive) and draw a picture of the vehicle that would take you there. Write about your experiences on another sheet of paper.

Things I Need to Take   **Vehicle**

_____

_____

_____

_____

_____

_____

_____

_____

_____

_____

Moon's "Faces"

As the moon orbits the Earth, we often see different amounts of the moon's lighted part. Sometimes it looks like a circle, half-circle or thin curved sliver. These different shapes are the moon's **phases**.

Directions:

Cut out the moon's phases (as seen from Earth) at the bottom of this page. Glue them next to the moon phase as seen from space. Label the pictures using the words in the Word Bank. Use a science book to help you.

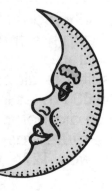

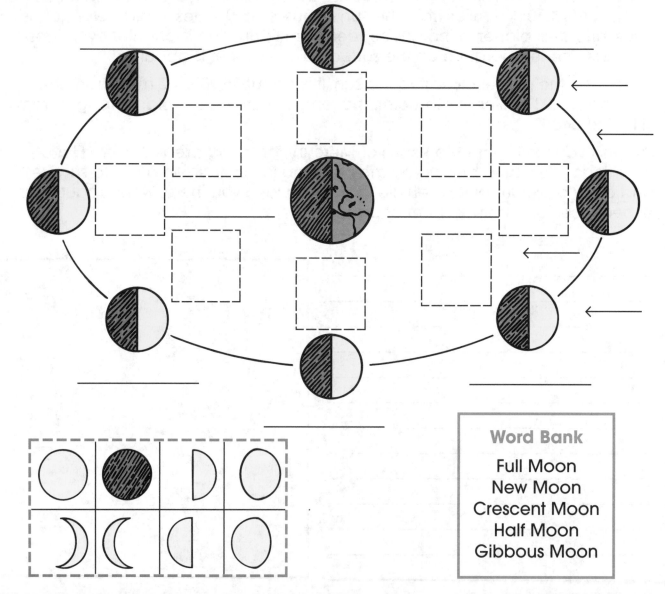

Word Bank

Full Moon
New Moon
Crescent Moon
Half Moon
Gibbous Moon

Moon Logs

Keep a log of the moon's phases.

You will need:

four sheets (8"x 12") of black construction paper
a stapler
a white crayon
a large calendar

Directions:

Create a moon log by folding four sheets of black
construction paper in half and stapling them together. Using a white crayon,
create a title and decorate the cover.

It is best to begin the moon observations with the "new moon." Observe the moon
twice a week (or every three days), weather permitting. If clouds interfere with
your planned dates to observe the moon, you may be forced to postpone it.

In your log, record the date of observation, and use half of a page on which to
draw the shape of the moon. Pay careful attention to which side of the moon is
illuminated. Be sure to draw it exactly as you see it. As the month progresses,
record your findings on a calendar.

Look up vocabulary such as waxing, waning, new, crescent, full, first quarter, etc.

Find out: Why the moon shines. Why its shape seems to change. Why we see only
one side of the moon. What does the surface of the moon look like from Earth?
What has NASA recently discovered regarding the moon?

When the log is complete and you are
observing another new moon, discuss with
your parent the amount of time that has
passed since you began logging the moon.
Relate the cycle of moon phases to the
calendar. Make predictions regarding
specific phases of the upcoming month (i.e.,
How much time will pass between the new
moon and the full moon? Predict the date we
will see the next full moon, etc.). You can add
the final touch to your log by writing a poem
about the moon and writing the final draft on
the inside cover of your moon log.

Moon Phases

You will need:

a ping-pong ball
heavy thread, needles
brass fasteners, a shoe box
scissors
a flashlight
index cards

Response Card				
Position	1	2	3	4
Phase				

Explain what conditions would be like when the moon is full. _____

_____

_____

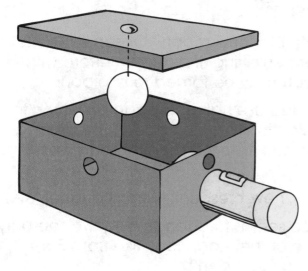

Directions:

Cut an opening at one end of a shoe box large enough for a flashlight to fit through from the inside of the box. Cut a 1" viewing hole on all four sides of the box. Thread a needle with heavy thread and tie a knot. Put the needle through the top of the ping-pong ball, through its opposite side and through the bottom of the box lid up through the top. Cut the thread off close to the needle. Put a fastener into the lid near where the needle entered. Tie the thread around the fastener so that the ball hangs into the box about an inch and a half.

Put the lid on the box. Turn on the flashlight. Number each side of the box 1, 2, 3, 4. Look through the viewing holes. Write which phase of the moon you see from each position on the card. Think of yourself as an observer on Earth, the flashlight as the sun, and the ball as the moon. Tell what conditions would actually be when you see each phase.

Space Shadows

Have you ever held your hand up in front of a bright light to make shadow pictures on the wall? The sun and moon can cast shadows on the Earth just like the light and your hand cast shadow pictures on the wall.

Sometimes the moon passes between the Earth and the sun in just the right place to cast a shadow on the Earth. The sky darkens. The air becomes cooler. It seems like the middle of the night. This is called a **solar eclipse**.

Directions:

Write "solar eclipse" on the picture which best shows one.

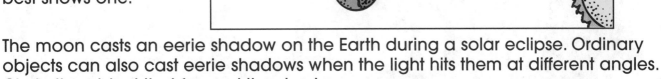

The moon casts an eerie shadow on the Earth during a solar eclipse. Ordinary objects can also cast eerie shadows when the light hits them at different angles. Circle the object that formed the shadow.

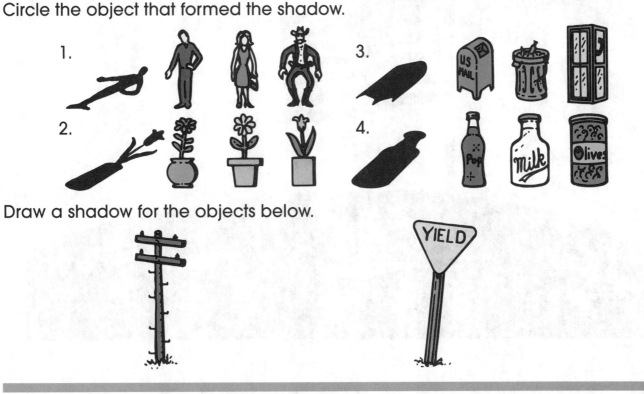

Draw a shadow for the objects below.

A Time Capsule on the Moon

Scientists have studied the rocky surface of the **moon**, our closest neighbor in space. By studying samples the astronauts have brought back to Earth, we know the moon is probably $4\frac{1}{2}$ billion years old! They also know the moon is very different from the Earth. Large holes on the surface of the moon are called **craters**. Scientists have discovered the moon has no air or gravity and no wind or water. Because of this, everything stays the same on its surface. The U.S. flag placed on the moon by our astronauts should stay for millions of years. That means future visitors on the moon will see it long after we're gone.

What do you think would be important to show millions of years from now? Design a space time capsule to be sealed and left on the moon. What will you put in it? Why?

Use some of these items and make a time capsule. Seal it until the end of the year.

Name _____

How Big?

Planets vary greatly in size. Look at the list of planets and their **diameters**.

Planet	Diameter
Mercury	3,000 miles
Venus	7,500 miles
Earth	7,900 miles
Mars	4,200 miles
Jupiter	88,700 miles
Saturn	74,600 miles
Uranus	31,600 miles
Neptune	30,200 miles

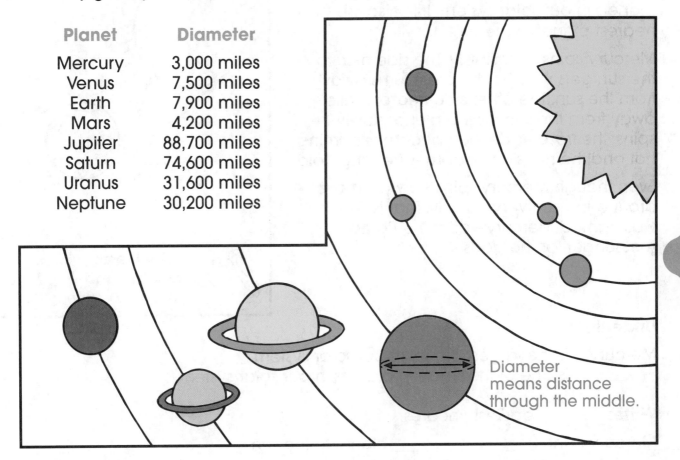

Diameter means distance through the middle.

Directions:

Write the names of the planets in order by size, starting with the planet that has the **largest** diameter.

1. _____
2. _____
3. _____
4. _____
5. _____
6. _____
7. _____
8. _____

Name _____

Mercury

Mercury is the smallest of the eight planets in our solar system. It is also the nearest planet to the sun.

Mercury spins very slowly. The side next to the sun gets very hot before it turns away from the sun. The other side freezes while away from the sun. As the planet slowly spins, the frozen side then becomes burning hot and the hot side becomes freezing cold.

Even though Mercury spins slowly, it moves around the sun very quickly. That is why it was named Mercury—after the Roman messenger for the gods.

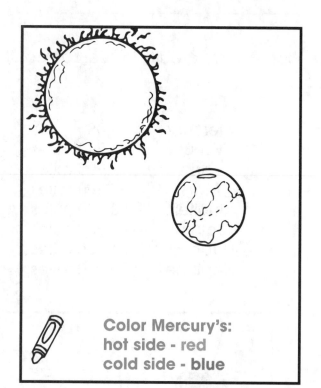

Color Mercury's:
hot side - red
cold side - blue

Underline:

Mercury   is the largest planet in our solar system.
            is one of the smallest planets in our solar system.

Write: darkest   nearest

Mercury is the_____ planet to the sun.

Match:

How does spinning slowly affect the temperature on Mercury?

The side next to the sun   is freezing cold.
The side away from the sun   is burning hot.

Circle:

Mercury moves   quickly   around the sun.   Mercury spins very   lightly.
                quietly   slowly.

Check:

Mercury was named for the ☐ famous Roman speaker.
                                  ☐ Roman messenger for the gods.

Name _____

Venus

Venus is the planet nearest to Earth. Because it is the easiest planet to see in the sky, it has been called the **Morning Star** and **Evening Star**. The Romans named Venus after their goddess of love and beauty. Venus is sometimes called "Earth's twin."

Venus is covered with thick clouds. The sun's heat is trapped by the clouds. The temperature on Venus is nearly 900°F!

Space probes have been sent to study Venus. They have reported information to scientists. But they can only last a few hours on Venus because of the high temperature.

Venus turns in the opposite direction from Earth. So, on Venus, the sun rises in the west and sets in the east!

West   East

Draw the sun rising on Venus.

Unscramble and Circle:

_____ is the friendliest / nearest planet to Earth.

   e s V u n
   2 5 1 4 3

Check:
It is called the
☐ Evening Sun
☐ Morning Star   because it is so easy to see.
☐ Evening Star

Circle:
The Romans named Venus for their:

goddess of love and beauty   god of light   goddess of truth

Circle Yes or No:

Half of Venus is frozen with ice and snow.	**Yes**	**No**
Space probes have reported information from Venus.	**Yes**	**No**
On Venus, the sun rises in the east and sets in the west.	**Yes**	**No**

Name _____

Mars

Mars is the fourth planet from the sun at 141,600,000 miles. The diameter of Mars is 4,200 miles. Mars is often called the Red Planet because rocks on its surface contain limonite, which is similar to rust. Mars has two moons.

Mars is dustier and drier than any desert on Earth. However, new evidence suggests that Mars may have once been a wetter and warmer planet. According to information gathered at the 1997 landing site of the Mars Pathfinder Mission, there may have been tremendous flooding on Mars about 2 to 3 billion years ago. Mars, then, may once have been more like Earth than was earlier thought.

Scientists are now pondering this question—if life was able to develop on Earth 2 to 3 billion years ago, why not on Mars too? What do you think about this? Explain your answer on the lines below.

_____

_____

_____

_____

_____

_____

_____

Fantastic Fact
Morning temperatures on Mars are much different than on Earth. If you were standing on Mars, your nose would be at least 68°F colder than your feet!

Name _____

Jupiter

Jupiter is the largest planet in our solar system. It has sixteen moons. Jupiter is the second-brightest planet—only Venus is brighter.

Jupiter is bigger and heavier than all of the other planets together. It is covered with thick clouds. Many loose rocks and dust particles form a single, thin, flat ring around Jupiter.

One of the most fascinating things about Jupiter is its Great Red Spot. The Great Red Spot of Jupiter is a huge storm in the atmosphere. It looks like a red ball. This giant storm is larger than Earth! Every six days it goes completely around Jupiter.

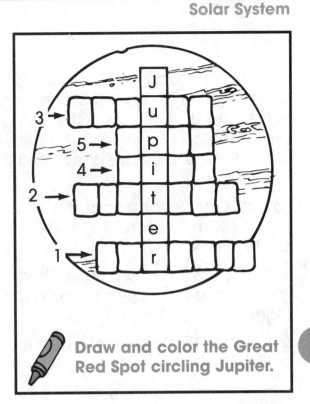

Draw and color the Great Red Spot circling Jupiter.

Unscramble and Write in Puzzle:

1. Jupiter is the _____ planet in our solar system.

   e t s l r g a
   5 7 6 1 3 4 2

2. Jupiter has _____ moons.

   t n x s e i e
   4 7 3 1 5 2 6

3. Jupiter is covered with thick _____.

   d s o c l u
   5 6 3 1 2 4

4. Loose rocks and dust form a _____ around Jupiter.

   g i r n
   4 2 1 3

5. The Great Red _____ of Jupiter is a huge storm.

   t s o p
   4 1 3 2

Circle and Write:

Jupiter is the second   largest
                         brightest   planet.

Jupiter is _____ and   lighter
              bigger   redder   heavier   than all of the planets together.

173

Saturn

Saturn is probably most famous for its rings. These rings are made of billions of tiny pieces of ice and dust. Although these rings are very wide, they are very thin. If you look at the rings from the side, they are almost too thin to be seen.

Saturn is the second-largest planet in our solar system. It is so big that 758 Earths could fit inside it!

Saturn is covered by clouds. Strong, fast winds move the clouds quickly across the planet.

Saturn has 18 moons! Its largest moon is called Titan.

Draw 18 moons around Saturn!

Circle:
Saturn is most famous for its

spots.   rings.

Write:
Saturn's rings are made of _____ and _____.
                              mud   ice   dust   moons

Check:
Saturn's rings are ☐ red, yellow and purple.
☐ wide, but thin.

Underline:

is the second-largest planet in our solar system.
is big enough to hold 758 Earths inside it.
is farther from the sun than any other planet.
is covered by fast, strong winds.
has 18 moons.

Unscramble:
Saturn's largest moon is called _____.
i T a n t
2 1 4 5 3

Name _____

The Large Planets

Jupiter is about 88,836 miles at its equator. Named after the king of the Roman gods, it is the fifth-closest planet to the sun at about 483,600,000 miles away. Jupiter travels around the sun in an oval-shaped (elliptical) orbit. Jupiter also spins faster than any other planet and makes a complete rotation in about 9 hours and 55 minutes.

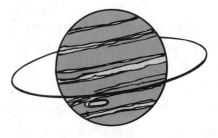

The surface of Jupiter cannot be seen from Earth because of the layers of dense clouds surrounding it. Jupiter has no solid surface but is made of liquid and gases that are held together by gravity.

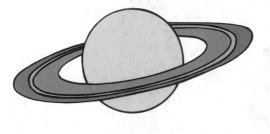

One characteristic unique to Jupiter is the Great Red Spot that is about 25,000 miles long and about 20,000 miles wide. Astronomers believe the spot to be a swirling, hurricane-like mass of gas.

Saturn, the second-largest planet, is well known for the seven thin, flat rings encircling it. Its diameter is about 74,898 miles at the equator. It was named for the Roman god of agriculture. Saturn is the sixth planet closest to the sun and is about 888,200,000 miles away from it. Like Jupiter, Saturn also travels around the sun in an elliptical orbit, and it takes the planet about 10 hours and 39 minutes to make one rotation.

Scientists believe Saturn is a giant ball of gas that also has no solid surface. Like Jupiter, they believe it too may have an inner core of rocky material. Whereas Saturn claims 18 satellites, Jupiter has only 16 known satellites.

Directions: Fill in the chart below to compare Jupiter and Saturn. Make two of your own categories.

Categories	Jupiter	Saturn
1. diameter		
2. origin of name		
3. distance from sun		
4. rotation		
5. surface		
6. unique characteristics		
7.		
8.		

Uranus

Did you know that Uranus was first thought to be a comet? Many scientists studied the mystery **comet**. It was soon decided that Uranus was a planet. It was the first planet to be discovered through a telescope.

Scientists believe that Uranus is made of rock and metal with gas and ice surrounding it.

Even through a telescope, Uranus is not easy to see. That is because it is almost two billion miles from the sun that lights it. It takes Uranus 84 Earth years to orbit the sun! Scientists know that Uranus has fifteen moons and is circled by ten thin rings. But there are still many mysteries about this faraway planet.

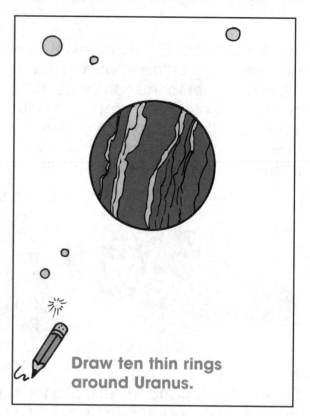

Draw ten thin rings around Uranus.

Circle:
Uranus was first thought to be a moon.
comet.

Write:
Uranus was the first planet to be discovered through a _____.
telescope   TV

Check:
Scientists believe that Uranus is made of:

☐ rock   ☐ oil   ☐ metal   ☐ oceans   ☐ gas   ☐ ice

Match:

two billion miles   . . . the number of Uranus's moons
84 Earth years   . . . the distance of Uranus from the sun
fifteen   . . . the number of Uranus's rings
ten   . . . the time it takes Uranus to orbit the sun

Name _____

Neptune

Neptune is the eighth planet from the sun. It is difficult to see Neptune—even through a telescope. It is almost three billion miles from Earth.

Scientists believe that Neptune is much like Uranus—made of rock, iron, ice and gases.

Neptune has eight moons. Scientists believe that it may also have several rings.

Neptune is so far away from the sun that it takes 164 Earth years for it to orbit the sun just once!

Scientists still know very little about this cold and distant planet.

Draw 8 moons around Neptune.

Write, Circle or Unscramble:

N eptune is the   sixth   planet from the sun.
                    eighth

E arth is almost three _____ miles from Neptune.
                          million   billion

P eople know very little about Neptune.
               very much

T elescopes are used to see Neptune. **Yes   No**

U ranus and Neptune are made of: rock   soap   gases   ice

N eptune is a _____ and _____ planet.
                 warm   cold   distant   near

E very orbit around the _____ takes Neptune 164 Earth years.

177

Name _____

The Twin Planets

1. Uranus and Neptune are similar in size, rotation time and temperature. Sometimes they are called twin planets. Uranus is about 1,786,400,000 miles from the sun. Neptune is about 2,798,800,000 miles from the sun. What is the difference between these two distances? _____

2. Neptune can complete a rotation in 18 to 20 hours. Uranus can make one in 16 to 18 hours. What is the average time it takes Neptune to complete a rotation? _____ Uranus?_____

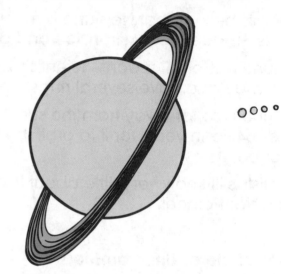

3. Can you believe that it is about -353°F on Neptune, and about -357°F on Uranus? Brrr! That's cold! What is the temperature outside today in your town?_____
How much warmer is it in your town than on Neptune?_____Uranus?_____

4. Uranus has at least five small satellites moving around it. Their names are Miranda, Ariel, Umbriel, Tatania and Oberon. They are 292, 721, 727, 982 and 945 miles in diameter, respectively. What is the average diameter of Uranus' satellites?_____

5. Neptune was first seen in 1846 by Johanna G. Galle. Uranus was first discovered by Sir William Herschel in 1781. How many years ago was Neptune discovered?_____Uranus?_____
About how many years later was Uranus discovered than Neptune? _____

6. Both Uranus and Neptune have names taken from Greek and Roman mythology. Use an encyclopedia to find their names and their origins.

_____

_____

_____

Pluto

Pluto used to be considered the ninth planet. Now, along with Ceres and Eris, it is considered a dwarf planet.

If you stood on Pluto, the sun would look just like a bright star in the sky. Pluto is so far away that it gets little of the sun's heat. That is why it is freezing cold on Pluto.

Some scientists think that Pluto was once one of Neptune's moons that escaped from orbit and drifted into space.

Pluto is so far away from the sun that it takes 247 Earth years just to orbit the sun once!

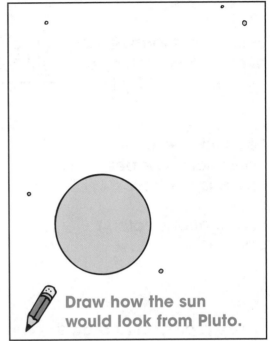

Draw how the sun would look from Pluto.

Unscramble and Circle:

_____ is farther / closer to the sun than Earth.

l t P o u
2 4 1 5 3

Pluto, Ceres, and Eris are large / dwarf _____ .

l a e n p t s
2 3 5 4 1 6 7

Check:

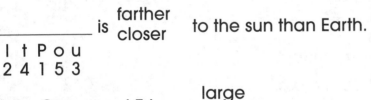

Pluto Facts

- [ ] On Pluto, the sun looks like a bright star.
- [ ] Pluto gets very little of the sun's heat.
- [ ] Pluto has very hot weather.
- [ ] Pluto takes 247 Earth years to orbit the sun.

Circle:

Some scientists believe that Pluto was once Neptune's sun. / moon.

Name _____

Pluto and Planet X

Pluto's orbit forms a long, thin oval shape that crosses the path of Neptune's orbit every 248 years. So, for about 200 Earth years, Pluto is actually closer to the sun than Neptune! Try this art project:

You will need:
construction paper
crayons or chalk
glue
yarn (various colors)
pencil

Directions:

1. Use a crayon to draw the sun in the center of the paper.
2. Use your pencil to draw each orbit, being careful to cross Pluto's with Neptune's.*
3. Color the planets along the orbits.
4. Trace the orbits in glue, then lay yarn on top.

*Only Pluto's and Neptune's orbits should cross.

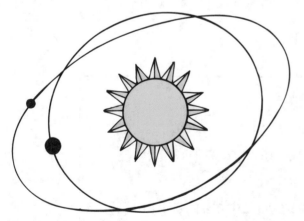

Imagine there is another planet called Planet X. Write a name for it below and use information about the other planets to estimate and create answers in the chart.

Planet Name	Diameter	Distance from Sun	Revolution	Rotation	Satellites

Name _____

Read My Mind

Pretend you have been contacted by NASA to serve as an astronaut on a secret mission. Because of its secrecy, NASA cannot give you your destination. Instead, you must figure it out using the clues below. After each clue, check the possible answers. The planet with the most clues checked will be your destination.

Destination Clues	Record Answers Here							
	Mercury	Venus	Earth	Mars	Jupiter	Saturn	Uranus	Neptune
It is part of our solar system.								
It is a bright object in the sky.								
It is less than 2,000,000,000 miles from the sun.								
It orbits the sun.								
It has less than 15 known satellites.								
There is weather there.								
It rotates in the opposite direction of Earth.								
It is the hottest planet.								
Its years are longer than its days.								
It is called "Earth's twin."								
It is closest to Earth.								

Secret Mission Destination is _____
I know this because _____

Solar System Match Game

You and a partner may enjoy checking your knowledge of the planets in our solar system by playing the Solar System Match Game found on the following pages.

Directions:

1. Study the fact cards (on page 187) for each object.

2. Cut out the cards and place them face down.

3. You and your partner should each have a game card.

4. Take turns with your partner flipping over one card and matching it with the correct object on your game card.

5. The first person to get 3 in a row, up and down, across or diagonally is the winner.

Solar System Match Game

Game Card

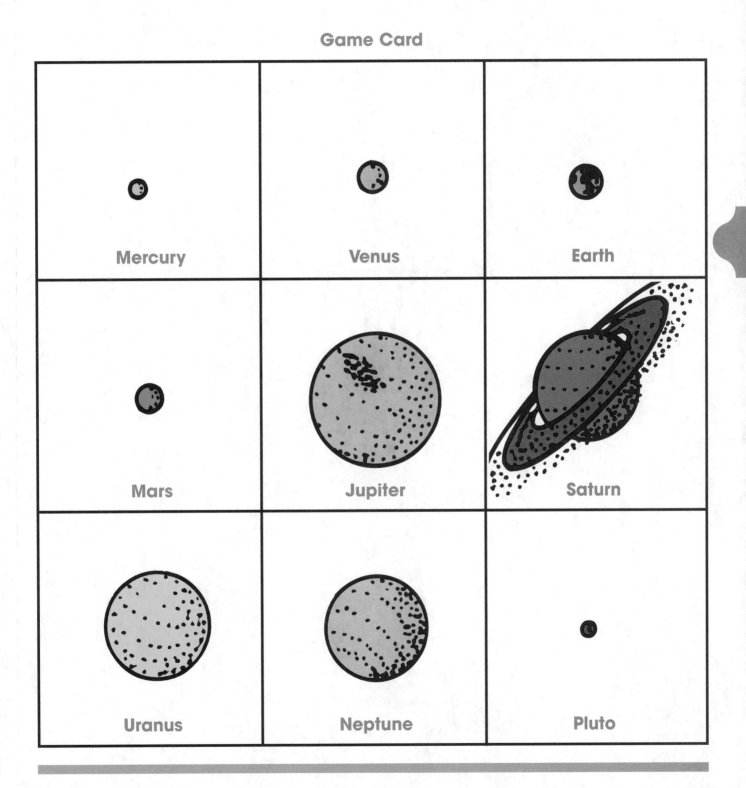

Mercury	Venus	Earth
Mars	Jupiter	Saturn
Uranus	Neptune	Pluto

This page intentionally left blank.

Solar System Match Game

Game Card

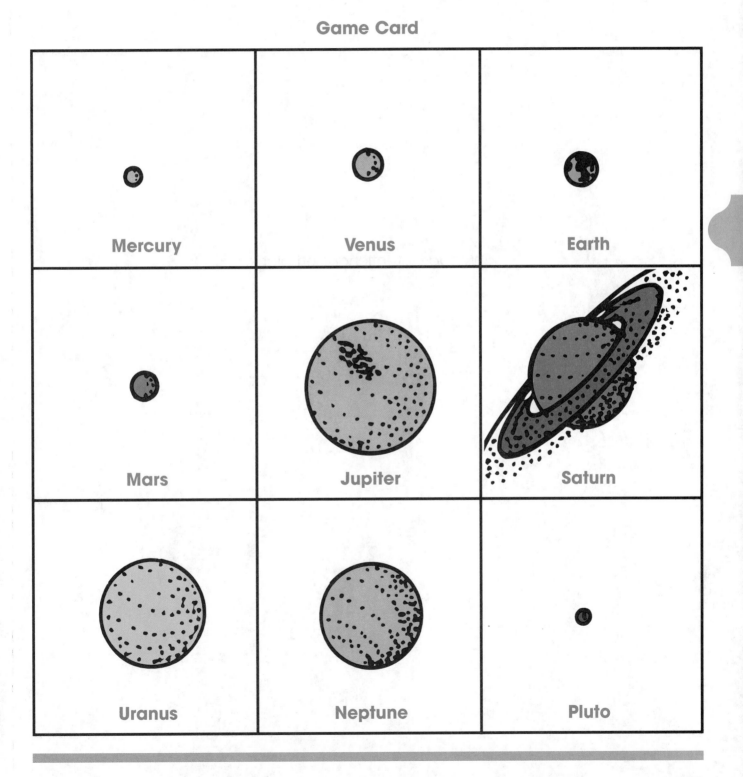

Mercury	Venus	Earth
Mars	Jupiter	Saturn
Uranus	Neptune	Pluto

This page intentionally left blank.

Solar System Match Game

Mercury	Closest planet to the sun	This planet orbits the sun in the fewest number of days—88
Venus	Known as "Earth's twin"	Earth's nearest planet neighbor
Earth	The only planet with life	Known as the "Blue Planet"
Mars	"The Red Planet"	Orbits the sun between Earth and Jupiter

Jupiter	Largest planet	Has a "red spot" caused by a huge storm
Saturn	Known for its beautiful rings	Second largest planet
Uranus	This planet was thought to be a comet.	Orbits between Saturn and Neptune
Neptune	Has eight moons and may have rings	Orbits between Uranus and Pluto
Pluto	Dwarf planet	Has the orbit farthest from the sun

This page intentionally left blank.

Name _____

Star Light, Star Bright

Lie on your back. Gaze up into the night sky. Which star is the brightest?
On a clear night you can see hundreds of stars—some are bright and others are dim.

Why are some stars brighter than others? Let's try to find out by looking at the picture on this page.

1. Look at the two streetlights in the picture. Which streetlight appears the brightest?_____

   Why?_____
   _____

2. Look at the bicycle and the truck. Which headlights appear the brightest? _____

   Why?_____

3. Some stars appear brighter than other stars for the same reasons as the lights in the picture. What are the two reasons?

   a. _____

   b. _____

Color Me Hot

Stars differ not only in brightness, but also in color. As the star gets hotter, the color changes.

Color these stars. Use the chart to find the correct color.

Star Color	
Temperature	**Color**
36,000°F	Blue
18,000°F	White
9,000°F	Yellow
5,400°F	Red

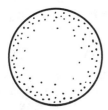

Spica
36,000°F

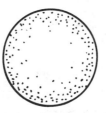

Sirius
18,000°F

Sun
9,000°F

Betelgeuse
5,400°F

Name _____

Constellations

On a clear night, you can see about two thousand stars in the sky. Scientists can use giant telescopes to see billions of stars.

Stars in groups form pictures called **constellations**. These constellations have been recognized for years. Ancient people named many constellations for animals, heroes and mythical creatures. Many of these names are still used.

Some constellations can be seen every night of the year. Others change with the seasons.

Since all stars are constantly moving, these same constellations that we now see will be changed thousands of years from now.

Connect the stars to form the constellation called the Little Dipper.

Write:

Stars in groups form pictures called _____.

telescopes   constellations

Check:

Ancient people named many constellations for:

☐ animals   ☐ heroes   ☐ oceans   ☐ mythical creatures

Match:

Billions of stars can be seen.
About two thousand stars can be seen.

Circle Yes or No:

Some constellations can be seen every night.   **Yes   No**
Some constellations change with the seasons.   **Yes   No**
In thousands of years, all constellations will be the same.   **Yes   No**

Pictures in the Sky

Color and cut out the constellations on this page. Make a mobile as pictured. Use a science book or other books to make pictures of other constellations for your mobile.

Cover a hanger with black paper and punch in holes to show some of your favorite constellations.

Orion

Cygnus

Gemini

Leo

Scorpio

This page intentionally left blank.

Create a Constellation

Thousands of years ago, people believed that there were many gods in the heavens above. They believed that the gods made the sun rise, the weather change, the oceans move and even made people fall in love! The people made up stories (myths) about the gods and their great powers. Many of the characters in these myths can be found in the shapes of the stars. These "star pictures" are called constellations. There are 88 constellations in the sky, but not all of them can be seen from one location. Some are only visible in the Southern Hemisphere while others can only be seen in the Northern Hemisphere. Some are also best observed only in certain seasons. Look at some of the constellations on page 195, Constellation Patterns. Pick one or create your own and write a myth about it. Follow the directions below.

1. On a lined sheet of 8 ½" x 11" paper, write your name, the title of your myth and the myth.
2. Glue the paper on the right side of a 12" x 18" piece of black construction paper.
3. In the box below, design your constellation using star stickers.
4. Connect the stars to show your constellation and add details.
5. Cut out and glue your constellation on the left side of the construction paper.

Name _____

Star Search

On a clear dark night, you can look up in the sky and see about 2,000 stars without the help of a telescope. But unless you know which stars form constellations, all you will be seeing are stars.

Carefully poke holes in the Constellation Patterns sheet on page 195, using a sharp pencil. Then, tonight, when it is dark, hold a flashlight behind the paper to make the constellations appear.

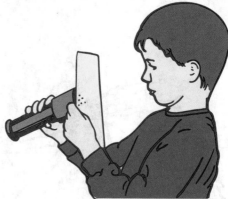

Below are star charts to further help you recognize the constellations. To use the charts, turn them until the present month is at the bottom. Depending on your position and the time of night, you should be able to see most of the constellations in the middle and upper part of the chart.

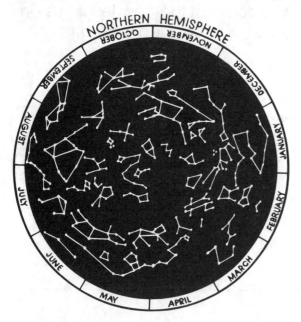

Directions:

1. Using the Constellation Patterns sheet to help you, label as many of the constellations in the chart as you can.

2. Which constellations should you be able to see tonight? _____

_____

3. When it is dark, go outside to look for constellations.

4. Which ones do you actually see?

_____

_____

5. On paper, draw the night sky you see. Draw a small **X** in the center. This should be the point in the sky directly above you.

Constellation Patterns

See Star Search, page 193, for directions.

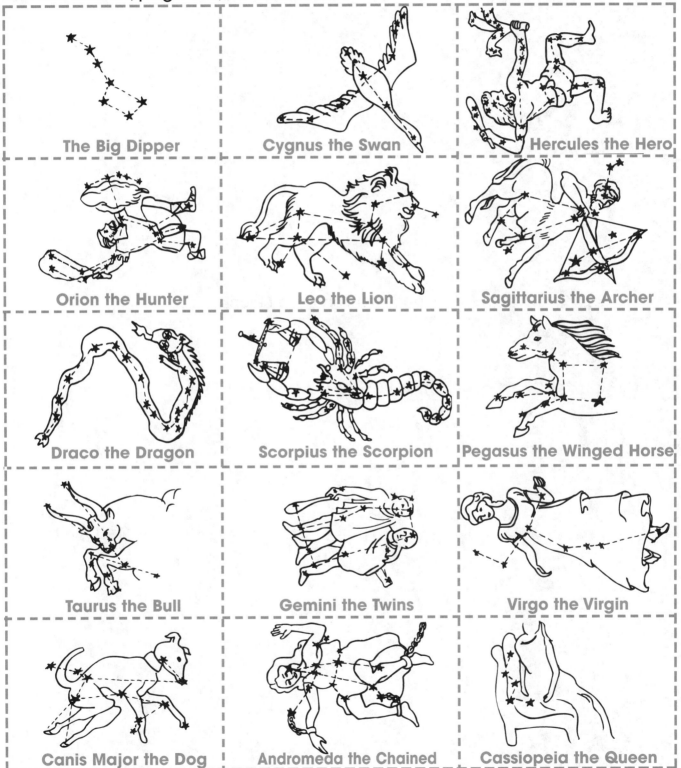

The Big Dipper

Cygnus the Swan

Hercules the Hero

Orion the Hunter

Leo the Lion

Sagittarius the Archer

Draco the Dragon

Scorpius the Scorpion

Pegasus the Winged Horse

Taurus the Bull

Gemini the Twins

Virgo the Virgin

Canis Major the Dog

Andromeda the Chained

Cassiopeia the Queen

This page intentionally left blank.

Ceiling Constellations

You will need:

a cylindrical oatmeal box with a lid
a pencil
flashlight
a thin nail
black tape
a black pen and scissors

Select a constellation visible in the Northern Hemisphere. Use a pencil to mark each star in the constellation on the box lid. Then, poke a hole for each star using a nail. Write the constellation's name on the side of the box using a pen. Next, cut a hole in the bottom of the box just large enough for a flashlight to fit through from the inside. Put the black tape around any air holes. Put the lid on. Darken the room and project your constellation on the ceiling.

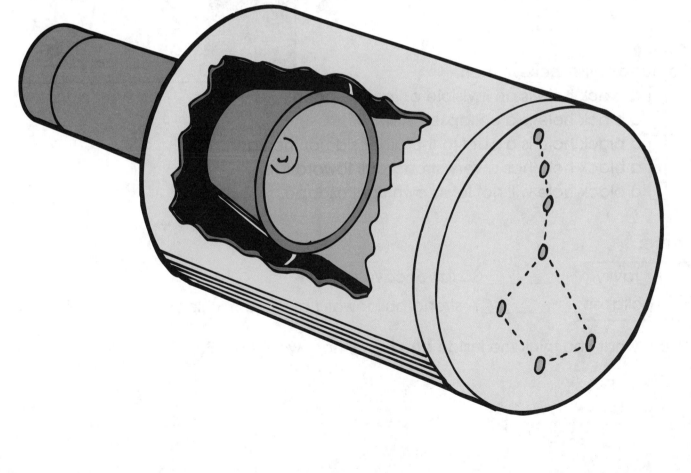

Name _____

A Black Hole

Have you ever heard of a mysterious black hole? Some scientists believe that a black hole is an invisible object somewhere in space. Scientists believe that it has such a strong pull toward it, called **gravity**, that nothing can escape from it!

These scientists believe that a black hole is a star that has collapsed. The collapse made its pull even stronger. It seems invisible because even its own starlight cannot escape! It is believed that anything in space that comes near the black hole will be pulled into it forever. Some scientists believe there are many black holes in our galaxy.

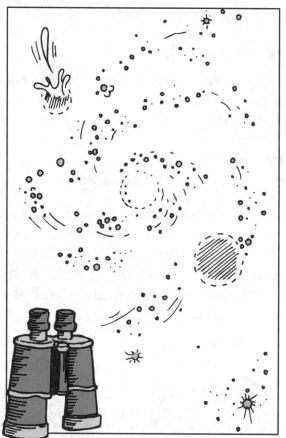

Check:

Some scientists believe that:

- ☐ a black hole is an invisible object in space.
- ☐ a black hole is a collapsed star.
- ☐ a black hole is a path to the other side of the Earth.
- ☐ a black hole has a very strong pull toward it.
- ☐ a black hole will not let its own light escape.

Write:

| A - gravity | _____ To fall or cave in |
| B - collapse | _____ A strong pull toward an object in space |

Draw what you think the inside of a black hole would be like.

Name _____

Space Snowballs

Planets and moons are not the only objects in our solar system that travel in orbits. Comets also orbit the sun.

A **comet** is like a giant dirty snowball that is ½ to 3 miles wide. It is made of frozen gases, dust, ice and rocks.

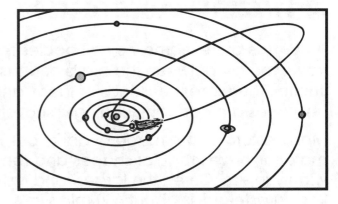

As the comet gets closer to the sun, the frozen gases melt and evaporate. Dust particles float in the air. The dust forms a cloud called a **coma**. The "wind" from the sun blows the coma away from the sun. The blowing coma forms the comet's tail.

There are more than 800 known comets. Halley's Comet is the most famous. It appears about every 76 years. The last scheduled appearance in this century was in 1985. When will it appear next?

Find the words from the Word Bank in the word search. When you are finished, write down the letters that are not circled. Start at the top of the puzzle and go from left to right.

Word Bank

dust	orbit
Halley	tail
coma	ice
snowball	sky
melt	shining
solar system	

```
S P M E L T L A N H E
O T S S H A C O M A V
L E N O R D B I T L S
A L O I K U E C I L R
R C W L E S S C O E M
S E B T S T H A V Y E
Y O A R O R B I T B I
S T L S S H A P E D L
T I L K T A I L E A F
E O O T I C E B A L L
M S K Y S H I N I N G
```

_____ _____ _____ _____ _____

_____ . _____ _____ _____

_____ _____ _ _____ .

Name _____

Amazing Asteroids

Asteroids are extremely small bodies that travel mainly between the orbits of Mars and Jupiter. There are thousands of them, and new ones are constantly being discovered.

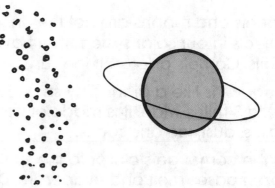

Many asteroids are made of dark, rocky material, have irregular shapes and range widely in size. Ceres, the largest and first-known asteroid, is about 600 miles in diameter. Hildago, another asteroid, is only about nine miles in diameter.

Because the asteroids' orbits change slowly due to the gravitational attraction of Jupiter and other large planets, asteroids sometimes collide with each other. Fragments from these collisions can cause other collisions. Any resulting small fragments that reach the surface of Earth are called meteorites.

Try your hand at personification. **Personification** means giving an inanimate (non-living) object human qualities. Draw a cartoon below of two asteroids colliding with each other. Give the asteroids names and write what they might say to each other.

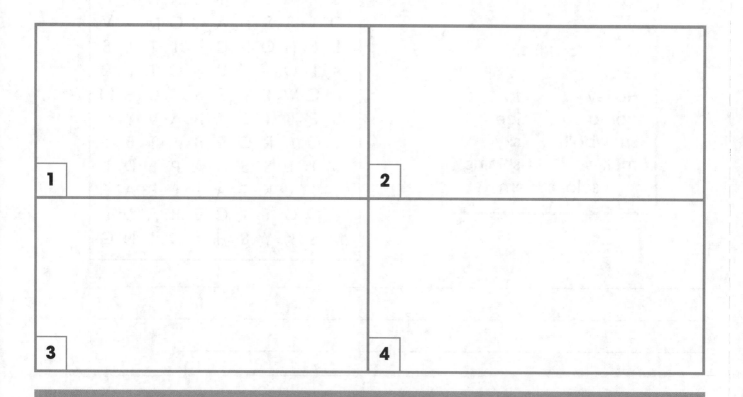

Name _____

The Milky Way Galaxy

The Milky Way galaxy is made up of the Earth, its solar system and all the stars you can see at night. There are over 100 billion stars in the Milky Way!

The Milky Way is shaped much like a C.D. It has a center which the outer part goes around.

The Milky Way is always spinning slowly through space. It is so large that it would take 200 million years for the galaxy to make one complete turn.

Many stars in the Milky Way are in clusters. Some star clusters contain up to one million stars!

Our solar system

Put a red circle around our solar system.

Check:

The Milky Way galaxy is made up of

☐ Earth.
☐ no sun.
☐ our solar system.
☐ 100 billion stars.

Circle Yes or No:

The Milky Way is shaped like a pencil.	**Yes**	**No**
The Milky Way is always slowly moving in space.	**Yes**	**No**
Many stars in the Milky Way are in clusters.	**Yes**	**No**
Some star clusters have one million stars.	**Yes**	**No**

Circle:

It would take   200
                 90   million years for the galaxy to spin once.
                 600

Underline.

Which object is the Milky Way shaped much like?

C.D.   ruler

201

Name _____

Weight and Gravity

Making a Scale

Directions:

1. Use a hole punch or scissors to punch two holes exactly opposite each other at the top of a clear plastic cup.
2. Cut a piece of fishing line 6" long. Tie one end to one hole and the other end to the opposite hole.
3. Tape a ruler to the top of a table so one end hangs over the edge. Then, tape a piece of tagboard to the side of the table.
4. Wrap a rubber band around the fishing line and loop it inside itself. Now hang the rubber band from the ruler. The cup should hang in front of the tagboard.

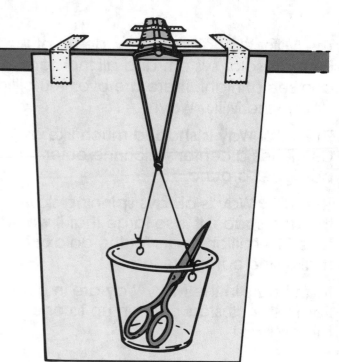

Comparing Weights

To weigh an object, place it in the cup. The heavier the object, the lower the cup will sag. To record its weight, put a mark on the tagboard even with the bottom of the cup and write the name of the object next to the mark.

Make a prediction. Put all the objects on the table. Line them up in order from the lightest to the heaviest. Now weigh the objects. Number them from lightest to heaviest, with 1 the lightest and 8 the heaviest.

_____ scissors   _____ small jar of water   _____ pencil   _____ coin
_____ stone   _____ crayon box   _____ eraser   _____ magnifying glass

How accurate was your prediction?

Extension:

Why is gravity important to humans? _____

_____

_____

What would happen if there were no gravity? _____

_____

_____

Name _____

"Lift-off"

"3-2-1, lift-off!" With a mighty roar, the Saturn V **rocket** leaves the **launch pad**.

Riding high on top of the Saturn V in the **Command Module** are the three Apollo astronauts. Below their Command Module is a Lunar Landing Module which will land two of the astronauts on the moon's surface.

Below this, the Saturn V has three parts, or **stages**. It takes a lot of power to escape the Earth's pull, called **gravity**. The spacecraft must reach a speed of almost 25,000 miles per hour. The bottom, or first stage, is the largest. After each stage uses up its **fuel**, it drops off, and the next stage starts. Each stage has its own fuel and **oxygen**. The fuels need oxygen, otherwise they will not burn.

The astronauts are now on their 3-day journey to the moon. Color each Saturn V section a different color. Color the key to match each section.

Fill in the spaces with the highlighted words from above. Then, use the numbered letters to answer the question.

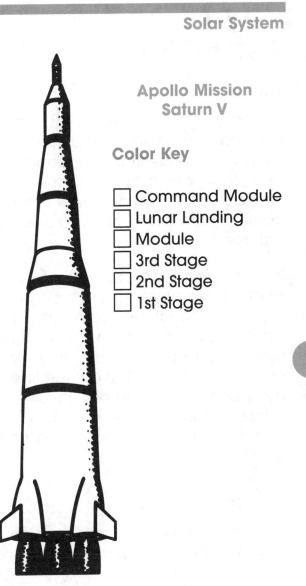

**Apollo Mission
Saturn V**

Color Key

☐ Command Module
☐ Lunar Landing
☐ Module
☐ 3rd Stage
☐ 2nd Stage
☐ 1st Stage

1. The Saturn V __ __ __ __ __ __ has three main parts, or __ __ __ __ __ __.
                13   1   5

2. Rocket engines burn __ __ __ __ and __ __ __ __ __.
                  10   8   6   16   7

3. The Earth's pull is called __ __ __ __ __ __ __.
                 16 11   14

4. "Lift-off." The Saturn V leaves the __ __ __ __ __ __ __ __.
                 9   2 12

5. The Apollo astronauts ride in the __ __ __ __ __ __ __ __ __ __ __ __ __.
                            3   15 4

What were the first words spoken from the surface of the moon on July 20, 1969?

" __ ,
  1 2 3 1   5   6 7 8   5 4 3 9 9   5 1 8 12   10 6 11   4 3 7

__ . "
  6 7 8 16 14 3 7 1   9 8 3 12   10 6 11   4 3 7 13 14 7 15

Neil Armstrong, Apollo II Commander

203

Astro-Flier

You will need:

a hole punch, scissors, coffee-can size lids, ruler, colored felt-tip pens, wire or string, pencils, short clear plastic drinking glasses, stencils, paper, tape, bottom of styrofoam egg carton, colored pipe cleaners, glue, colored toothpicks, colored ribbon, glitter, colored yarn

You may want an adult to help you. Make a stencil by tracing around it on paper, cutting it out and punching two holes in it where the small circles are drawn. Put the stencil on a plastic lid. Using a pencil, draw around its outline and holes. Cut out the lines you have made on the lid and punch holes. Run a string or a wire across the room. Tie pieces of yarn from which to hang the astro-flier.

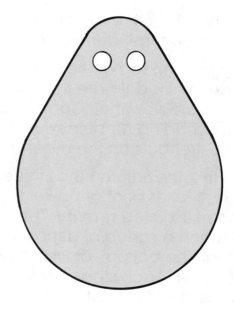

Directions:

1. Divide a plastic lid into quarters. Cut it apart. On each of the quarters, cut off the rim of the lid.

2. Use a stencil to mark the holes with a pencil in each pointed end. Punch out the holes.

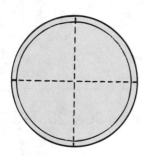

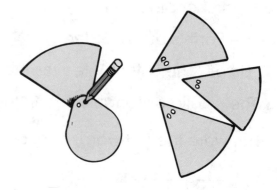

Astro-Flier

3. Using scissors, make two holes in the bottom of the plastic glass. Cut a piece of yarn 10" long. Put the yarn in one hole from the outside of the glass, and put it through the other hole from the inside of the glass. Tie the yarn ends together to make a loop for hanging.

4. Set the plastic glass upside-down over the middle of the plastic lid. Trace around the glass using a pencil. Cut out the inner circle, cutting just inside the circle you traced.

5. Divide the ring into quarters. Use the stencil to make four sets of holes on the ring. Punch them out.

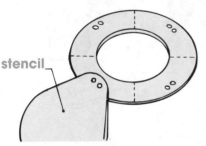

stencil

6. Cut out six $\frac{1}{4}$" x 2$\frac{1}{4}$" strips from the plastic lid. (Make sure the strips are a little wider than the holes on the stencil. Otherwise, they won't hold the pieces described on page 206 together.)

actual size →

7. Use four plastic strips to attach the wings under the ring at the holes. Set the other two strips aside. Match up a pair of holes in the wings with a pair on the ring. Put one end of the strip through one hole and the other end through the other hole of the pair.

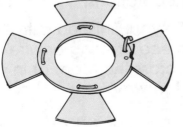

8. Pull the glass up from the bottom through the big center hole. Tape the glass to the ring underneath.

Astro-Flier

9. Use the stencil to mark two sets of holes in the ring between wings BC and wings AD. Punch them out.

10. Cut off the rim of another plastic lid, the same size as the one that made the ring. Place it under the first ring and mark the two sets of holes in the ring on it. Punch them out. Set this ring aside.

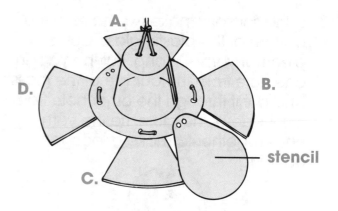

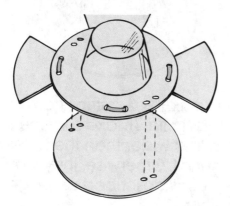

13. Put the ring with the astronaut under the first ring. Line up the holes. Use the last two plastic strips to fasten the circle to the plastic ring.

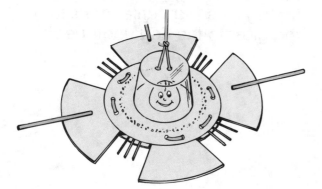

11. Cut out one egg section from a carton. Cut around it so that it is flat on the bottom. Draw a face on it.

12. Tape the astronaut (face) onto the center of the flat ring you set aside.

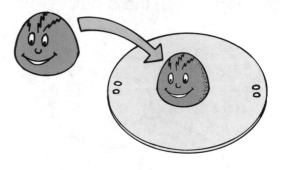

14. Use pipe cleaners for antennae, ribbons for streamers, toothpicks for decorations or antennae, glitter for sparkle, etc. You can glue them on or poke very small holes in the glass in which to stick the decorations.

15. Tie your finished astro-flier to the piece of string or wire hanging across the room or in an open doorway.

"Live Via Satellite"

"This program is brought to you live via satellite from halfway around the world." Satellites are very helpful in sending TV messages from the other side of the world. But this is only one of the special jobs that satellites can do.

Most satellites are placed into orbit around the Earth by riding on top of giant rockets. More recently some satellites have been carried into orbit by a space shuttle. While orbiting the Earth, the giant doors of the shuttle are opened, and the satellite is pushed into orbit.

This satellite relays TV signals from halfway around the world.

Satellites send information about many things. Use the code to find the different kinds of messages and information satellites send.

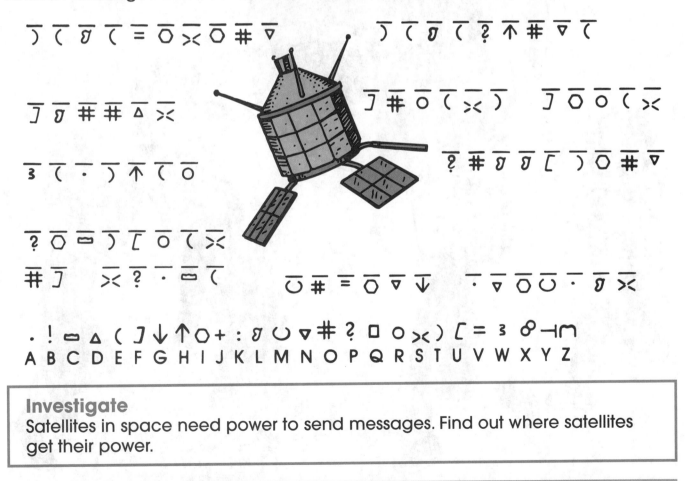

Investigate
Satellites in space need power to send messages. Find out where satellites get their power.

Section 8
Earth

Believe It or Not!

Thousands of years ago, people made up stories to explain things that happened in their world. Those stories are called **myths**. Below are some examples of myths.

1. Some ancient cultures believed that Earth was held by huge figures. For example, the Greeks believed that Atlas carried the sky on his shoulders. When he shrugged his shoulders, an earthquake took place. An early California Native American legend says that seven sea turtles hold up the land. An earthquake happens when one of these turtles gets restless and wants to move.

2. Another Greek legend says that when Poseidon, the sea god, was angry, he banged the sea floor with his trident (or spear), thus causing storms at sea.

3. A Japanese myth says the wriggling of a giant catfish causes earthquakes.

4. Aerial views of craters look like giant eyes. Mount Vesuvius's crater may have inspired the Greek myth of the Cyclops, a tribe of one-eyed giants.

5. It is said that the powerful goddess, Pele, lives in the crater Halemaumau at the summit of Kilauea on Hawaii and makes mountains, melts rocks, destroys forests and builds new islands.

6. The Aztecs believed the gods were angry at the Spanish conquistador who looted their temples, so they caused Popocatepetl to erupt.

Extension:
Look up natural disasters in almanacs and/or encyclopedias and write a myth to explain its event. Give the main characters (quakes, volcanoes, gods, animals, etc.) human characteristics and motions. The name of your story should be the name of a natural disaster.

Magnificent Mountains

Directions: Use the outlines of continents on the next page to locate the mountain ranges of the world. Cut out, label and post the continents on a large sheet of paper. Write the names of some of Earth's mountains on small index cards. Some are listed below for your convenience.

Aconcagua
Alps
Andes
Appalachian Mountains
Atlas Mountains
Catskills
Cotopaxi

Kilimanjaro
Lassen Peak
Mauna Loa
Mount Etna
Mount Everest
Mount Hood
Mount Rainier

Mount Saint Helens
Paricutín
Rocky Mountains
Sierra Nevada
Stromboli
Teton Range
Vesuvius

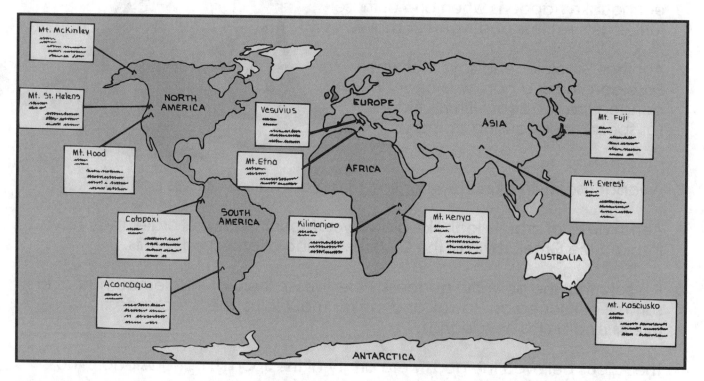

Select an index card with the name of a mountain on it. Find out what you can about it—its kind (volcanic, fold, dome, etc.), location, composition, formation, etc. and write about it on the index card. Put the cards around the map and use string to connect each card to its location.

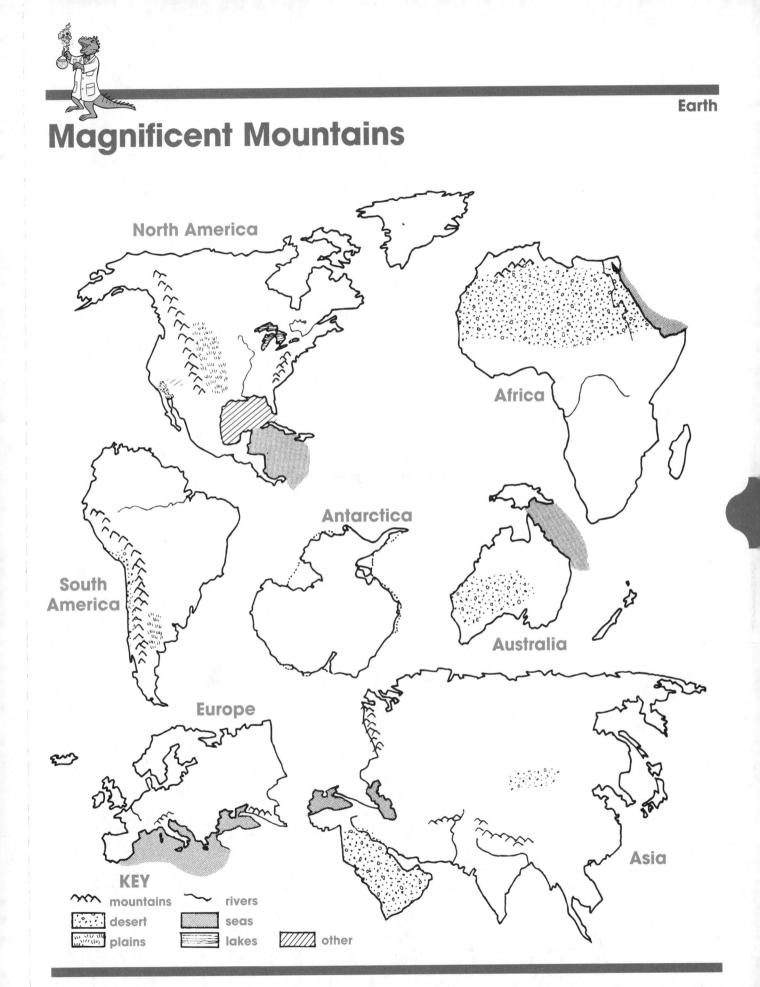

Magnificent Mountains

North America

Africa

Antarctica

Australia

South America

Europe

Asia

KEY

mountains   rivers

desert   seas

plains   lakes   other

This page intentionally left blank.

From the Inside Out

This activity should help you understand the Earth's composition.

You will need:

green, blue, red, gray, white and yellow plasticine clay; knives; a lemon, a small apple, an orange, a small grapefruit (or their equivalent sizes); paper; pen or chalk

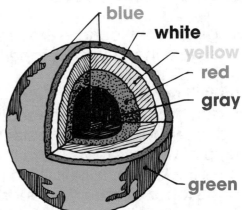

Directions: Put the fruit on display. Make the Earth's inner core using gray plasticine. Roll it into a ball about the size of a lemon. Then, add red plasticine around it to make the outer core. The total size should now be equal to that of an apple. Next, add yellow clay to make the mantle. When this is added, the clay should be about the size of an orange. The last layer of the Earth is the crust. Put a $\frac{1}{4}$" white layer of clay around the mantle. Next, put on what is visible—a thin layer of blue (water) and green (continents). Cut out a wedge to show the cross section of the Earth's different layers.

Sampling the Earth

Collect rocks from a safe and permissible area. Set the number and size of rocks to collect. You may want to visit more than one location. Take a bag, masking tape, notebook, pencil, colored pencils and marking pen with you.

Directions:

Collect rocks at the chosen site. Put a piece of tape on each rock you find and number it using a marking pen. In your notebook, you should enter each rock on a separate page. Then, write its number and precisely where it was found. Next, draw a picture of it using colored pencils. If more than one site is visited for collection purposes, use a different color marking pen for numbering rocks at each place.

Rock Sleuths

Using the rocks found in the previous activity, you can also investigate the physical properties of the rocks.

You will need:
an adult, rocks, a balance scale with weights, your field notebook, a penny, a steel knife or nail, a piece of window glass (bind the edges with thick tape), thick tape, a steel file, a piece of steel, quartz, topaz or emery paper, silicon carbide paper, a pencil, a magnifying glass, reference books on rocks and minerals, paper, vinegar, small cereal bowls, three to four 6" x 6" white unglazed porcelain tiles

Use the Hardness Chart on page 215. Follow the directions on that page.

1. **Weight:** Put the same weight on the scale for all rocks. Put enough similar rocks on the scale to equal the weight. Make a notation in your notebook under the rock's number comparing one of the rocks to others. (Example: It takes a smaller amount of rocks to equal the weight of this rock than it did of rock 2, 4 and 6.) If you did not include the rock being studied in your collection, write another number in your notebook and continue notations for this rock under a new number. Also, since your rock numbers will not coincide, you will have to refer back to its number in your notebook.

2. **Hardness:** Rate the hardness of rocks. Scratch a rock from each group. (Or scratch the designated material with a rock.) Use the hardness chart to determine its level of hardness. Record it in your notebook.

3. **Acid Test:** Put a rock in a small box. Pour a little vinegar over it. If it fizzes, it has carbonates in it. You may have to put your ear close to it to hear the noise. Record your finding in your notebook.

4. **Streak Color Test:** On the back side of the white porcelain tile, draw a line using a rock from each group. It may leave a colored streak which would be characteristic of the mineral(s) in the rock. Record the color of the streak if there is one.

5. Look for rocks in reference books. Match them with your rocks and minerals. Record your findings and the reasons why you believe they match.

Rock Sleuths

Hardness Chart

A mineral will scratch anything as hard as or softer than itself. It can be scratched by anything as hard as or harder than itself. The lower the number of hardness, the softer the rock.

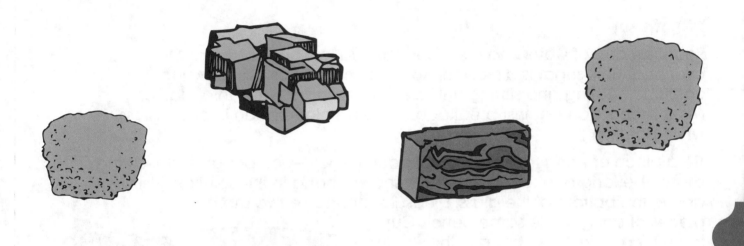

Hardness #	Activity to Check Hardness
1.	Rock can be scratched easily by fingernail.
2.	Rock can be scratched by fingernail.
3.	Rock can be scratched by a penny.
4.	Rock can be scratched easily by a steel knife or nail.
5.	Rock can be scratched with difficulty by a steel knife or nail.
6.	Rock can be scratched by a steel file or it can scratch a piece of glass.
7.	Rock can be scratched by flint or can scratch a piece of glass or steel.
8.	Rock will scratch a piece of quartz.
9.	Rock will scratch a piece of topaz, or it can be scratched by emery paper.
10.	Rock can be scratched by a diamond (not recommended) or it will scratch silicon carbide paper.

Crystal Rock Candy

You will need:

an adult, 4 cups of sugar, water, a string, pencils, glasses that will not break when hot water is added, saucepans, spoons, measuring cups, magnifying glass, food coloring, a stove, a pen, scissors, a stainless steel spoon, 9" x 12" sheets of drawing paper cut into four equal pieces

Directions:

Pour one cup of water into a saucepan. Add two cups of sugar. Stir over heat until sugar is dissolved. Add two more cups of sugar and continue heating and stirring until clear. Pour sugar water into glasses. (As a precaution against breakage, put a stainless spoon in each glass while pouring.)

Tie a piece of string to the center of each pencil—one per glass. The string should be long enough so that the string will hang in the solution, just above the bottom of the glass. Measure off and tie two more pieces of string to the same pencil. Cut them off and let them hang in the solution, too. Add food coloring if you want the crystals to have color.

In a few hours, examine the string in the glass. Some crystals should have formed. Look at them with a magnifying glass and draw a picture of them. Taste one. If you like it, you can eat it.

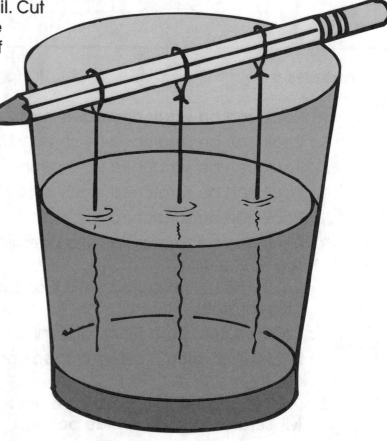

Disastrous Shapes

Write a descriptive shape poem about a type of natural disaster.

Directions:

List different kinds of natural disasters (i.e., tornado, flood, monsoon, volcanic eruption, earthquake, typhoon, hurricane, etc.). Under each one, name words associated with that disaster.

Pick one of the natural disasters about which to write a shape poem. Use the words listed, other words of your choosing or made-up words that help evoke the picture you want. Share the poem.

Toothpaste Magma

Magma is liquid molten material that rises from within the Earth. Use a half-empty, unrolled tube of toothpaste and a pin to visualize this earthy material.

Directions:

1. With the cap on the tube of toothpaste, press the tube until all the paste is at the top of the tube. Roll up the bottom of the tube. Observe what happens when the cap is removed. Then, press the tube and observe the difference.

2. Poke two or three holes in the closed tube with a pin. Press the tube. Next, take the cap off and press the tube. Observe the rate at which the paste comes out and where it comes out.

3. Discuss the above activities with an adult. Equate what happened with magma finding weak spots in the Earth's crust.

Out of This World

You will need:

an adult, 2 large bowls (one that can go in the freezer), a rolling pin, a wooden spoon, a large wooden cutting board, a saucepan, measuring spoons, a long sharp knife, paper plates, plastic forks, the ingredients listed below.

Cover the inside of the bowl that will go in the freezer with a nonstick spray.

INGREDIENTS:

Crust
- 4 tablespoons powdered sugar
- ½ cup butter
- 2 cups graham crackers

Mantle
- ½ cup crushed, unsalted peanuts
- chocolate ice cream

Outer Core
- orange, red and yellow sorbet
- M&M's™

Inner Core
- vanilla ice cream
- red and green food coloring

—— crust
—— mantle
—— outer core
—— inner core

CRUST: Crush graham crackers on the cutting board. Mix powdered sugar with melted butter in a bowl. Line all sides of sprayed bowl with the mixture. Pat it inside the bowl to about ¼-½" thickness. Put it in the freezer until frozen.

Make layers in the order shown above, one layer at a time. Freeze each layer in the bowl before you go on to the next step. (Before mixing and adding each layer, let the ice cream soften, without completely melting.)

When the Earth's cross section is frozen, take it out of the freezer. Cut it in half and then in fourths. Remove one quarter at a time. Slice it like a cake so that each serving has a little of each of Earth's layers. Put it on plates and serve.

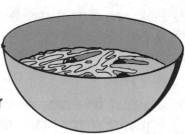

Voom!

You will need:
vinegar, red food coloring, a large cardboard box, baking soda, a narrow plastic beaker, sand, a paper towel tube, scissors, clay, a flat box (3-4" high), an X-acto™ knife, masking tape

Cut and tape a flat box together so that it is about 10" square. Color the vinegar with red food coloring. Wear old clothes for the eruption.

Directions:

1. Fill half of a beaker with baking soda.

2. Cut two or three holes in the paper towel tube. Put it over the beaker.

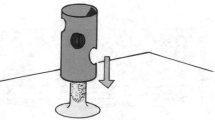

3. Mold clay around the tube. Leave the top and the holes you poked open.

4. Make tunnels out of clay that lead down to the holes.

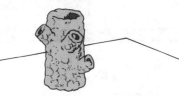

5. Put the beaker with the tube molded with clay in the large box. Pile damp sand around the clay volcano. Pat it to make it into a volcano shape. Leave the top and tunnels exposed.

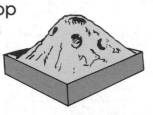

6. When it is time to make it erupt, take it outside. Pour red vinegar into the beaker. Stand back. **VOOM!**

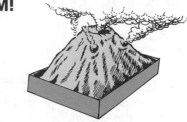

Name _____

Water

Much of the Earth is covered with **water**. Try the following activity to examine some properties of water.

You will need:

several objects that will react differently when put into a basin of water (i.e., a block of wood, a paper clip, a pencil, sugar, salt, a sponge, a piece of fabric, a rubber band, an eraser, baking soda, nylon netting, a paper towel, a nail, a pair of scissors, etc.), a large basin of water, the chart below

Predict what will happen to each object when it is put into a basin of water. Record this information on the chart. Conduct the experiments and record what actually happened. Compare your predictions with the actual results.

Object/Item	Predictions of what will happen	Results of what happened

Twist and Turn

To observe how rocks within the Earth shift when broken off inside Earth and how that movement can be felt on Earth, try the following demonstration.

You will need:

½" wide elastic, a black pen, a ruler, a stapler, heavy-duty tape (duct tape), drinking straws, scissors

Directions: Cut a piece of elastic 3" long. Using a black pen, make a mark 6" from one end of the elastic. Make 11 more marks, one every 2". Place a straw across each mark, perpendicular to the elastic. Staple the center of each straw to the elastic. Tape one end of the elastic to the top of a door frame.

Hold the bottom of the elastic strip. Gently pull it down about a foot. Twist the bottom straw halfway around and then release it.

Observe the motions of the straws. Twisting straws can be compared to the strain placed on rocks within Earth's crust.

• •

POW!

Seismic P-waves are movements in the Earth's crusts often caused by earthquakes. Use marbles, masking tape, string, a ruler, a table with overhang and scissors to observe how seismic waves are transmitted through Earth.

Directions: Cut five pieces of string, each 12" long. Tape each piece of string to a marble. Place the free end of the string even with the top of a table. Tape it to the edge of the table. Do this for each of the four strings. Adjust the length of the strings so that the marbles are exactly the same height and are touching each other.

Raise one of the end marbles to the side and release it. Observe what happens. Energy transferred from the initial blow and was spread out in waves.

Take It Away!

Here is an activity to help you understand the effects of erosion on Earth.

You will need:

dirt, five 12" square pieces of thick cardboard, 5 roasting-type pans (you may wish to purchase disposable ones), grass seed, small rocks, leaves, twigs, paper towels, a small watering can, water, a quart-size jar

Directions:

Moisten dirt and cover the 5 pieces of cardboard with at least an inch or two of the dirt. Then, do one of the following with each piece of cardboard:

1. Leave one piece of cardboard as is.

2. Set the leaves into the dirt in one.

3. Set the twigs into the dirt in one.

4. Set the rocks into the dirt in one.

5. Plant grass seed in one. Water it and wait for a good crop of grass to grow. When the board is dry and there is a good crop of grass, follow the directions below.

Lean the cardboard against the inside of a pan. Fill a quart jar with water and pour it into a watering can. Holding the spout about 2" above the cardboard, sprinkle water over it and observe the water flowing over the dirt into the pan.

To compare the amount of dirt that has been eroded, fold a paper towel into a cone shape. Place it in the mouth of the jar and pour the muddy water from the pan into it. Compare what each piece of cardboard looks like and the amount of dirt on the paper towels. Why do you think there are differences?

Whole Earth

Use this activity to help recognize definitions of geological words. You can play by yourself or with several people.

You will need: paper, one copy of the gameboard (per person) on page 225, pens, game markers

earthquake—sudden movement of Earth's crust caused by the release of pressure from inside Earth

epicenter—point on Earth's surface directly above the occurrence of an earthquake

erosion—combination of weathering and the movement of weathered material

fault—a break in Earth's crust

fault-block mountain—formed when sections of Earth's crust cracked and/or shifted up or down

folded mountains—formed when sections of Earth's crust have pushed together

hydrosphere—the liquid surface of Earth; the oceans, lakes, rivers and Earth's other bodies of waters

igneous—rock formed when magma finds its way from the inside of Earth and then cools and hardens

inner core—solid iron and nickel

lava—hot liquid rock that breaks through Earth's surface

lithosphere—Earth's crust and upper mantle

magma—hot liquid rock inside Earth

mantle—second layer of Earth's interior; a thick layer of solid rock

metamorphic—rock formed when igneous and sedimentary rocks are changed by heat and the weight of the crust pressing on them

minerals—inorganic substances with different chemical composition that make up Earth's crust

outer core—melted iron and nickel

Pangaea—a giant land mass that may have existed 200 million years ago

Richter scale—number system used to measure amount of shaking of an earthquake

sedimentary— rock formed by layers of loose materials deposited by water, wind and/or glaciers

seismograph—an instrument that measures and records waves produced by earthquakes

strata—layers of rock

tectonic plates—about 20 large, moving pieces of Earth's crust and upper mantle

tsunami—giant ocean wave caused by an earthquake under the ocean floor

volcano—opening in Earth's crust that releases gases and molten rock

weathering—process where rocks are worn into smaller pieces due to physical and chemical changes

Whole Earth

Directions:

After each person copies the words (not the definitions) in random order onto his/her individual gameboard, tell him/her to give each word a value of 1, 2 or 3 (not more than nine of each of the numbers) and write the number in the lower right-hand corner of the word box. Appoint a caller. The caller reads the definitions of one of the words. Players put a marker on the word whose definition was read. The first person to cover five across, down or diagonally in a row calls "Whole Earth." If all answers are correct, that person adds up the number of points (the five numbers in the boxes that make up the winning row), writes down the total and becomes the next caller. If two players call "Whole Earth" at the same time, the one with the higher score becomes the caller. At the end of the game, players add up their scores. The one with the most points is the winner.

Option:

Use this activity for one. To do this, make one gameboard. Write the definitions from the list in each box. Make 25 cards the size of the gameboard square. Write one of the words defined on each of the cards. Make a copy of the words and their definitions. Put everything in a manila folder or box. Put the words on the correct definitions. When the card is filled, check your answer against the answer sheet.

Whole Earth Gameboard

Copy one gameboard per player.

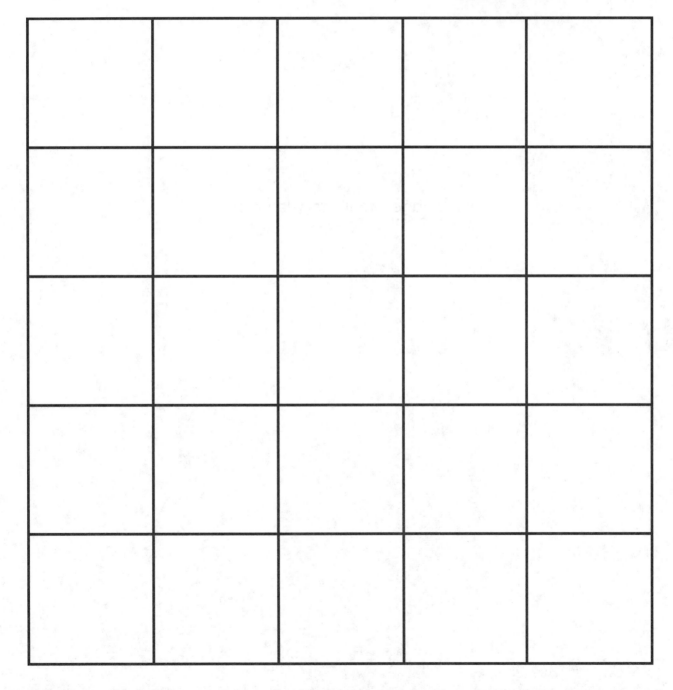

This page intentionally left blank.

Section 9
Weather

Cloud Coverage

You will need:

cotton balls, dryer lint or gray flannel, glue, 11" x 18" sheet of tagboard, a pencil, crayons, markers, white paint, paintbrushes, glitter, the book *Cloudy With a Chance of Meatballs* by Judi Barrett, other fiction and nonfiction books about clouds, a stapler

You can become more familiar with three major types of clouds when you complete this project. This activity should be completed over a period of a week or so.

To begin the project, use a pencil to divide the tagboard into six sections. (You can do this with an adult.) You will use the three top sections to simulate the three major types of clouds by following the directions below.

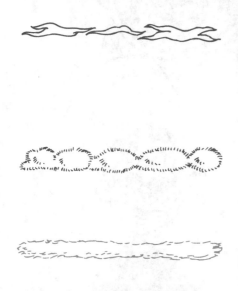

1. **Cirrus Clouds**—high, white clouds with a feathery appearance. To create this type of cloud, paint white streaks at the very top of your paper and sprinkle glitter sparingly while the paint is still wet to represent the ice that may be present in these high clouds.

2. **Cumulus Clouds**—puffy, white, low clouds with flat bottoms. In the second top box, glue cotton balls of various sizes approximately $\frac{1}{3}$ of the way down the paper.

3. **Stratus Clouds**—wide, often gray, low clouds that can drip snow flurries and drizzle. Glue dryer lint or gray flannel across the top of the third top box covering the length of the box.

After each of the three major cloud types is completed, draw pictures in the box underneath each cloud. The pictures should show activities you could do if you were to observe that particular type of cloud on any given day.

At some point in the week, read *Cloudy With a Chance of Meatballs*. Then, imagine that it rained something other than water or food. "What would come out of the clouds? What would this type of cloud look like? What would your umbrella look like? What would you do on a 'rainy' day?" Write your own story answering these questions. When the final draft is completed, staple it to the bottom of the cloud chart.

Cloud Families

You will need:

9" x12" sheets of gray paper, scissors, cotton, glue, a black felt-tip pen, practice paper, wire, a hole punch, string

Select the name of a type of a cloud (i.e., cumulus, stratus, cirrus). Include the name of the cloud in the title of your poem. Write a double cinquain poem about the chosen cloud.

Pattern for double cinquain poem:

first line = 4 syllables   **fourth line** = 16 syllables

second line = 8 syllables   **last line** = 4 syllables

third line = 12 syllables

First, write your poem on practice paper. When it is finished, cut out a cloud from gray paper and copy the poem on it using a black pen. Next, punch a hole in the top center of the cloud. Cut a piece of string long enough to tie one end to the cloud and the other end to the wire strung across the room. Stretch pieces of cotton out so that they are airy and fluffy. Put glue around the outside edge of the cloud on the same side on which your poem is written. Lightly press cotton onto the glue. Hang the cloud poem from the wire.

Cloud Watching

On a partly cloudy day, go to a park near home. Lie on your back to watch the clouds move and notice their shapes. What did you observe? With a drawing board, a piece of paper and pastel chalk, select a cloud to draw.

Rainmaker

You will need:

empty juice or jelly jars with lids, sandpaper, a nail, a hammer, water, index cards, a pencil, ice cubes, a stove, a measuring cup, a saucepan, potholders, a candle, salt

Have an adult available to help supervise this activity.

Directions:

Rub sandpaper on the lids of the jars until the paint is removed and the lids are shiny. Using a hammer and nail, make five- or six-inch dimples on the inside of the lid so that the points stick up on the top side of the lid. If you poke a hole in the lid, seal it on the inside using candle wax.

Pour a cup of water into the saucepan. Bring it to a boil. Use potholders to remove the pan from the stove. Pour the hot water into the jar. Place its lid upside-down on the jar's opening. Put ice cubes in the lid. Add a little water and salt and stir the mixture with your finger. Let the jar stand a few minutes. Write what happened on index cards and explain why that happened.

How Wet Is Wet?

Make several gauges and place them in different areas outside. Use the chart below to compare how much it has rained in different areas. Compare the amount of precipitation with that of the U.S. Weather Bureau (found in the newspaper or on the news).

You will need:

clear plastic glasses, a ruler with sixteenths, clear tape, an index card, masking tape, a pen

Directions:

To make a rain gauge, place the ruler so that it is just at the "floor" of your glass. (You want to measure the water that falls into the glass and not include its base.) Tape the ruler in place. Put your rain gauge in a flat, open area. After a rainfall, record the amount of water in the glass.

SNOW: You can use a ruler and a coffee can to measure snowfall. Put the coffee can in an open area. After snowfall, measure the inches of snow in the can using a ruler. Bring the can of snow inside. Let it melt. Pour it into a rain gauge. Write your observation on an index card.

Precipitation					
Name _____					
Address _____					
Date	Amount	Official	Date	Amount	Official

Rain in the Rainforest

At least 80 inches of rain falls, and thundershowers may occur for 200 or more days each year in a rainforest. **Rainforests** need a lot of rain so that the plants native to them do not dry out. Fill in the precipitation graph below with the average rainfall of a typical tropical rainforest. The amounts are listed beneath the graph.

	0 2 4 6 8 10 12 14 16 18 20 22 24 26 28 30
JANUARY	
FEBRUARY	
MARCH	
APRIL	
MAY	
JUNE	
JULY	
AUGUST	
SEPTEMBER	
OCTOBER	
NOVEMBER	
DECEMBER	

J	F	M	A	M	J	J	A	S	O	N	D
24"	20"	13"	11"	10"	7"	8"	9"	9"	11"	14"	18"

What was the total rainfall for the year in this rainforest? _____

What is the total rainfall for a year in your area? _____

Name _____

Lightning

Lightning is a flash of light caused by electricity in the sky. Clouds are made of many water droplets. All of these droplets together contain a large electrical charge. Sometimes these clouds set off a large spark of electricity called **lightning**. Lightning travels very fast. As it cuts through the air, it can cause thunder.

Lightning takes various forms. Some lightning looks like a zigzag in the sky. Sheet lightning spreads and lights the sky. Ball lightning looks like a ball of fire.

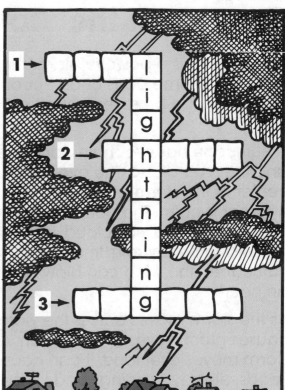

Underline:

Lightning is a flash of light

1. caused by sunshine.

2. caused by electricity in the sky.

Circle Yes or No:

Sometimes clouds set off a huge spark of electricity.	**Yes**	**No**
Lightning is caused by dry weather.	**Yes**	**No**
Lightning travels very fast.	**Yes**	**No**
Lightning can cause thunder.	**Yes**	**No**

Unscramble and write in the puzzle above:

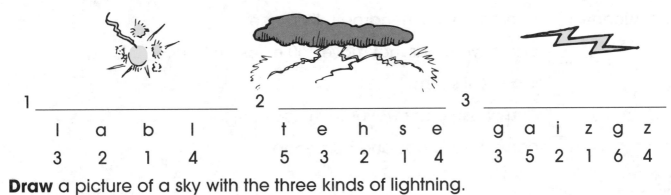

1 _____   2 _____   3 _____

l a b l   t e h s e   g a i z g z
3 2 1 4   5 3 2 1 4   3 5 2 1 6 4

Draw a picture of a sky with the three kinds of lightning.

Name _____

The Eye of the Storm

A **hurricane** is a powerful storm that forms over some parts of an ocean. A hurricane can be several hundred miles wide.

A hurricane has two main parts: the **eye** and the **wall cloud**. The eye is the center of the storm. In the eye, the weather is calm. The storm around the eye is called the wall cloud. It has strong winds and heavy rain. In some hurricanes, the wind can blow 150 miles an hour!

As the storm moves across the water, it causes giant waves in the ocean. As the storm moves over land, it can cause floods, destroy buildings and kill people who have not taken shelter.

Circle:

A hurricane has two main parts: tornado   wall cloud   eye

Match:

The calm center of the hurricane _____ .   wall cloud

The wind and rainstorm around the eye _____ .   eye

Check:

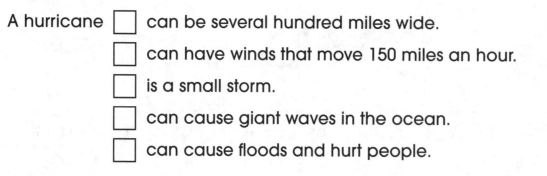

A hurricane ☐ can be several hundred miles wide.

☐ can have winds that move 150 miles an hour.

☐ is a small storm.

☐ can cause giant waves in the ocean.

☐ can cause floods and hurt people.

Wind and Weather

Make a weather vane to determine if wind direction is a prediction of weather.

You will need:

a pencil with an eraser, a drinking straw, a straight pin, a small, round wooden bead, construction paper, scissors, the tail pattern (below), tape, red paint, a paintbrush

Directions:

Paint the tip of the drinking straw red. This will be the pointer. Push the straight pin through the straw (about $\frac{1}{4}$ distance from the tail end), through the bead and then into the pencil eraser. Make a paper tail using the pattern and tape it to the end of the straw. For a period of a month, use this weather vane each day to determine the direction of the wind. You can use the chart above to record this data. Also, record the weather which follows the next day.

Did you notice any patterns? Try this experiment in different seasons to see if patterns change or if they are the same.

Wind Weather Chart	
Month _____	
Wind Direction	Weather
Day 1	
Day 2	
Day 3	
Day 4	
Day 5	

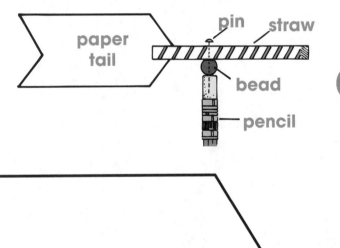

paper tail · pin · straw · bead · pencil

tail pattern

This page intentionally left blank.

A Funnel Cloud—Danger!

Did you know that a tornado is the most violent windstorm on Earth? A **tornado** is a whirling, twisting storm that is shaped like a funnel.

A tornado usually occurs in the spring on a hot day. It begins with thunderclouds and thunder. A cloud becomes very dark. The bottom of the cloud begins to twist and form a funnel. Rain and lightning begin. The funnel cloud drops from the dark storm clouds. It moves down toward the ground.

A tornado is very dangerous. It can destroy almost everything in its path.

Circle:

A thunder / tornado is the most violent windstorm on Earth.

Check:

Which words describe a tornado?

❑ whirling   ❑ twisting   ❑ icy   ❑ funnel-shaped   ❑ dangerous

Underline:

A funnel shape is:

Write and Circle:

A tornado usually occurs in the_____ on a cool / hot day.

autumn   spring

Write 1 - 2 - 3 below and in the picture above.

◯ The funnel cloud drops down to the ground.

◯ A tornado begins with dark thunder clouds.

◯ The dark clouds begin to twist and form a funnel.

Watch That Wind!

To depict how wind can be helpful and/or harmful, use paper, crayons, markers and newspaper weather articles to make the following display.

Divide a large sheet of paper in half. Label one side **Destructive Wind Forces** and the other side **Helpful Wind Forces**. Draw illustrations with appropriate captions or find newspaper weather articles to enter on both sides of the paper.

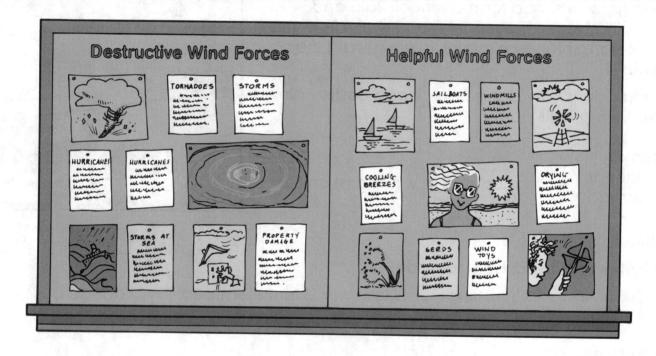

Windy Weather

Most people know of the dangerous aspects of wind—hurricanes, tornadoes, property damage, trees down, electric wires and telephone wires down, windstorms at sea, etc. Brainstorm some of the helpful aspects of wind, such as creating energy as in windmills, cooling you off on a hot day, moving sailboats, drying wet areas, transporting seeds, etc.

Weather Personalities

Talk about "weather personalities" such as Jack Frost and Punxsutawney Phil. Or, make up some of your own like Harry Cane, Ike Cicle, Gail Stone or MacLoud.

Pick or design a weather personality of your choice. Then, write a short story about the personality giving it human characteristics. Draw a picture of the personality in action. Then, put his/her story and picture inside a piece of 12" x 18" paper folded in half. On the outside, write the title of the story and your name as the author.

Speaking Weather

Write the weather expressions below or others of your own on a sheet of paper.

cool cat

hot number

razor-sharp winds

Snow White

thundering hooves

dancing raindrops

head in the clouds

greased lightning

fair-weather friend

cold shoulder

Write sentences using the expressions on the paper. Select one about which to write more.

Experiments With Air

You can demonstrate that air takes up space.

You will need:

a deep container such as an aquarium, a water glass, a sheet of paper towel or a paper napkin, paper, pencils

Directions:

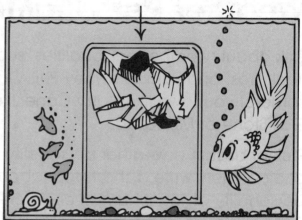

Read over the questions for observation #1 and #2 at the bottom of the page and make predictions. Then, do the demonstration below.

Fold the sheet of paper towel or paper napkin so that you can force it into the bottom of the glass. Make sure that it will not fall out when the glass is inverted. Next, lower the glass, mouth downward into the container of water. Lower it until the glass is completely submerged making sure that the mouth of the glass remains downward. Hold the glass in this position for several seconds. Withdraw the glass from the container keeping the mouth downward. After the glass has been completely removed from the water, remove the paper and examine it. Answer observation #1 questions.

Observation #1

1. Was the paper wet or dry?

2. Why do you think the paper was in that condition?

3. What was in the glass besides the paper?

4. How do you know?

Repeat the experiment. This time, tilt the glass a little at a time. Then, remove the glass and examine the paper. Answer observation #2 questions.

Observation #2

1. What do you see in the container of water when you tilt the glass?

2. Was the paper wet or dry?

3. Why?

4. How do you know?

Can You Pour Air?

Directions:

Lower a water glass (mouth downward) into a basin filled with water. Next, lower another glass of exactly the same size into the container of water. Tilt the second glass until it fills up with water. Still holding both glasses under water, turn the glass filled with water up so that the mouths of both glasses are together. Now, turn the first glass upward and watch the air pour from the first glass into the second. Holding both glasses under water, continue to pour the air from one glass into the other. Was either glass empty at any time?

Heavy or Light Air

Follow the directions and make a barometer to use for weather predictions.

You will need:

a glass or jar with a wide mouth, a balloon, a rubber band, a broom straw, scissors, tape, a black felt-tip pen, paper, tagboard

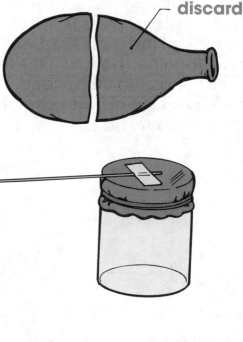

discard

Directions:

1. Blow up a balloon. Let the air out. Cut the balloon in half and throw away the part with the neck. Stretch the top part over the mouth of the jar. Secure it with a rubber band.

2. Tape a broom straw on top of the stretched balloon.

3. Cut a piece of tagboard a little taller than the jar. Set it up against a wall. Put the barometer next to it with the straw in front of the tagboard.

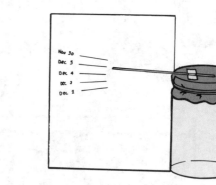

Each time you read the barometer, make an extension of the broom straw and write the date and time after it using a marker. If the broom straw is higher than the last time the barometer was read, mark an up arrow (↑) on the weather chart. If it is lower, mark a down arrow (↓). If it is the same, write **steady**. Predict what the weather might be in the next 24 hours.

Higher air pressure usually indicates fair or sunny weather. Lower air pressure usually indicates an approaching change in the weather, maybe precipitation.

Weather Station

Name _____

Watch a national broadcast of weather on television every day. Using the information that you gather watching the television weather and checking the weather in the local newspaper, keep the Weather Station chart below. After several days, compare the reports. Do you see any patterns?

DATE	TIME OF DAY	WEATHER PREDICTION	TEMPER-ATURE	ACTUAL WEATHER	PRECIP-ITATION	BAROMETRIC PRESSURE	WIND DIR.	WIND SPEED	U.S. REPORT

Whirly Wind

Make an instrument to measure the wind's speed.

You will need:

tennis balls of like color, small nails or tacks, a long, thin nail, a 2" square stake which is 6' tall, grease, enamel paint, paintbrushes, turpentine, an empty jar, a stopwatch, ¾-1" trim, a small saw, a drill with ⅜-¼" bit, a ruler, a pencil, a hammer

Have an adult available to help supervise this activity.

Directions:

1. Cut two pieces of trim. Measure and mark 12" on each piece of trim. Using a saw, cut them to this length.

2. Cut two tennis balls of like colors in half. Paint one of the halves a different color. Let it dry.

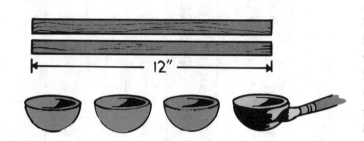

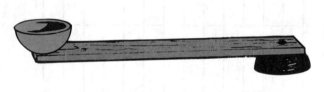

3. Nail the tennis ball halves to the end of the 12" strips of wood. The outside of each tennis ball should touch the wood. One-half should face one way, and the other half should face the other way. In other words, the halves will be on opposite sides of the strips.

4. Drill a hole in one end of the stake. Put grease in it to cut down on friction.

5. Cross the two wood strips with the balls attached so that the hollow of the balls are all facing the same direction. Have someone hold the stake. Put the balls on top of the stake. Drive the stake into the ground outside, away from anything that could block the wind from reaching it. Drive a long, thin nail though the wood strips and onto the hole in the stake.

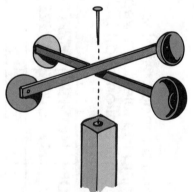

It takes two people to measure the wind speed. One person controls the stopwatch. That person starts the watch and at the same time says, "Count." The other person counts the number of revolutions (number of times the painted ball goes around) until the person with the stopwatch says "Stop" (30 seconds). Divide the number of revolutions by five to determine the wind speed.

Let the Wind Blow

You will need:

a globe
dry-erase markers
an index card
a pencil
cloth

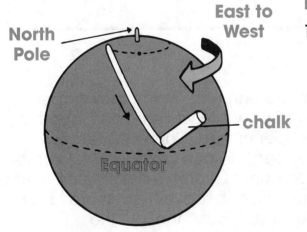

Directions:

1. Put one hand on top of the globe and slowly turn it from east to west. As the globe turns, draw a line straight down from the North Pole to the equator. Stop the globe. Look at the line you drew. Draw a picture of it on an index card. Draw an arrow to show its direction. Explain from which direction to which direction the line travels. Label this side of the card **Trade Winds**.

2. Put one hand on top of the globe and slowly turn it again, only this time turn it west to east. As the globe turns, draw a line straight up from the equator to the North Pole. Stop the globe. Look at the line you drew. On the other side of the index card, write **Prevailing Winds**. Draw a picture of the line you made with an arrow to show its direction. Explain from which direction to which direction the line travels. Compare trade winds to prevailing winds.

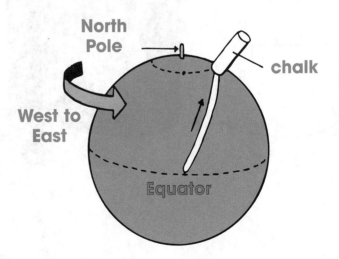

Cool Color

Does color have anything to do with temperature?

You will need:

2 identical glasses
one 9" x 12" sheet of black paper
one 9" x 12" sheet of white paper
masking tape
an index card
a pencil
a pen
an outside thermometer
water
scissors

Copy the Cool Color chart information onto the index card.

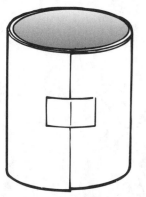

Cool Color

Name _____

Directions:

Wrap one glass with black paper and one with white paper. Tape the paper closed. Cut off the excess paper. Fill each glass with the same amount of water. Set both glasses in a sunny spot. Leave them there for at least an hour. Then, put the thermometer into each glass and record the temperature of each on the Cool Color chart. Also write on the chart what you concluded from this experiment. Do this experiment at least two more times to verify your conclusion. Try other colors to see if there is any difference.

Note: The water in the jar wrapped with black paper should be warmer because the black paper absorbs more heat than the white.

Sailboat Race

Put two toy boats in a large tub of water. Have one person use a feather to create wind while another person uses a piece of cardboard. Predict which boat will win the race. Try to sail the boats. Try some other materials to create wind and "sail" the boats.

Dry That Spot

Using a sponge or paper towel, put two equal-sized wet spots on a chalkboard. Let one dry by itself and fan the other one using a piece of cardboard. Predict which one will dry faster. Discuss the other ways wind can be used to do work. Illustrate one of them.

Section 10

Environment

Keep Earth Green!

Make a Healthy Environment book by using the charts and information on pages 249-255.

You will need: 9" x 12" sheets of construction paper in a variety of colors, scissors, a stapler, a black felt-tip pen, a black pen, green posterboard paint, paintbrushes, glue, the picture of Earth (below), the Survey sheet found on page 253, the Survey Results sheet found on page 255.

Directions: Cut out the picture of Earth. Use a black pen to outline the land masses. Paint the land masses green. Glue the globe to one piece of construction paper. With markers, write **Keep** on the left side of the globe and **Green** on the right.

This page intentionally left blank.

Keep Earth Green!

Survey your home. On a blank survey form (you will need a copy for each family member who will be participating), have each person fill in each category. Follow the instructions in each section of the survey sheet.

Estimate how much water was used by the family using the chart "Amount of Water Used" at the right. Decide the precise number of gallons (average) you will use to figure for each. (A typical person uses about 70 gallons of water a day.) Fill in the blanks in the study summary letter (page 255). Then, glue it, as well as all tally sheets onto separate sheets of construction paper. Staple the title page and all others (survey sheets and summary letter) together to complete the Keep Earth Green book.

Amount of Water Used

- Each time a toilet is flushed, about 3 gallons of water are used.

- Each time a bath is taken, 30-40 gallons of water are used.

- Each 10-minute shower uses about 50-70 gallons of water.

- Each load in a washing machine uses about 30 gallons of water.

- Each load of dishes in a dishwasher uses about 10 gallons of water.

Invisible Pollution

Check out how much cars pollute the air. You will need an automobile and an old white sock. Put a sock over a cold tailpipe of the car. An adult will then run the motor for one minute. Take the sock off the tailpipe and look at the sock. What you see is air pollution which normally cannot be seen. Imagine what is being put in the air by millions of cars every day. Then, write a "jingle" telling people to leave their cars at home and travel by other means of transportation.

Three R's of Conservation

Use posterboard, colored markers, a pencil, a ruler, assorted colored paper, scissors, glue and scratch paper to check out the 3 R's.

Teach your child the 3 R's: **reduce** the use of anything detrimental to the environment or that is not needed, **reuse** whatever possible and **recycle** as much as possible.

Make a poster emphasizing the 3 R's of conservation. First, lay out the design of your poster on paper using a pencil. Then, use markers and/or construction paper and cut it into any letters and shapes you want. The cut paper will have to be glued into place on the posterboard. Hang the poster where all can see.

Ecology Password

Use this activity to practice what you have learned about ecology. You will need small slips of paper, a paper bag and a marker.

On a separate slip of paper, write nouns relating to the environment (i.e., rainforest, acid rain, landfill, etc.). Place all of the strips in a bag and shake them up. Select a strip from the bag. Take five minutes to think of ten words to describe your word. Then, share those clues with others, giving them three guesses. Continue until you have had the opportunity to describe several nouns.

Name _____

Keep the Earth Green! Survey

TRASH

List what you throw away each day in the appropriate column.
Circle the items that you recycle.

MONDAY	TUESDAY	WEDNESDAY	THURSDAY	FRIDAY	SATURDAY	SUNDAY

USING RECYCLED MATERIALS

List the recycled items you use. There are two ways to tell if something has been recycled: it could have a logo or it may be gray or brown—never white. (Examples: inside of a cereal box, writing paper, greeting cards, etc.)

_____
_____
_____
_____
_____
_____
_____
_____
_____
_____
_____
_____

WATER USAGE

Make a tally mark under the appropriate day each time you did one of the following:

	M	T	W	TH	F	SA	SU
Flushed Toilet							
Took Bath							
*Took Shower							
Ran Washing Machine							
Ran Dish-washer							

*Write the number of minutes you ran water to take a shower.

This page intentionally left blank.

Keep Earth Green! Survey Results

Dear _____,

Here are the results of my survey. In our household during the time it was surveyed, we threw out _____

_____

_____

and recycled _____

_____.

In recycled material, we used _____

_____.

We flushed our toilets ___ times, using approximately ___ gallons of water. We took ___ baths (___ gallons). We took ___ minutes of showers (___gallons). The washing machine was run ___ times (___ gallons) and the dishwasher was run ___ times (___ gallons). Our household used approximately ___ gallons of water in the time period measured.

Thank you for participating in the survey. Let's talk over the results. Let's see if there is something more we can do in our home to help keep Earth healthy.

_____

signed

This page intentionally left blank.

To Stay Or Not To Stay

Check out what is, or is not, **biodegradable** with this long-term activity.

You will need: an adult, trowel, apple cores, large lettuce leaves, plastic packing, styrofoam cups, tongue depressors, pencils

Directions:

1. Find a spot where it is all right to dig 4 holes. Dig all about the same size —2" deep by 3" square.

2. Put the item for each hole in the hole and cover it with dirt.

3. Then, write the name of the item buried on a tongue depressor and stick it in the ground above the spot where the item is buried.

4. In a month, go back and dig up the items. Discuss with an adult what was discovered.

Where Are the Apples?

What happens to food thrown away outside? Try this activity to help answer that question.

You will need: apple cores, 9" x 12" sheet of paper, a pencil

This activity will take a few days or weeks. Put two or three apple cores in a corner of your yard. Fold a piece of paper into sixths. Number each box. Look at the apple cores every day. Write, in order in the boxes, the dates you looked at the cores. You should use both sides of the paper. A second sheet can be used if the activity goes on longer. In each section, draw a picture of what the cores look like each day and write a sentence or two about what you observed.

Acid Action

Using three plants, watch to see how acid water affects growth.

You will need: 3 quart jars, 3 similar plants, vinegar, tape, a pencil, water, paper, a marker

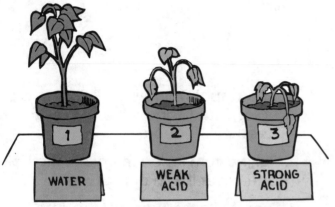

Directions:

Fill one jar with water, one with a little vinegar and the rest water, and one with mostly vinegar and a little water. On a piece of tape write **1. WATER**. Put the tape on the jar filled with water. On another piece of tape, write **2. WEAK ACID**. Put it on the jar filled with a little vinegar (weak acid). On yet another piece of tape, write **3. STRONG ACID** and put it on the jar filled with mostly vinegar (strong). On three pieces of tape write **1.**, **2.** and **3.** Tape a number on each plant. Water the plants as follows: #1 with water, #2 with weak acid and #3 with strong acid. Observe how the plants grow under these conditions. Record the results on a piece of paper.

Trash Hunt

Designate a day "Neighborhood Clean-Up Day." You will need trash bags for this activity.

Take a walk in your neighborhood to pick up litter. Put the litter in bags. One at a time, have each person who helped empty his/her collection of trash in the center of the circle. Look at it and classify it generally according to paper, glass, metal, etc. Or, classify it more specifically (i.e., ice-cream wrappers, broken toys, school papers, etc.). You can then make a bar graph that shows what you found.

On another day, go for another "trash hunt" around another child's home. Compare the amount and kind of litter picked up in the two areas or that were found at two different times.

Twice Around

Make some recycled paper.

You will need: old paper that is not shiny (newspaper, egg cartons—not styrofoam, old envelopes, etc.), a blender or beater, a bowl, a dishpan or large, deep pan, a piece of window screen, paper towels, sections of the newspaper, pens, a measuring cup, a large board, water, tape

Put tape around the edges of the screen. Follow the directions below. An adult should work with you for the activity after the first soaking (#1).

Directions:

1. Tear enough old paper into tiny pieces to fill six cups. Put them in a pan. Cover the paper with water. Soak this overnight.

2. Blend or beat a small handful of the soaked paper with two or three cups of water. Add water if blending or beating is too difficult. Empty the pulp into a large bowl. Continue making small batches of pulp.

3. Add enough water to the pan so that when you stir the mixture with your fingers, you cannot feel the pulp.

4. Tilt the screen and slide it to the bottom of the pan. Using your fingers, spread the pulp evenly over the screen. Let it settle a minute.

5. Open a section of newspaper to its center. Cover one side of it with paper towels.

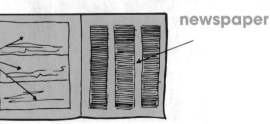

newspaper

paper
towels

6. Lift the screen straight up over the pan. Let it drain.

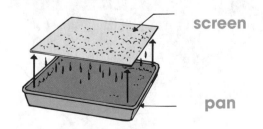

screen

pan

Twice Around

7. Place the screen with the pulp onto the side of newspaper without towels. Close the paper making sure the towels are over the screen.

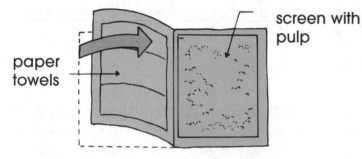

paper towels

screen with pulp

8. Carefully flip the entire newspaper section so that the screen is on top of the pulp.

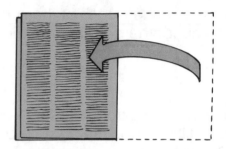

9. Put the board on top of the newspaper. Press on it to squeeze out the excess water.

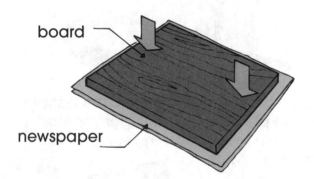

board

newspaper

10. Open the newspaper. Remove the screen. Carefully remove the paper towel with the pulp on it to a dry piece of newspaper. Let it dry.

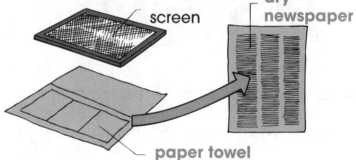

screen

dry newspaper

paper towel

11. When dry, carefully peel the pulp away from the paper towel.

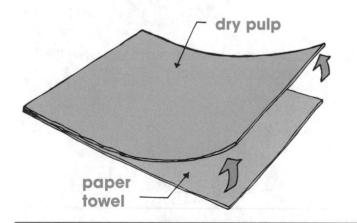

dry pulp

paper towel

12. Write a message about recycling on it.

RECYCLE OLD PAPER

SAVE A TREE

Conservation Wise

This game will help you learn ways to help keep the environment safe.

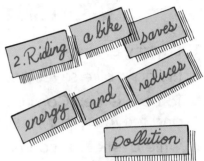

You will need: tagboard, a paper cutter, a black felt-tip pen, an index card, a manila envelope, writing paper, pens, a copy of the sentences on page 262, scissors

Write the first half of each sentence and its number on page 262 on tagboard. Cut these apart. Write the last part of each of the sentences on tagboard. Write the number of each sentence's first half on the back, making sure the number does not "show through." Cut them apart.

Directions: Match up the phrases so that they make sense and make 20 sentences. These sentences will tell you 20 things you can do to help keep the environment safe. Check your work by seeing if the number on the back of the second half matches the number on the front of the first half.

• •

Save Earth!

You will need: chart paper, a black pen, 18" x 24" sheets of colored paper, scraps of assorted colors of paper, scissors, glue, a pencil, drawing paper scraps, a copy of *My Teacher Flunked the Planet* by Bruce Coville.

Make two lists—one containing good things about Earth and the other containing things that could be improved on Earth. Select one of the things that needs fixing and design a poster stating a concern and/or solution for the problem. When your poster is planned, select a large piece of paper

for its background. Then, cut out letters and/or figures using the scraps of colored paper. Set the letters/figures on the poster and glue them in place. Put your poster up in the neighborhood.

Conservation-Wise Sentences

1. Buy dry groceries in cardboard boxes / made from recycled material.

2. Riding a bike saves / energy and reduces pollution.

3. To be a Green Consumer, refuse to buy excessively packaged products / and reuse and recycle what you can.

4. Write a letter to a company doing something environmentally / harmful and ask its people to change their ways.

5. Help reduce needless waste by not / purchasing products with excessive packaging.

6. Mix waste foods with dirt to make a compost / pile that will help plants grow.

7. Know what you want from the refrigerator before you open the door so / energy won't be wasted by the door being open too long.

8. Look for spray bottles rather than aerosols which are non-recyclable, / fill up landfills and contribute to air pollution.

9. Lessen water pollution by eating vegetables that don't have / chemicals sprayed on them which can often be washed into streams.

10. Dispose of hazardous waste materials / at a site set aside for them.

11. Just because you are outside on a picnic / doesn't mean you have to use throwaway plates and cups.

12. Reduce your heating bill and energy usage / by sealing off drafts and checking the insulation in your home.

13. Recycle paper by using the back / of a sheet of paper.

14. Plant a tree to help / hold the ground.

15. Batteries contain hazardous materials which can leak / into landfills when thrown away, so use rechargeable ones.

16. Set up a recycling center in your home and / recycle newspapers, glass and aluminum.

17. Take bags to the store when you shop and fill them with what you buy / rather than taking more bags home and throwing them away.

18. Turn tap water on and off as / you need it when brushing your teeth.

19. Turn off lights when you are not using them to cut down / on your electric bill and energy usage.

20. You can tell if a product or package is made from recyclable materials / if it is gray or dark brown—not white.

Save Earth! Careers

You will need: paper, a black pen, reference books, pens

Look at the names of jobs below that help save Earth. Feel free to add to the list.

solid waste technician	geologist
air pollution inspector	ecologist
sewage plant worker	forester
pollution scientist	oceanographer
city planner	marine biologist
park ranger	forest naturalist
forest ranger	conservationist

Select from the list above a career about which you would like to learn and write a report about it. If someone in the community holds one of those jobs, you should write the person to ask for an interview and/or on-site visit, or ask if they might send information about their job. You may also learn about environmental careers from reference books or by obtaining material from one of the organizations below.

Air and Waste Management Association
Gateway Center, 3rd Floor
Pittsburgh, PA 15222

American Forests
1516 P Street NW, P.O. Box 2000
Washington, D.C. 20005

American Geological Institute
4220 King Street
Alexandria, VA 22302

American Institute of Architects
1735 New York Avenue NW
Washington, D.C. 20006

American Water Works Association
6666 W. Qunicy Avenue
Denver, CO 80235

Conservation Fund
1800 N. Kent Street, Suite 1120
Arlington, VA 22209

Save Earth! Careers

Ecological Society of America
Arizona State University
Center for Environmental Studies
Tempe, AZ 85287-3211

Environmental Protection Agency
401 M Street SW
Washington, D.C. 20460

International Oceanographic Foundation
4600 Rickenbacker Causeway
P.O. Box 499900
Miami, FL 33149-9900

National Ocean Industries Association
1120 G Street NW, Suite 900
Washington, D.C. 20005

National Park Foundation
1101 17th Street NW, Suite 1102
Washington, D.C. 20036

National Recreation and Park Assoc.
2775 S. Quincy Street, Suite 300
Arlington, VA 22206-2204

National Solid Wastes Management Assoc.
4301 Connecticut Avenue NW, Suite 300
Washington, D.C. 20008

The Nature Conservancy
1815 N. Lynn Street
Arlington, VA 22209

U.S. Forest Service
14th Street and Independence Ave. SW
P.O. Box 96090
Washington, D.C. 20090

U.S. Geological Survey
120 Sunrise Valley Drive
Reston, VA 22092

Seeing is Believing

Arrange for one or more tours to the following:

| aquarium | national park | disposal plant |
| science museum | landfill | sewage plant |

Visit a place that has something to do with keeping the environment safe. After the trip, make a cumulative list of the many things being done to protect the environment.

Section 11
Magnets

Name _____

The Invisible Force

Hold a magnet close to a piece of metal. Do you feel a pulling force? Magnets are attracted to certain metals. The invisible force is called **magnetism.**

What kinds of objects will a magnet pull? The best and the most fun way to find out is to experiment. Gather some of the objects listed below. Hold a small magnet next to these objects. Which objects will the magnet pull? Add some of your own objects to the list.

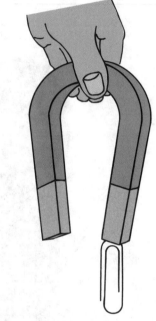

Object	Magnet Attracts	Magnet Does Not Attract
scissors		
wood ruler		
eraser		
paper clip		
thumbtack		
paper		
aluminum foil		

Magnets do not attract all metals. Find the six metals in the word search. The metals that are written "up and down" are attracted to magnets. The metals written "across" are not attracted. List each metal in the correct group.

```
B N B R A S S X
Z I K L N T I A
A C O P P E R D
N K T R O E O S
T E K G N L N P
A L U M I N U M
```

Attracted By Magnets	Not Attracted By Magnets
_____	_____
_____	_____
_____	_____

Fantastic Fact

Magnets were named after a shepherd called Magnes. According to legend, magnets were first discovered when Magnes stood on a rock. His sandals stuck to the rock when the nails in his sandals stuck to the "magic" rock. The magic rock was lodestone, a natural form of a magnet.

Name _____

Magnetic Attraction

Try to pick up each of these objects with your magnet. Circle the ones it picks up.

scissors   eraser   ruler   pencil   crayon

paper clip   thumbtack   toothpick   pen

A magnet will only pick up an object made of _____.

Investigate:

List all the objects you can find which your magnet picks up or is attracted to.

1. _____   6. _____

2. _____   7. _____

3. _____   8. _____

4. _____   9. _____

5. _____   10. _____

Is the magnet attracted to any non-metal object?

Extension:

Hold a piece of tagboard between the magnet and each object you listed in the "Investigate" section. List each one the magnet is still attracted to.

_____

_____

Place each of the objects the magnet is still attracted to in a cup of water.

Hold the magnet against the outside of the cup.

Which items was the magnet still able to attract? _____

_____

What other materials can a magnet attract objects through, besides tagboard and water? _____

Maggie the Magnet

You will need:

an iron rod
a horseshoe magnet
two pipe cleaners
several pieces of yarn
construction paper
writing paper
tape
a shoe box
crayons
scissors
the story on the following pages

Before you begin, create Maggie Magnet and Iggie Iron. To do this, tape a few pieces of yarn onto a horseshoe magnet to create Maggie, and wrap pipe cleaners around the iron rod to create short hands and legs for Iggie. Next, create a setting for the story. To do this, stand a shoe box on its side. Cut off three sides of the box so that a wall is created. Tape the wall to a table or desk. Next, read the story, "Maggie the Magnet" on the following pages without using the characters, setting and illustrations.

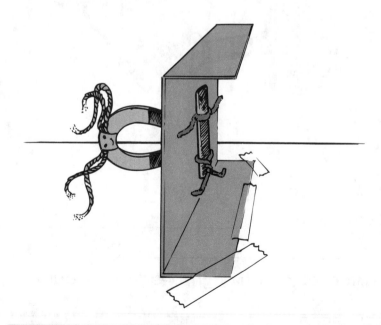

Reread the partial story again, this time using the characters and setting you created earlier to create a reenactment of the story. Illustrate each scene. Complete the story by solving the problem using your knowledge of magnets, and unite Maggie and Iggie. Cut apart and assemble the pages to create the book. You can create a cover using construction paper. Use the "stage" you created to perform the completed story with a friend.

Maggie the Magnet

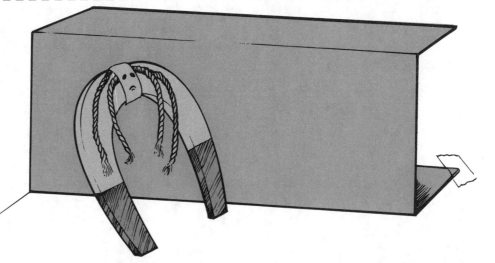

Once upon a time, in a faraway land, lived Maggie the Magnet. Maggie the Magnet was extremely upset. She wanted to see her friend Iggie Iron who lived on the other side of the wall.

"The wall is much too high for me to climb," cried Iggie Iron.

"Oh Iggie!" exclaimed Maggie the Magnet, "I wish so much to see you! If only we could think of a way to get you over this wall!"

This page intentionally left blank.

Maggie the Magnet

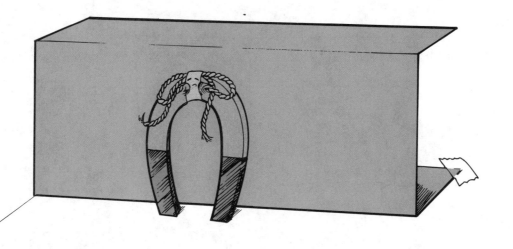

Maggie leaned against the wall and began to cry in despair. Suddenly, she heard Iggie give a yell. "Whooooaa!" cried Iggie with surprise. Then, there was a loud "thump" followed by silence.

"Iggie, are you all right?" shouted Maggie with fear.

"I think so, Maggie . . . but I'm stuck to the wall!" Iggie responded in a high-pitched voice, unsure of what had happened.

This page intentionally left blank.

Name _____

Magnets

You will need:

a magnet
several objects made of various
    materials (i.e., paper clips, staples,
    rubber bands, paper fasteners,
    coins, aluminum foil, a gold ring, a
    silver ring, a piece of copper wire,
    several non-magnetic metals)
a marker
paper

Object	Magnetic	Non-Magnetic

Predict which objects would be attracted to a magnet. Draw a simple chart to classify your predictions (see above). Place the objects for which the predictions have been made in the correct column on the chart. After all the objects have been classified, test them with a magnet. Rearrange misclassified objects. Think about why these objects may have been misclassified. Scientific experiments are much more accurate than just guessing.

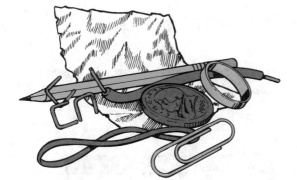

Magnetic Magician

The force of a magnet may pass through certain objects. Perform this activity to find out what materials work.

You will need: one strong magnet, paper clips, a sheet of paper, a piece of cardboard, a plate, a glass, a thin piece of wood, a piece of fabric, aluminum foil, a sheet of plastic, the lid of a large tin can, a plastic lid

Place some paper clips on the top of each of the materials listed above. Move a magnet under the materials. Watch to see if the magnet moves the clips through the paper, the wood, the glass, etc. If the clips can be moved, the force of the magnet is working through the material. Through experimentation, you will discover that magnetism will not pass through materials which are themselves magnetic. Why do you think this is so?

Name _____

Push and Pull

The ends of a magnet are called its **poles.** One pole is called the north-seeking pole or north pole; the other is the south-seeking pole, or south pole.

When the poles of two bar magnets are put near each other, they have a force that will either pull them together or push them part. If the poles are **different**, then they will pull together, or **attract** each other. (One pole is a south pole and one pole is a north pole.) If the poles are the **same**, then they will push apart, or **repel** each other. (They are either both south poles or both north poles.) The push and pull force of a magnet is called **magnetism.**

1. If these magnets are brought toward each other, will they attract or repel each other?

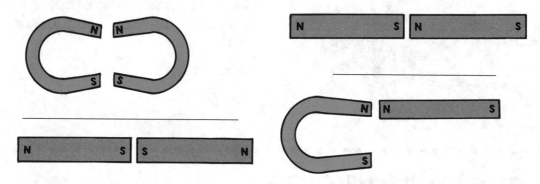

2. Look at each picture. Does the ? show a north pole or a south pole?

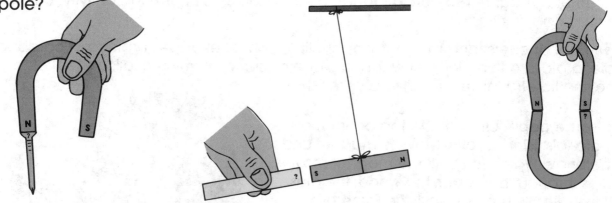

Fantastic Fact
If a magnet is broken into pieces, each piece will have a north pole and a south pole.

Name _____

Magnet Magic

It is a lot of fun to play with magnets. In the pictures below are some "tricks" that you can do to amaze your friends. Under each picture, explain why each of these amazing things happens.

The Magic Dollar

_____
_____
_____

The Unfriendly Needles

_____
_____
_____

The Trained Paper Clip

_____
_____
_____

The Magic Push

_____
_____
_____

Investigate

Magnets are attracted to the metal nickel, but are they attracted to a "nickel" (5¢ coin)? Try picking up a U.S. 5¢ nickel with a magnet. Now try to pick up a Canadian 5¢ nickel. What did you find? Why did this happen?

Which Magnet Is Stronger?

You will need:

2 horseshoe magnets
paper clips
a nail
2 bar magnets
a ruler

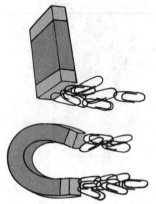

Directions:

1. Use the two horseshoe magnets to pick up paper clips. Record how many paper clips each magnet picks up. Repeat this with the two bar magnets and record the results. Does each magnet pick up the same number of clips each time?_____Does one magnet pick up more clips than the other at each try?_____Which one appears to be stronger? _____

   Why? _____

   _____

2. Use two horseshoe magnets. Put a nail between the poles of the two magnets. Pull the magnets apart slowly. The nail will remain with one magnet. Which magnet do you think is stronger?_____

   Why do you think so? _____

   _____

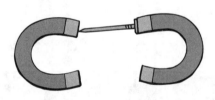

3. Use the two bar magnets. Place a nail on top of a ruler near its end. Move the magnet very slowly toward the nail. Note the point at which the nail will start to move toward the magnet. (What makes the nail move toward the magnet?) Now, repeat this with the second magnet. Note the distance at which the nail starts to move toward this magnet. Which magnet do you think is stronger? _____

   Why do you think so?_____

   _____

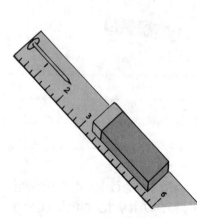

Name _____

The North Pole

The Earth is like a big magnet and has magnetic poles just like a magnet. The Earth's magnetic poles are near the Earth's **true poles.**

A **compass** is a free-turning magnet. Compasses that you buy are made with a thin magnet, called a **needle,** that turns freely inside a case. The case is made of a non-magnetic material. The north-seeking pole of the magnet is attracted toward the Earth's **magnetic north pole.** The other end points to the **magnetic south pole.** A compass helps you find the directions north and south.

There is a **compass rose** in the corner of Elgin's map. The compass rose gives the eight compass directions: North (N), South (S), East (E), West (W), Northeast (NE), Southeast (SE), Southwest (SW) and Northwest (NW).

Follow the directions to find where the secret treasure is buried. Each box is equal to one step.

Directions:

1. Start at the star.
2. Go North 5 steps.
3. Go East 9 steps.
4. Go Southwest 4 steps.
5. Go East 2 steps.
6. Go South 2 steps.
7. Go Northeast 4 steps.
8. Dig here. You have reached the secret treasure!

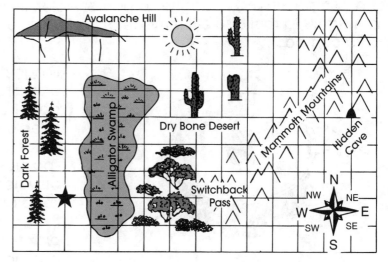

Challenge
While leaning against his dad's car, Elgin noticed that his compass would not point to north. What was the problem?

Make a Magnet

You will need:

a nail
a bar magnet
some paper clips

Directions:

Using a bar magnet, pick up the paper clips. Next, try to pick up the paper clips using the nail. Does it work? Now, you will try to turn the nail into a magnet. Stroke the nail in one direction (not back and forth) with one end of the magnet about 25-30 times. Now, try to use the nail to pick up the paper clips. The nail has been magnetized. How many clips will it pick up? Is it as strong as the bar magnet? Drop the nail on the floor a few times. Will it still pick up as many clips? What does this tell you about the effect of dropping a magnet?

Which Way Is North?

Make a compass using a magnet, a pan of water, a long sewing needle (test it first with a magnet to make sure it is made of iron), a slice of cork, candle wax and a standard compass.

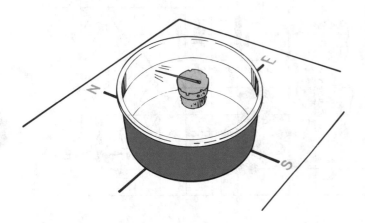

Magnetize the needle by stroking it in one direction with a strong magnet about 25-30 times. Place the magnetized needle on a slice of cork and keep it in place using a drop of candle wax. This "pointer" should next be floated in a pan of water. It is important to remember to keep all objects made of iron away from the compass as iron objects in close proximity will cause deviation in the compass.

The needle of the compass should be pointing north. Check this with a standard compass. Are both compasses pointing in the same direction? They do because a magnetic needle compass always points in the north-south direction towards the magnetic north and south poles.

Name _____

Electromagnets

Some of the most powerful magnets are made with electricity. These magnets are called **electromagnets**. A strong magnet can be made by winding wire around an iron bar. As soon as the current from a battery is switched on, the bar becomes a strong electromagnet. The magnet can be switched off by stopping the flow of current.

Larry and Eddie each made an electromagnet. Only one of them worked.

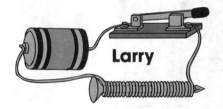
Larry

Eddie

1. Whose electromagnet worked? _____

2. Why wouldn't the other electromagnet work? _____

_____

3. Electromagnets have many uses and can be found in many places.

Circle and list the objects in the word search which use electromagnets.

1. _____
2. _____
3. _____
4. _____
5. _____
6. _____
7. _____
8. _____

```
T D O O R B E L L L T
E T A B E K J S R A A
L X O L F V R E L P P
E S T E R E O T R E E
V A E L I T H O N R R
I M L O G U A R B E E
S P E R E N O G L C C
I X P L R K A M I O O
O R H R A D I O T R R
N R O L T U P R O D D
B A N M O T O R K E E
S H E L R M U S L R R
```

Investigate
Make an electromagnet like the one in the picture above.

1. What happens to the strength of your electromagnet if you use more turns of wire?

2. Is your electromagnet still magnetic when you disconnect it from the battery?

279

Working with Electromagnets

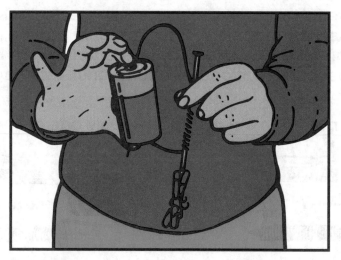

Investigate with an adult:

1. Strip 1 inch of insulation from each end of a 2-foot-long piece of thin wire.

2. Wrap the wire around a nail 30 times, leaving most of the extra wire dangling at one end.

3. Touch one bare end of the wire to the top of a battery.

4. Touch the other bare end of the wire to the bottom of the battery.

5. Hold the nail near some paper clips. How many paper clips did the electromagnet pick up?_____

Making the electromagnet stronger:

Wrap the wire around the nail 30 more times.

How many paper clips will the electromagnet pick up now? _____

Tape two batteries together with the top of one battery touching the bottom of the other.

How many paper clips will the electromagnet pick up now? _____

Wrap as many coils around the nail as you can.

How many paper clips can you pick up now? _____

Name two ways to make an electromagnet stronger._____

_____

Electricity

Name _____

Charge It!

Have you ever scuffed your feet as you walked across the carpet and then brought your finger close to someone's nose? Zap! Did the person jump? The spark you made was **static electricity.**

Static electricity is made when objects gain or lose tiny bits of electricity called **electrical charges.** The charges are either positive or negative.

Objects that have electrical charges act like magnets, attracting or repelling each other. If two objects have **like charges** (the same kind of charges), they will repel each other. If the two objects have **unlike charges** (different charges), the objects will attract each other.

Directions:

Find out more about static electricity by unscrambling the word(s) in each sentence.

1. Flashes of (ghtlining) _____ in the sky are caused by static electricity in the clouds.

2. Electrical charges are either (ospivite) _____ or (givnatee) _____.

3. Small units of electricity are called (srgache) _____.

4. Two objects with unlike charges will (arcttat) _____ each other.

5. Sometimes electric charges jump between objects with (unkile) _____ charges. This is what happens when lightning flashes across the sky.

Look at the pictures below to see how static electricity affects objects.

1. Name the two objects that are interacting in each picture.

2. Tell whether the two objects have like charges or unlike charges.

Objects: _____ _____ _____

Charges: _____ _____ _____

Something Special

Hold this paper against a wall and rub it with 50 quick strokes with the side of your pencil. Take your hand away. Presto! The paper stays on the wall because of the static electricity you have made.

Name _____

The Charge of Electricity

Read a poem about inventions. Then, create your own poetry project.

You will need: a copy of the book *Where the Sidewalk Ends* by Shel Silverstein, writing paper, a pen, assorted colors of construction paper, scissors, a black pen, glue, the appliance patterns below

Directions:

Cut out the appliance patterns below. Glue them on different-colored construction paper.

Read the poem "Invention" by Shel Silverstein. Visualize the "invention." Then, write a poem about an electrical device or machine. The poem should describe the device, tell its function and make its sounds. The object may be an actual appliance or one you make up. When your poem is finished, cut it out and glue it on a piece of construction paper with the appliance shape.

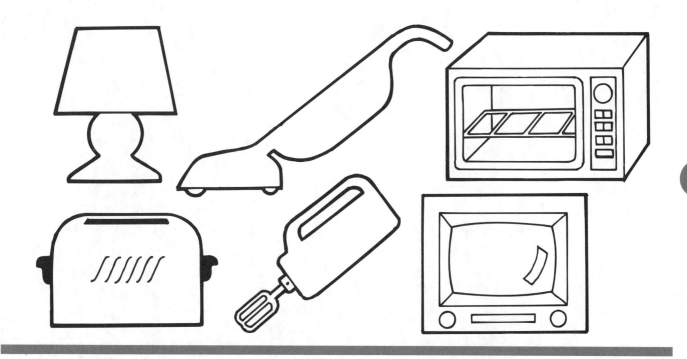

This page intentionally left blank.

Name _____

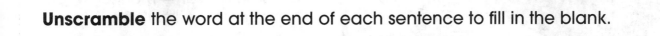

Power Paths

A **circuit** is a path along which electricity travels. It travels in a loop around the circuit. In the circuit pictured below, the electricity travels through the wire, battery, switch and bulb. The electricity must have a source. What is the source in this circuit? You're right if you said the battery.

If the wire in the circuit was cut, there would be a **gap.** The electricity wouldn't be able to flow across the gap. Then, the bulb would not light. This is an example of an **open circuit.** If there were no gaps, the bulb would light. This is an example of a **closed circuit.**

Directions:

1. Draw in the wire to the battery, switch and bulb to make a closed circuit.

2. Draw in the wire to the battery, switch and bulb to make an open circuit.

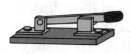

Unscramble the word at the end of each sentence to fill in the blank.

3. Even the tiniest _____ can stop the electricity from flowing. (apg)

4. A _____ is a path along which electricity flows. (ricituc)

5. If there are no gaps, or openings, a _____ circuit is formed. (sodelc)

6. A battery is a source of _____ in some circuits. (treleciytci)

> **Fantastic Fact**
> If all of the circuits in a small personal computer were made out of wire and metal switches, the computer would fill an average-sized classroom. Today, these circuits are found in tiny chips called microchips.

Electricity—Light the Bulb

Follow the directions below to make an electrical circuit.

You will need:

An adult
2 flashlight batteries
a flashlight bulb
a bulb holder
2 wires
aluminum foil

Directions:

1. Scrape off the covering of both ends of the two wires. Screw the bulb into the bulb holder. Attach the end of one wire around the screw of the bulb holder. Attach the end of the other wire around the other screw of the bulb holder. Complete the circuit using the two loose wire ends. Hold one on the bottom of the battery and the other wire on the top of the battery. Watch the light go on.

2. Put the second battery on top of the first battery so that the bottom of the second one is touching the top of the first one. Complete the circuit in the same manner. What happens to the light? Why?

3. Now use aluminum foil instead of the wires. Does the bulb light? What does this tell you about aluminum foil? (If you don't have the answer to this question, look at the lesson on page 290.)

Find a Match

You will need: an adult, a 9" x 12" piece of cardboard, 8 pieces of wire (cut back approximately $\frac{3}{4}$" of insulation from each end), a dry cell, a flashlight bulb in a bulb holder, 10 short screws and 10 nuts, 2 coffee stirrers (wood), 2 paper clips, tape, 2 stick probes

Directions:

Put 10 screws through the piece of cardboard as shown in illustration **A**. Put the nuts on the back of the board as shown in illustration **B**. Number and initial the nuts as indicated. Attach the wires firmly between points by twisting the ends around the screws and tightening the bolts to connect the wires as follows:

Point **1** to Point **C**

Point **2** to Point **A**

Point **3** to Point **E**

Point **4** to Point **D**

Point **5** to Point **B**

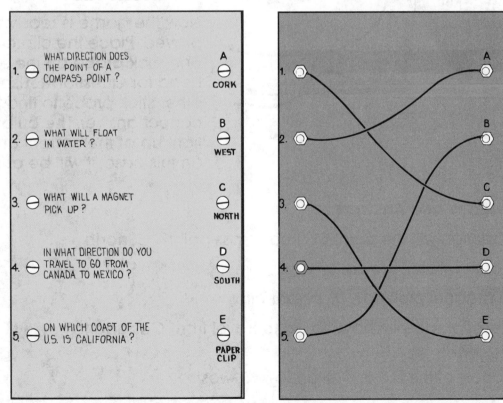

A. FRONT

1. WHAT DIRECTION DOES THE POINT OF A COMPASS POINT?

2. WHAT WILL FLOAT IN WATER?

3. WHAT WILL A MAGNET PICK UP?

4. IN WHAT DIRECTION DO YOU TRAVEL TO GO FROM CANADA TO MEXICO?

5. ON WHICH COAST OF THE U.S. IS CALIFORNIA?

A CORK

B WEST

C NORTH

D SOUTH

E PAPER CLIP

B. BACK

Find a Match

Connect a wire from one pole of the dry cell to one screw of the bulb holder. Prepare two stick probes for use in playing the game by attaching a paper clip to each wood stirrer. Connect a wire from the other end of the bulb holder to the paper clip of one stick probe and secure with tape. Make sure the wire is long enough to cover the entire gameboard. Connect the last wire from the other end of the dry cell to the paper clip of the second probe and secure with tape. Again, make sure the wire is long enough to cover the entire gameboard. (See diagram.)

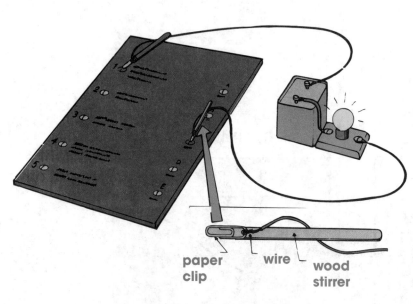

paper clip   wire   wood stirrer

Prepare a list of five questions and write them at points 1 to 5. Put the answers on the lettered spots as follows:

Answer to **#1** will be at Point **C**
Answer to **#2** will be at Point **A**
Answer to **#3** will be at Point **E**
Answer to **#4** will be at Point **D**
Answer to **#5** will be at Point **B**

Now the game is ready to be played. Place the clip end of one stick probe on the screw head for Question 1. Use the other stick probe to find the correct answer. The bulb will light up at the correct answer. (In this case, it will be answer C.)

Sample Questions and Answers:

1. In which direction will the point of a compass point? C. north

2. What will float in water? A. cork

3. What will a magnet pick up?   E. paper clips

4. In which direction do you have to go to travel from Canada to Mexico?   D. south

5. On which coast of the U.S. is California?   B. west

Series or Parallel?

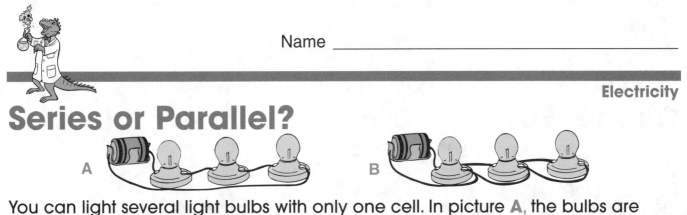

A

B

You can light several light bulbs with only one cell. In picture **A**, the bulbs are connected in a **series circuit.** What would happen to the circuit if you unscrewed one bulb? All the lights would go out. In picture **B**, the bulbs are connected in a **parallel circuit.** What would happen if you unscrewed a light bulb in a parallel circuit? The other lights would still burn.

Dry cells can also be connected in series and parallel circuits. However, cells are usually connected in series. A series of cells increases the amount of power that flows in a circuit. A series of cells will make a light bulb burn brighter.

C

D

1. In which picture above are the cells connected in a series?_____

2. In which picture above will the bulb light more brightly?_____

3. When one light burned out on Sally's Christmas tree, the rest of the lights went out, too. In what kind of circuit were the bulbs connected?_____

4. Do you think the electric lights in your house are connected in a series circuit or a parallel circuit?_____How do you know?_____
_____

5. How are the batteries connected in the flashlight below? In a series or parallel?
_____

6. Some flashlights have four or five cells. How would the brightness of the light from this kind of flashlight compare with one that has only one or two cells?

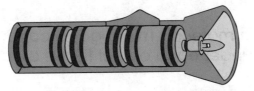

Fantastic Fact

A single dry cell is often called a battery, but it really isn't a battery. A battery is two or more cells connected together. You can buy batteries that look like a single cell, but they are really two or more cells connected together and put inside one case.

Name _____

Fill the Gap

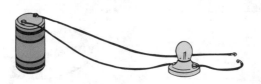

The bulb won't light in the circuit above. What's wrong with the circuit? It has a gap. How could you fill the gap to make a closed circuit? The easiest way would be to connect the two wires, but with what?

What would happen if you placed a paper clip across the gap? How about a nail? The bulb would light up. The nail or paper clip would form a bridge across the gap. The nail and paper clip carry, or **conduct**, electricity. They are both **conductors.**

Some materials will not carry the electricity well enough to make the bulb light. Try a rubber band. The bulb won't light. Rubber is a poor conductor of electricity. It is called an **insulator**.

Directions:

Find the different materials hidden in the wordsearch. The materials listed "up and down" are conductors. Those written "across" are insulators. List these materials in the correct group.

C	O	T	T	O	N	P
O	K	G	T	S	O	R
P	A	P	E	R	X	K
P	L	A	S	T	I	C
E	U	D	T	O	R	D
R	M	K	E	L	O	S
T	I	X	E	R	N	N
N	N	G	L	A	S	S
R	U	B	B	E	R	Z
K	M	G	R	X	Z	P

Insulator

_____

_____

_____

_____

_____

Conductor

_____

_____

_____

_____

Now that you know which materials make good conductors and which make good insulators, write **C** under each object that is a conductor and **I** under each object that is an insulator.

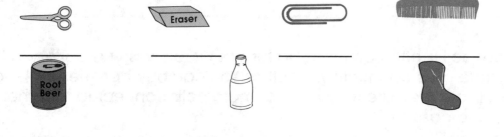

Name _____

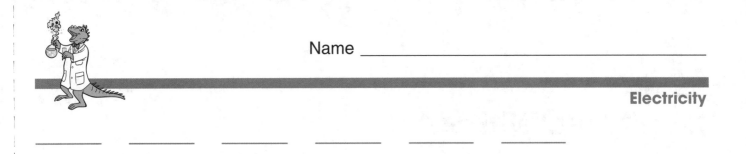

In 1877, Samuel Morse used electricity to make the first telegraph. This invention allowed people to communicate directly with one another over long distances.

Study the picture of the simple telegraph. Notice how the switch, light bulb, battery and wire form a circuit. Use the symbols in the key to draw a diagram of the telegraph.

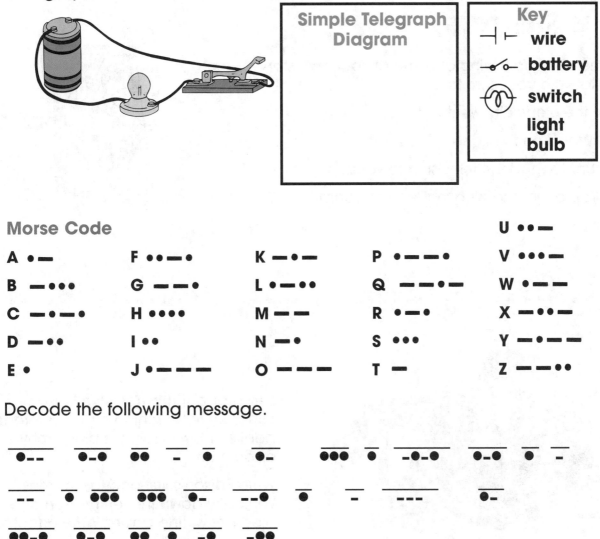

Simple Telegraph Diagram

Key
⊣⊢ **wire**
⊸⌒⊸ **battery**
⊸Ⓜ⊸ **switch**
light bulb

Morse Code

				U •• —
A • —	F ••—•	K —•—	P •——•	V •••—
B —•••	G ——•	L •—••	Q ——•—	W •——
C —•—•	H ••••	M ——	R •—•	X —••—
D —••	I ••	N —•	S •••	Y —•——
E •	J •———	O ———	T —	Z ——••

Decode the following message.

•—— •—• •• — • | •— ••• — —•—• •—• • —

—— • •••• ••• •— ——• • — ——— •—

••—• •—• •• • —• —••

Extension:

In 1876, Alexander Graham Bell used his new invention, the telephone, to make the first telephone call. He said, "Mr. _____, come here, I want to see you." To find the name of the first person to receive a telephone call, decode the title of this page.

Can't Live Without It

Make a list of as many things as you can that use electricity. Then, choose one of the items and write about why you could not live without it.

• •

Story Starters

Use some of the following or some of your own story starters to write your own tale.

The day the electricity went out, . . .

When I turned on the lights . . .

Mother unplugged the television to vacuum . . .

Sparks flew out of the plug in the living room . . .

• •

T. A. E.

Learn about Thomas Alva Edison either by researching him in reference books or by reading a biography about him.

Write Edison's first and last names vertically down the left margin of a piece of writing paper. Write a fact about Edison (in sentence form) that begins with each letter of his name.

Name _____

Light Up Your Life

A light bulb changes electricity into light. Electricity passes through the very thin wire, called a **filament**, inside the bulb. As electricity flows through the filament, the wire gets hot and gives off light.

Look very closely at the filament in a light bulb. It is made of tiny coils of wire. By using coils, more wire can be put in the bulb—so more light can be made.

Directions: Label the parts of the light bulb using the words from the Word Bank.

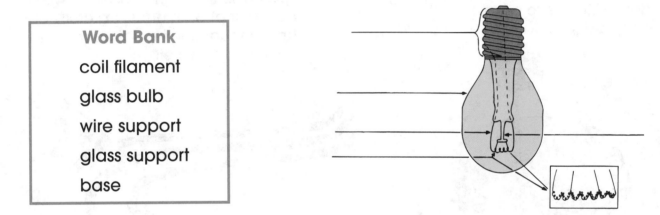

> **Word Bank**
> coil filament
> glass bulb
> wire support
> glass support
> base

On the top of a light bulb, you will see numbers and letters, such as **60W** or **100W**, or **60 watts** and **100 watts**. This tells you how much power the bulb uses. The more power the bulb uses, the brighter it glows.

1. Which light bulb uses the most electricity? _____

2. Which light bulb would make a good night light in your bedroom? _____

3. Which light bulb would glow the brightest? _____

4. Which light bulb would be a good light for reading? _____

> **Investigate**
> The first light bulb ever made had a filament made out of cotton! It burned brightly, but didn't last long. Find out who invented the first light bulb and when it was invented.

Light of My Life

Find out how a light bulb works by making one.

You will need: an adult, a 6-volt lantern battery, insulated bell wire, copper-strand lamp wire, a switch, a birthday candle, a wide-mouth jar with lid, masking tape, soda bottle cap, matches, a hammer, a nail, scissors, paper, a lantern light bulb, a small plastic bag, a large spoon, work gloves

Directions:

1. Turn the lid of the jar upside down. Make two holes 1½" - 2" apart using a hammer and a nail.

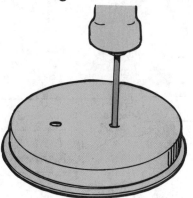

2. Cut three 12" pieces of bell wire. Use scissors to strip 1 inch of each wire's cover off of both ends. Carefully cut only through the insulation (not the wire) and pull it off.

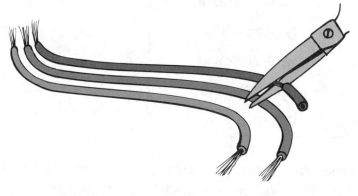

3. Put the ends of the two wires through the jar lid from the outside. Bend the ends of two wires onto the inside of the lid and then bend them so the rest hangs straight down into the jar. Tape the wires to the lid.

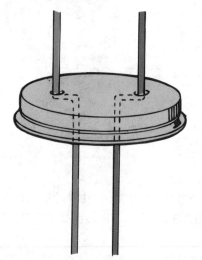

4. Remove one 12" copper strand from lamp wire. Coil it around a nail. Then, remove the nail.

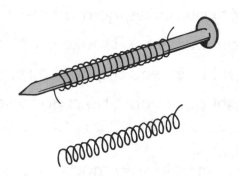

Light of My Life

5. Twist one end of the coil to the end of one wire hanging down from the lid and the coil's other end to the other wire hanging down.

6. Connect one wire extending from outside the lid to a terminal on the battery. Connect the other wire outside the lid to one of the screws on the switch.

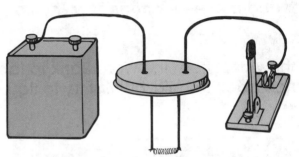

7. Connect the third bell wire to the free terminal on the battery and to the other screw on the switch.

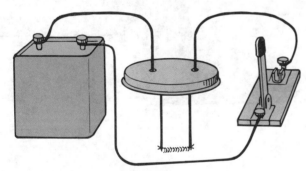

8. Light a candle. Let a couple of drops of wax fall into the bottle cap. Set the candle in it. Put the candle in the jar. Relight it if it is still not burning. Screw on the lid.

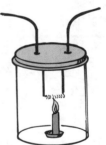

9. As soon as the candle goes out, turn on the switch. (This indicates that there is no oxygen left in the jar.)

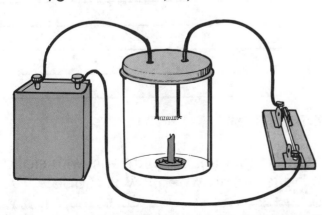

10. Compare what you have made with the inside of a light bulb.

Portable Power

Steve and Lenny really enjoyed listening to the radio while they fished. Radios need electricity to work. Where did Steve's radio get its power? From a **dry cell battery**, of course. Dry cells are sources of portable power.

Most portable radios use dry cells. A dry cell makes electricity by changing chemical energy into electrical energy. Chemicals in the dry cell act on each other and make **electrons** flow. The flow of electrons is called **electricity.**

Directions:

Use the words from the Word Bank to label the parts of the dry cell. You can use a science book to help, but first try to figure out each part by yourself.

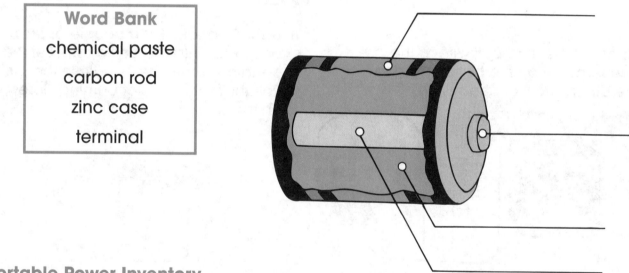

Word Bank

chemical paste

carbon rod

zinc case

terminal

Portable Power Inventory

List the appliances, tools or toys in your house that are powered with dry cells.

_____   _____
_____   _____
_____   _____
_____   _____
_____

Investigate
Before batteries were invented, scientists did all their experiments with static electricity. Find out who made the first battery and when it was made.

Name _____

Making Electricity

Where does the electricity that is in your house come from? It all begins at a large **power plant.** The power plant has a large **turbine generator.** High-pressure steam spins the turbines and the generator that is attached to the turbine shaft. As the generator spins, it produces hundreds of megawatts of electricity.

Directions:

Below is a picture of a power plant where electricity is generated. Label each part using the terms found in the Power Bank below.

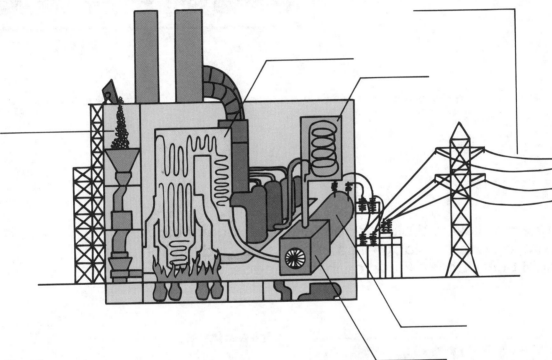

Power Bank

FUEL — Fuel, such as coal, enters the power plant.

BOILER — The burning fuel heats water in the boiler, making high-pressure steam.

TURBINE — High-pressure steam spins the blades of the turbine up to 3,000 times a minute.

CONDENSER — Steam is cooled in the condenser and is turned back into water. The water is sent back to the boiler.

GENERATOR — The generator attached to the turbine turns, producing hundreds of megawatts of electricity.

POWER LINES — Electricity is sent to your home through wires.

Bright Ideas

Think of an electrical gadget you wish you had (i.e., homework machine, room picker-upper, money maker, etc.). Design this gadget. Label each part and explain how your invention works.

Electrifying Words

You will need: yellow and black paper, a large piece of black posterboard, a pencil, a black felt-tip pen, scissors and the lightning pattern, light bulb patterns found on the next page

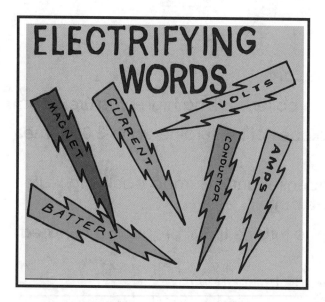

Directions:

Use a large sheet of black posterboard. Cut out the letters for the title from yellow paper. Attach the title diagonally across a piece of posterboard going from the top left corner to the bottom right.

Cut out the lightning pattern and the light bulb pattern and use them to trace more of the shapes on yellow paper. Make as many of the shapes and write as many words as you can think of related to electricity and glue or tape them on the black posterboard.

Electrifying Word Patterns

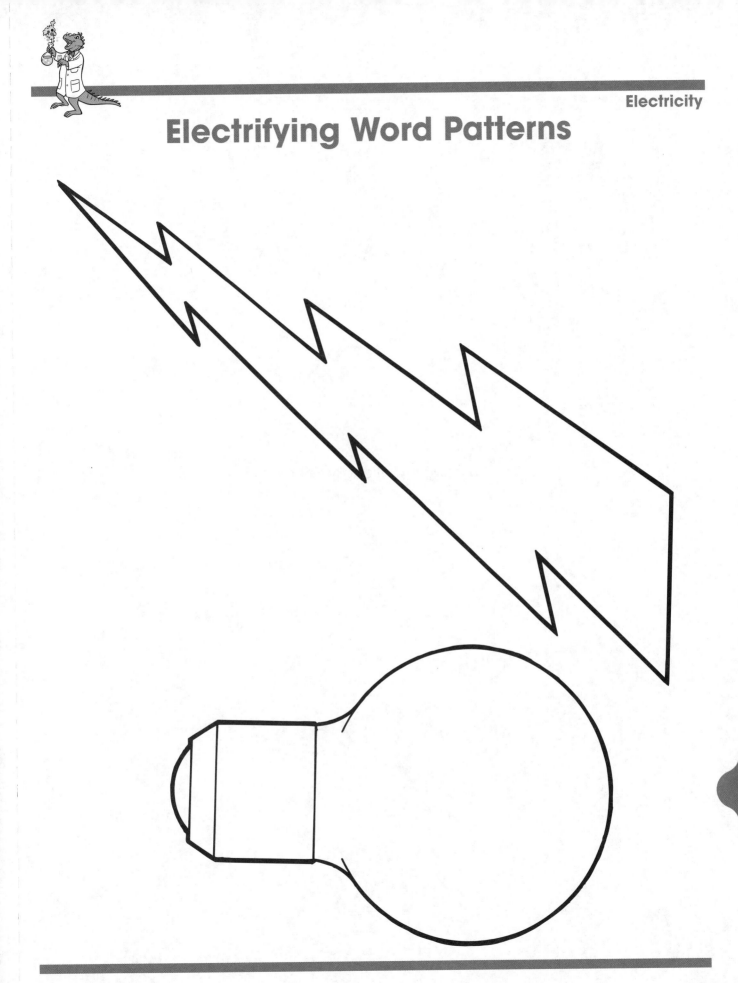

This page intentionally left blank.

Conserving Electricity

"Jane, did you remember to turn off the TV?" Jane's parents want Jane to remember to conserve electricity. It takes a lot of fuel to make electricity. We have to be careful not to waste electricity.

Your house has an **electric meter** that measures the amount of electricity your family uses. The meter measures the electricity in **kilowatt hours**. It would take one kilowatt hour to light ten light bulbs (100 watts each) for one hour. Would a 75-watt light bulb use more or less power than the 100-watt light bulb?

Look carefully at Jane's home. How could Jane conserve electricity?

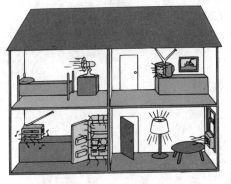

1._____

2._____

3._____

4._____

5._____

6._____

The electric meter on Jane's house is shown in Picture **A** below. It reads 2,563 kilowatt hours. Picture **B** shows Jane's electric meter after one month. Write the number of kilowatt hours shown on the meter. Then, figure out the number of kilowatt hours Jane's family used in one month.

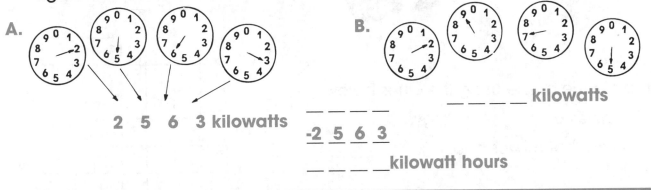

A.

2 5 6 3 kilowatts

B.

_ _ _ _ _ **kilowatts**

_ _ _ _
-2 5 6 3
_ _ _ _ _ **kilowatt hours**

Investigate

Read your electric meter at home. Have an adult help you. Record the number of kilowatts. Read your meter one day later to find out how much electricity your family has used. Keep a record every day for one week. On which days did you use the most electricity?

Name _____

Energy

Do you feel tired after raking the lawn? You feel tired then because work takes a lot of energy. **Energy** is the ability to do work.

There are many forms of energy. Food contains **chemical energy**. Your television uses **electrical energy**. The furnace in your house gives you **heat energy**. The moving parts of your bicycle have another form of energy called **mechanical energy**. Anything that moves has mechanical energy.

Energy can be changed from one form to another. Your radio changes electrical energy into sound energy. Your parents' car may change chemical energy into heat energy, and the heat energy into mechanical energy.

What kind of energy is being used to do work in each of these pictures?

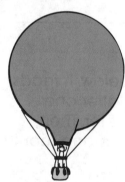

Directions:

Complete the puzzle using the clues below.

1. A fire gives us _____ energy.

2. Anything that moves has _____ energy.

3. _____ is the ability to do work.

4. Energy can be _____ from one form into another form.

5. Food contains _____ energy.

Simple Machines

Push and Pull

Look at the children in the picture. How are they moving their friends? A push or a pull on something is called a **force.** Forces can cause an object to move, slow down, speed up, change direction or stop.

Directions:

You use pushing and pulling forces every day to move objects. List five ways that you use each of these forces.

Pushing Forces

1. _____
2. _____
3. _____
4. _____
5. _____

Pulling Forces

1. _____
2. _____
3. _____
4. _____
5. _____

It takes more force to move some objects than it does to move others. Circle the object in each picture which would take more force to move.

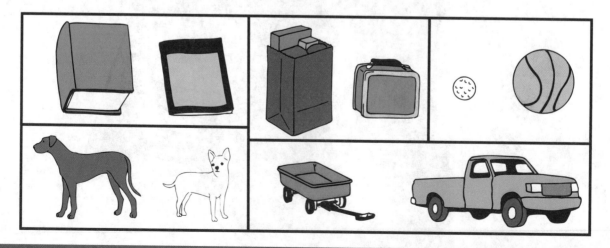

Machines of Old

Simple machines have been used for hundreds of years. The builders of the famous castles in Europe did not have modern machines. But they did have some simple machines to help them make their fabulous castles.

Directions:

Look carefully at the men building the castle. They are working hard, but their simple machines are missing. Draw in the missing machines. The Picture Bank at the bottom of the page will help you.

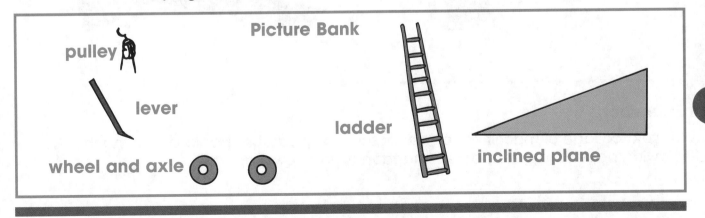

Mild-Mannered Machines

Machines help to make work like pushing, pulling and lifting easier. A machine is often made up of different parts that move, is sometimes big and complicated and is other times small and simple.

Here are some examples and definitions of some simple machines.

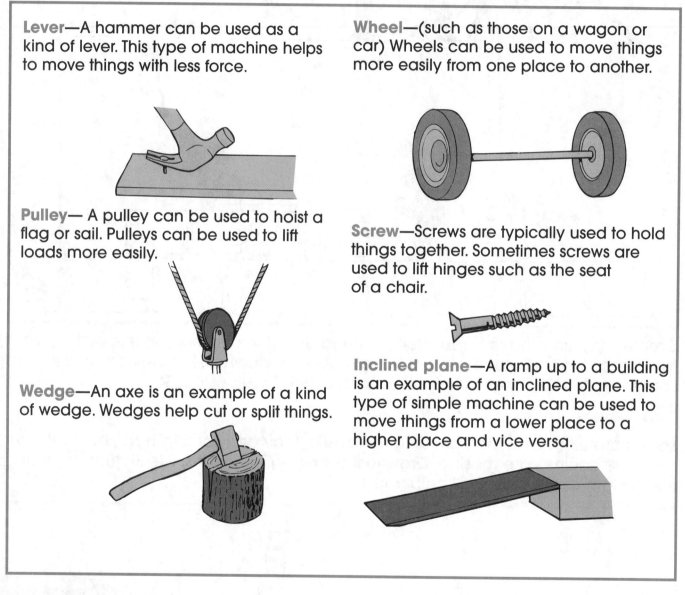

Lever—A hammer can be used as a kind of lever. This type of machine helps to move things with less force.

Pulley— A pulley can be used to hoist a flag or sail. Pulleys can be used to lift loads more easily.

Wedge—An axe is an example of a kind of wedge. Wedges help cut or split things.

Wheel—(such as those on a wagon or car) Wheels can be used to move things more easily from one place to another.

Screw—Screws are typically used to hold things together. Sometimes screws are used to lift hinges such as the seat of a chair.

Inclined plane—A ramp up to a building is an example of an inclined plane. This type of simple machine can be used to move things from a lower place to a higher place and vice versa.

Extension:

Make a collage of machines you use or see every day. Use books about machines, drawing paper, crayons, markers, magazines and newspapers.

"Inventing" the Wheel

You will need:

a textbook
string
a rubber band
3 pencils

Directions:

Put a piece of string through a thin rubber band. Then, tie the string around a chosen textbook. Putting one finger into the rubber band, pull the book along any flat surface. Observe the following: the book is hard to pull because it rubs or drags on the surface of the table, desk or floor; the rubber band stretches very far as the book is pulled. The rubbing is called friction. Friction makes things hard to move.

A simple machine can be used to help reduce friction and make the work easier. Predict which simple machine introduced earlier could be used. You will use three pencils as wheels. Putting "wheels" under the book reduces friction and makes it easier to pull the book along the surface using the rubber band and one finger.

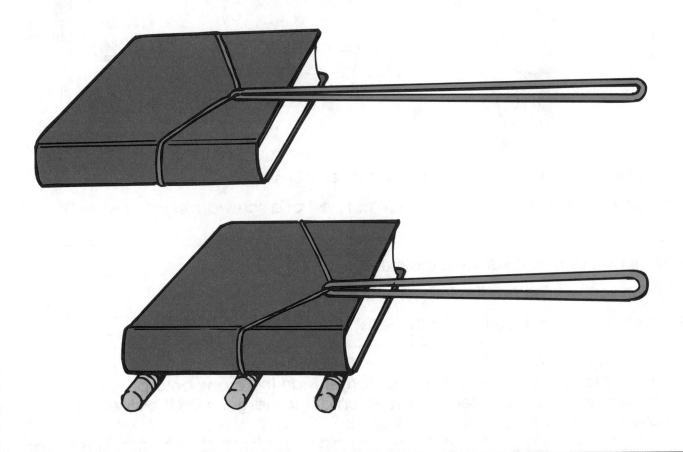

Name _____

Around and Around

A doorknob is a simple machine you use every day. It is a **wheel and axle machine**. The wheel is connected to the axle. The axle is a center post. When the wheel moves, the axle does, too.

Opening a door by turning the axle with your fingers is very hard. But by turning the doorknob, which is the "wheel," you use much less force. The doorknob turns the axle for you. The doorknob makes it easy because it is much bigger than the axle. You turn the doorknob a greater distance, but with much less force.

Sometimes the "wheel" of a wheel-and-axle machine doesn't look like a wheel. But look at the path the doorknob makes when it is turned. The path makes a circle, just like a wheel.

Directions:

Color only the wheels of the wheel-and-axle machines below.

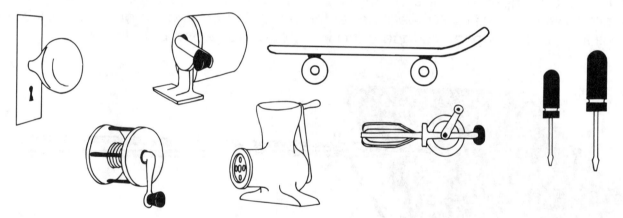

Look at the pictures above and answer these questions.

1. A screwdriver is a wheel and axle. What part of a screwdriver is the wheel?

_____

2. What part of a screwdriver is the axle? _____

3. Which screwdriver has the largest wheel? _____

4. Which screwdriver would take the least amount of force to turn? _____

> **Challenge**
> Why is the crank on a meat grinder larger than the crank on a pencil sharpener? Why is the steering wheel on a truck larger than the steering wheel on a car?

Name _____

Gearing Up

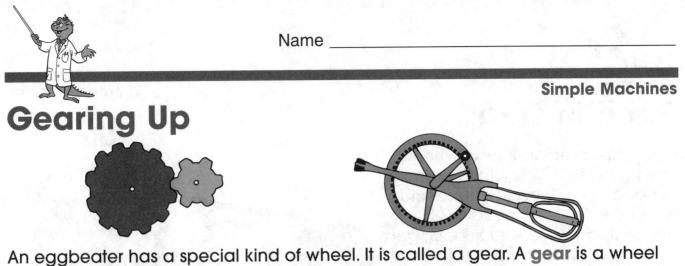

An eggbeater has a special kind of wheel. It is called a gear. A **gear** is a wheel with teeth. The teeth allow one gear to turn another gear.

Gears are often used to increase or decrease speed. If the large gear in the picture turns one time, how many times will the small gear turn?

Directions:

Gears are found in many machines. Circle all of the machines you can find in the puzzle. Then, list only the machines that use gears.

```
S T K N Z O R K G
H A M M E R U T K
O P S O R E R C N
V G Z V F A O T S
E B O I C L G X Z
L Z N E C B Z E K
D K X P W I Y G L
C K T R U C K G K
R R M O X Y T B G
A T N J S C U E H
K N R E R L V A Z
E G S C Q E W T R
P L K T G Z T E S
Z K P O H O X R T
Z U T R A M P N P
```

Machines with Gears

_____

_____

_____

_____

_____

_____

_____

Look at the picture to the right.

1. Draw an arrow on the picture showing the direction gear **B** will turn.

2. If gear **A** is turned one time, how many times will gear **B** turn?_____

Challenge
Look at the gears to the right. What will
happen if gear **A** is turned?

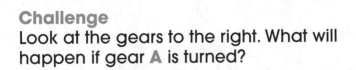

Put It in Gear!

Gears are special kinds of wheels that have teeth. If possible, examine the gears of a bicycle. You should note how the large pedal is connected with the small back gear by a chain. Push the pedal to show how the chain makes the small gear in the back work.

You will need:
one copy of the gears on the
  following page
construction paper
markers
crayons
scissors
brass fasteners
a bicycle (if possible)

Directions:

Cut out the gears on page 311. Then, fold up the points of **Gear B.** Attach the gears to the construction paper with brass fasteners so that the teeth of Gear A interlock with the folded-up teeth of **Gear B.** When **Gear A** is turned, Gear B should also turn.

Finally, draw a toy or machine that will move around on the gears you have attached to the construction paper. Create a name for the invention.

Gear Patterns

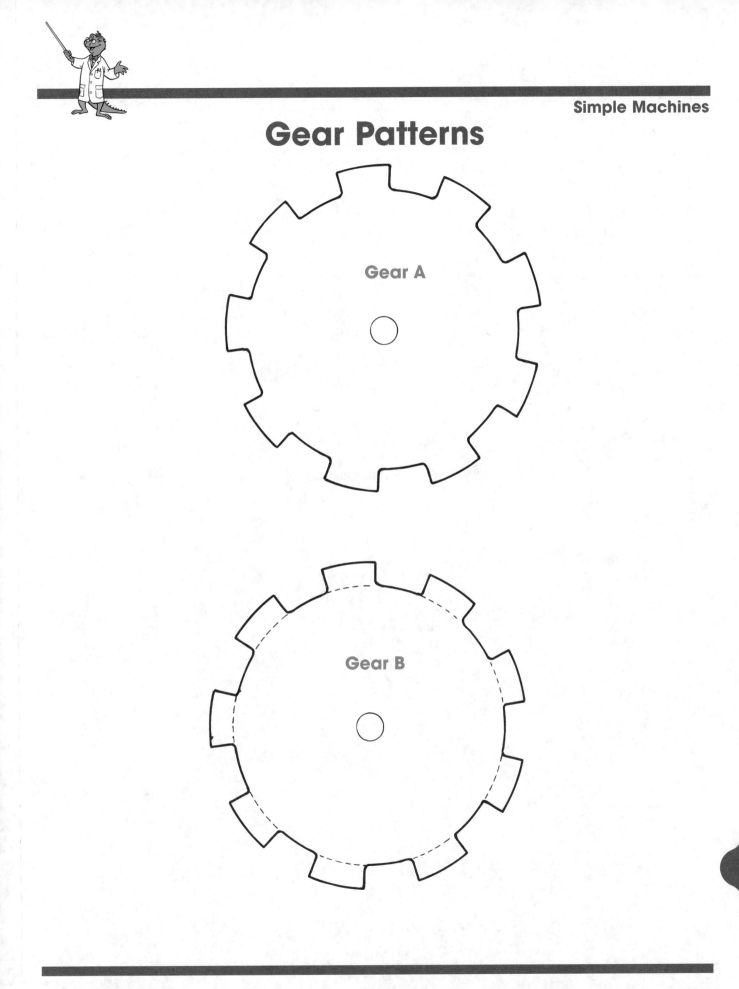

Gear A

Gear B

This page intentionally left blank.

Ramps, Hills and Slopes

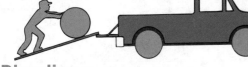

Word Bank

machine	easier
force	inclined
shorter	longer

Directions:

Fill in the blanks with words from the Word Bank.

Simple machines help people do work. In the picture above, the ramp makes the man's work a lot _____. The ramp is a simple _____ called an inclined plane.

An _____ plane makes work easier. It lessens the amount of force needed to move a load. By using the ramp, the man moves the barrel with much less force than if he tried to lift the barrel himself. With the ramp, the man moves the barrel a _____ distance, but with much less force. By just lifting the barrel onto the truck, he would move it a _____ distance, but would need to use much more _____.

Ramps are used in many places to help people in wheelchairs get around more easily. List some places where ramps are used in your community.

1. _____

2. _____

3. _____

The angle of an inclined plane affects the amount of force needed to lift an object. The longer and less steep the inclined plane is, the less force it takes to lift an object.

Study the pictures below and then answer the questions.

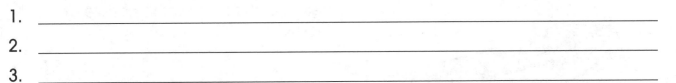

1. On which ramp will the barrel have to travel the farthest to get on the truck?___

2. On which ramp will the least amount of force be needed to roll the barrel onto the truck?___

3. How does the angle of the ramp affect the force needed to move the barrel?

_____

Investigate
How did the early Egyptians use inclined planes to build the great pyramids?

Tall Ramps, Short Ramps

Experiment with the heights of ramps and the distance an object can roll.

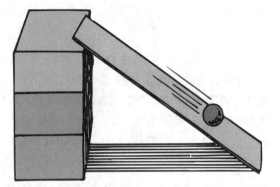

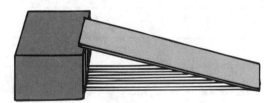

You will need:

long blocks or long pieces of cardboard (to create a ramp)

rectangular blocks or books (to rest the ramp upon)

matchbox cars or anything else that will roll (i.e., a can, a pencil, a marble, etc.)

the data sheet on the next page

Before you begin this lesson, discuss with an adult the scientific process or method. This lesson is designed to emphasize the concepts of "variables" and "constants." Use the data sheet on the next page. The variable in this experiment will be the height of the ramp (or the angle of incline).

Create a ramp, measure the height of the ramp and then roll one object down the ramp. Next, measure the distance the object rolled. Record your findings on the data sheet. The same object should be rolled two more times at this height. Change the variable, or the height, of the ramp, roll the object down again and measure it. The same object should be rolled again two more times, with the observer taking and recording measurements. Discuss your findings.

Tall Ramps, Short Ramps

Experiment with ramps, heights and distances. You can choose the materials you want to use.

Problem: To find out what ramp height allows an object to roll the farthest.

Procedure: Create two ramps of different heights by using a different number of blocks to lay each ramp on. Then, roll an object down each ramp three times and measure how far the object rolled each time.

Variable: The height of the ramp

Observations:

	Height of Ramp	Object Rolled
Trial One		
Trial Two		
Trial Three		
	Height of Ramp	Object Rolled
Trial One		
Trial Two		
Trial Three		

Conclusion(s):

I think _____

because _____.

Name _____

Special Inclined Plane — Wedge

"Poof!" Leroy just shrank himself again in his "Super Electro Shrinking Machine." He is trying to decide which would be easier—climbing around and around the threads of a screw to get to the top or just climbing straight up the side of the screw. He found that the distance up the winding ramp is a lot farther, but the traveling is much easier than going straight up the side. The winding ramp of the screw is like a spiral stairway.

Directions:

Answer these questions.

1. Would you travel a farther distance climbing a spiral stairway up three floors or climbing a ladder straight up three floors? _____

2. Which would take more force to climb—the stairway or the ladder?_____

3. When you climb a spiral stairway, you travel a greater _____, but you use less _____.

A screw is a special kind of inclined plane. A spiral stairway is also an inclined plane. Two or more inclined planes that are joined together to make a sharp edge or point form a wedge. A **wedge** is a special kind of inclined plane. A wedge is used to pierce or split things. A knife is a wedge. Can you name some other wedges?

Some special inclined planes are pictured below. Label each picture either a wedge or a screw.

_____   _____   _____   _____

_____

Find these special inclined planes in the puzzle to the right.

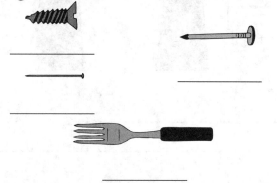

W	G	T	P	I	N	O	K
E	X	W	B	D	Z	K	N
D	A	Z	K	F	E	N	I
G	S	C	R	E	W	P	F
E	A	S	K	A	X	E	E
J	R	F	T	U	N	K	L
P	A	T	O	N	A	I	L
S	T	A	I	R	W	A	Y
V	R	T	N	O	K	O	T

nail   stairway
fork   screw
pin   axe
knife   wedge

_____

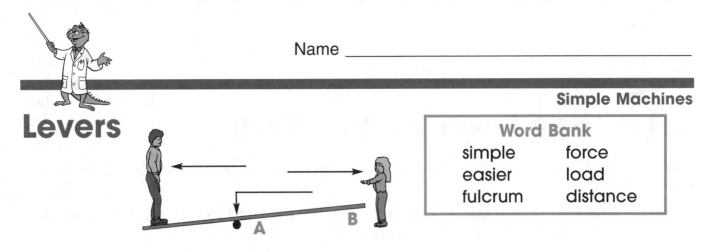

Name _____

Levers

Word Bank

simple	force
easier	load
fulcrum	distance

Directions: Use the words from the Word Bank to complete the sentences.

Mandy wants to try to lift her dad off the ground. Where should Mandy stand on the board? By standing on point ___, Mandy can lift her dad.

The board resting on the log is an example of a _____ machine called a lever. A **lever** has three parts—the **force**, the **fulcrum** and the **load**. Mandy is the force. The point on which the lever turns is called the _____. And Mandy's dad, the object to be lifted, is called the _____. The greater the _____ between the _____ and the fulcrum, the _____ it is to lift the load. The closer the distance between the **force** and the **fulcrum**, the harder it is to lift the load.

Label the picture of Mandy and her father with these words: **load**, **force** and **fulcrum**.

1. Fulcrum far away from load

2. Fulcrum close to load

The distance between the **load** and the **fulcrum** also affects the force needed to lift a load. The closer the fulcrum is to the load, the easier it is to lift the load.

Look at the pictures above to answer these questions.

1. Matt wants to move a large rock with a lever. Which lever would let him use the least amount of force to move the rock?

2. Which lever would have to be moved the greatest distance to move the rock?

3. Why is a lever called a simple machine?

Label the **force**, **fulcrum** and **load** of the levers below.

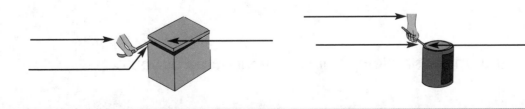

Let a Little Lever Do the Work

You will need: scissors, tongs, a nutcracker, a shovel, a ruler, a block or an eraser, a toy wheelbarrow

When you use a lever, you can lift a heavy load without pushing very hard. A lever is a bar which may be made out of metal, wood or other hard material.

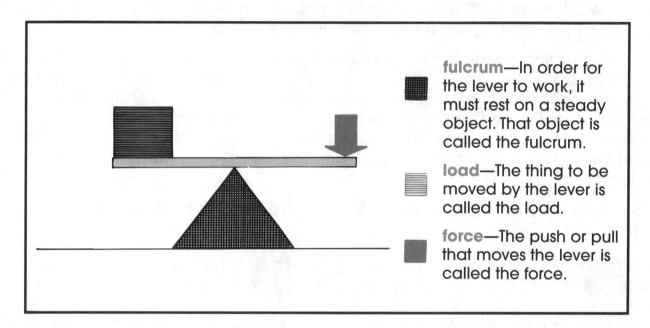

fulcrum—In order for the lever to work, it must rest on a steady object. That object is called the fulcrum.

load—The thing to be moved by the lever is called the load.

force—The push or pull that moves the lever is called the force.

Examine some everyday examples of levers such as scissors, tongs, nutcrackers, shovels and even your arms. Then, create a lever using your ruler. Use a block, eraser or any object as the load. Experiment with your lever. Try different lengths of levers. Experiment with the two levers and to compare the amount each lever can lift. Also, vary the position of the fulcrum. The longer the lever, the more that can be lifted, and the closer the fulcrum is to the load, the easier it is to lift.

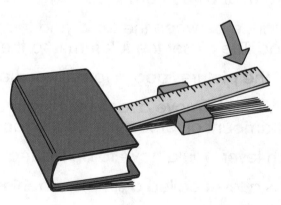

Extension: Find and list as many simple machines in your home as you can.

Simple + Simple = Compound

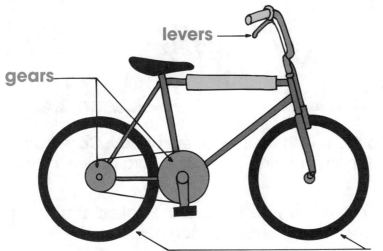

levers

gears

wheel and axle

Many of the machines that you use each day are made up of two or more simple machines. What simple machines can you find in Mandy's bicycle? Find the gears, the wheel and axle machines and the levers. Machines that are made up of two or more simple machines are called **compound machines**.

Directions:

Look carefully at the compound machines pictured on this page. Find the simple machines that make up each compound machine. Label the simple machines you find.

Challenge
Find a compound machine in your home. Show someone in your family why it is a compound machine.

Work Savers

People use machines to help them with their work every day. Cars, trucks, sewing machines and bicycles have many moving parts. They are called **compound machines**.

Some machines have few or no moving parts. They are called **simple machines**. A hammer, a pulley and a ramp are all simple machines.

A simple machine makes work easier. It lets you do the work with less force, but you have to move the object a greater distance.

Directions: Look at the machines in the picture above. List each machine in the correct group.

Simple Machines	**Compound Machines**
_____	_____
_____	_____
_____	_____
_____	_____
_____	

Unscramble these mixed-up sentences.

1. work machines make easier. _____

_____

2. machines compound many have parts moving. _____

_____

3. force machines less do with you let work. _____

_____

4. machines no few or parts have moving simple. _____

_____

Pulley Power

Volunteer for a community service and learn about another simple machine. Perform a service for your community while learning about the power of pulleys.

Perhaps you could volunteer to help raise and lower the American flag in front of a local building. Then, with a parent, set up a schedule to assist the person normally in charge of this task. Note that a pulley is a small wheel with a groove. The rope fits into the groove of the wheel. As the rope is pulled, the wheel turns and helps to lift an object (in this case, the flag).

This is a great way for you to see a simple machine being used in everyday life and to perform a service for your community.

A

antigen: substance that stimulates production of antibodies in the bloodstream

asteroid: extremely small bodies that travel mainly between Mars and Jupiter

auditory nerve: receives sound vibrations through the ear and sends them to the brain

axis: the imaginary pole on which the Earth rotates

C

carnivorous: meat-eating

central nervous system: the brain and the spinal cord

chrysalis: the hard shell in which a caterpillar changes to a butterfly

circuit: complete path of electrical current

circulatory system: the network of organs and tissue that moves the blood throughout the body

coma: cloud of dust around the nucleus of a comet

conservation: prevention of decay, waste or loss, as with Earth's forests, lands and water

constellations: pictures formed by groups of stars

cotyledon: primary leaf of the embryo of seed plants

D

digestive system: the group of organs that work together to gain fuel from the food we eat

E

electromagnet: device with an iron or steel core magnetized by electric current in a surrounding coil

embryo: early stages of development

energy: capacity for work, available power

G

germinate: begin to grow or develop

gravity: strong pull from an object in space

H

hurricane: violent tropical storm that forms over water

I

invertebrate: animal which has no backbone

M

metamorphosis: changes that take place in an insect's life cycle

N

nucleus: core; central part of a cell

nutrient: that which supplies nourishment

O

optic nerve: sends messages from the eye to the brain

P

paleontologist: scientist who studies fossils

petroglyph: a carving or line drawing on a rock

photosynthesis: process by which plants use sunlight, carbon dioxide and water to make food for plants

potential energy: energy which is possible; energy not used

R

refraction: the change of direction of a ray of light, heat or sound

respiratory system: group of organs which work together to take in oxygen for the body's use

S

solar system: the sun together with all the planets and the other bodies that revolve around it

static electricity: a stationary electric charge

T

tornado: funnel-shaped, violent windstorm

V

vertebrate: animal which has a backbone

vitreous humor: the clear jelly filling the eyeball

ANSWER KEY

Science Essentials
Grades 3 & 4

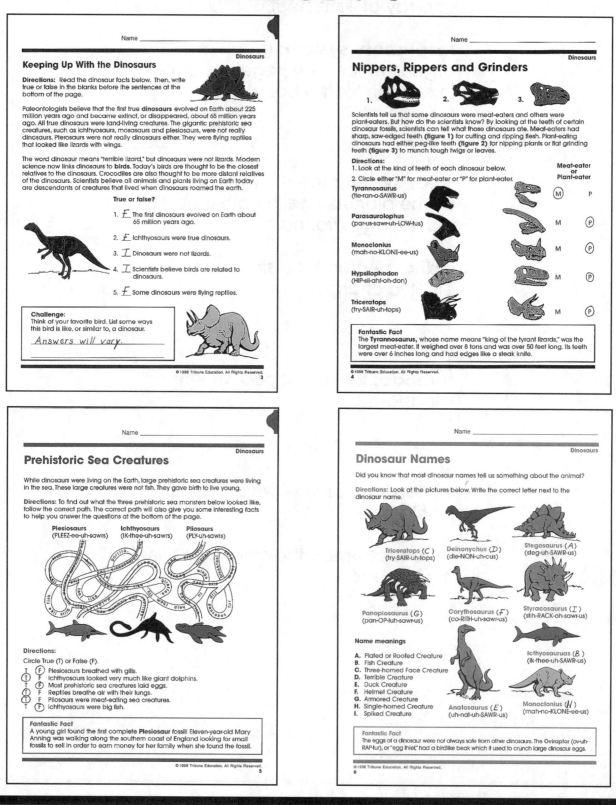

Name _____

Dinosaurs

Keeping Up With the Dinosaurs

Directions: Read the dinosaur facts below. Then, write true or false in the blanks before the sentences at the bottom of the page.

Paleontologists believe that the first true **dinosaurs** evolved on Earth about 225 million years ago and became extinct, or disappeared, about 65 million years ago. All true dinosaurs were land-living creatures. The gigantic prehistoric sea creatures, such as ichthyosaurs, mosasaurs and plesiosaurs, were not really dinosaurs. Pterosaurs were not really dinosaurs either. They were flying reptiles that looked like lizards with wings.

The word dinosaur means "terrible lizard," but dinosaurs were not lizards. Modern science now links dinosaurs to **birds**. Today's birds are thought to be the closest relatives to the dinosaurs. Crocodiles are also thought to be more distant relatives of the dinosaurs. Scientists believe all animals and plants living on Earth today are descendants of creatures that lived when dinosaurs roamed the earth.

True or false?

1. _F_ The first dinosaurs evolved on Earth about 65 million years ago.

2. _F_ Ichthyosaurs were true dinosaurs.

3. _T_ Dinosaurs were not lizards.

4. _T_ Scientists believe birds are related to dinosaurs.

5. _F_ Some dinosaurs were flying reptiles.

Challenge:
Think of your favorite bird. List some ways this bird is like, or similar to, a dinosaur.

Answers will vary.

© 1998 Tribune Education. All Rights Reserved.
3

Name _____

Dinosaurs

Nippers, Rippers and Grinders

1.   2.   3.

Scientists tell us that some dinosaurs were meat-eaters and others were plant-eaters. But how do the scientists know? By looking at the teeth of certain dinosaur fossils, scientists can tell what those dinosaurs ate. Meat-eaters had sharp, saw-edged teeth (figure 1) for cutting and ripping flesh. Plant-eating dinosaurs had either peg-like teeth (figure 2) for nipping plants or flat grinding teeth (figure 3) to munch tough twigs or leaves.

Directions:
1. Look at the kind of teeth of each dinosaur below.
2. Circle either "M" for meat-eater or "P" for plant-eater.

	Meat-eater or Plant-eater
Tyrannosaurus (tie-ran-o-SAWR-us)	(M) P
Parasaurolophus (par-us-sawr-uh-LOW-fus)	M (P)
Monoclonius (mah-no-KLONE-ee-us)	M (P)
Hypsilophodon (HIP-sil-ahf-oh-don)	M (P)
Triceratops (try-SAIR-uh-tops)	M (P)

Fantastic Fact
The **Tyrannosaurus**, whose name means "king of the tyrant lizards," was the largest meat-eater. It weighed over 8 tons and was over 50 feet long. Its teeth were over 6 inches long and had edges like a steak knife.

© 1998 Tribune Education. All Rights Reserved.
4

Name _____

Dinosaurs

Prehistoric Sea Creatures

While dinosaurs were living on the Earth, large prehistoric sea creatures were living in the sea. These large creatures were not fish. They gave birth to live young.

Directions: To find out what the three prehistoric sea monsters below looked like, follow the correct path. The correct path will also give you some interesting facts to help you answer the questions at the bottom of the page.

Plesiosaurs (PLEEZ-ee-uh-sawrs)   **Ichthyosaurs** (IK-thee-uh-sawrs)   **Pliosaurs** (PLY-uh-sawrs)

Directions:
Circle True (T) or False (F).

I (F) Plesiosaurs breathed with gills.
(T) F Ichthyosaurs looked very much like giant dolphins.
(T) F Most prehistoric sea creatures laid eggs.
(T) F Reptiles breathe air with their lungs.
(T) F Pliosaurs were meat-eating sea creatures.
T (F) Ichthyosaurs were big fish.

Fantastic Fact
A young girl found the first complete **Plesiosaur** fossil! Eleven-year-old Mary Anning was walking along the southern coast of England looking for small fossils to sell in order to earn money for her family when she found the fossil.

© 1998 Tribune Education. All Rights Reserved.
5

Name _____

Dinosaurs

Dinosaur Names

Did you know that most dinosaur names tell us something about the animal?

Directions: Look at the pictures below. Write the correct letter next to the dinosaur name.

Triceratops (C) (try-SAIR-uh-tops)
Deinonychus (D) (die-NON-uh-cus)
Stegosaurus (A) (steg-uh-SAWR-us)
Panoplosaurus (G) (pan-OP-luh-sawr-us)
Corythosaurus (F) (co-RITH-uh-sawr-us)
Styracosaurus (I) (stih-RACK-oh-sawr-us)
Ichthyosauruas (B) (ik-thee-uh-SAWR-us)
Anatosaurus (E) (uh-nat-uh-SAWR-us)
Monoclonius (H) (mah-no-KLONE-ee-us)

Name meanings

A. Plated or Roofed Creature
B. Fish Creature
C. Three-horned Face Creature
D. Terrible Creature
E. Duck Creature
F. Helmet Creature
G. Armored Creature
H. Single-horned Creature
I. Spiked Creature

Fantastic Fact
The eggs of a dinosaur were not always safe from other dinosaurs. The Oviraptor (ov-uh-RAP-tur), or "egg thief," had a birdlike beak which it used to crunch large dinosaur eggs.

© 1998 Tribune Education. All Rights Reserved.
6

326

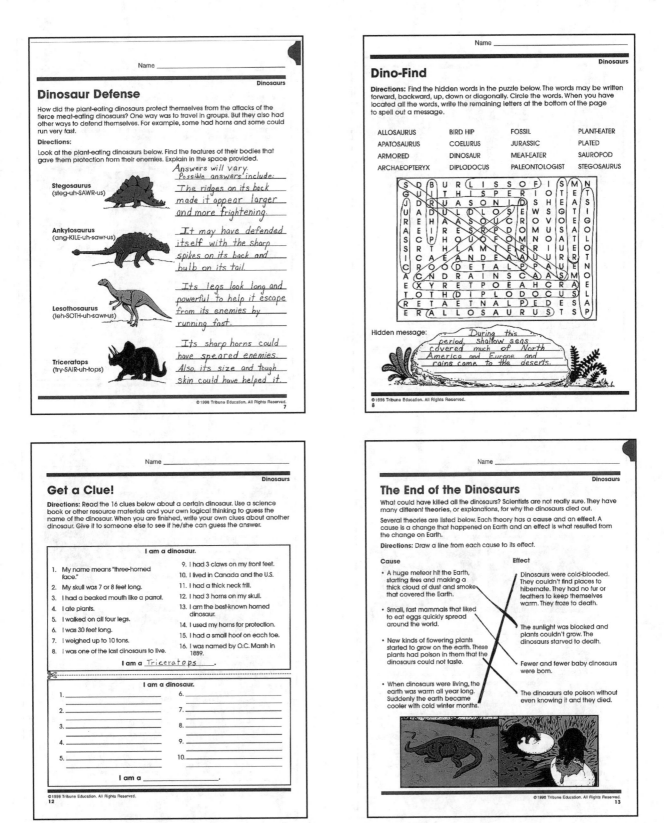

Name _____

Dinosaurs

Dinosaur Defense

How did the plant-eating dinosaurs protect themselves from the attacks of the fierce meat-eating dinosaurs? One way was to travel in groups. But they also had other ways to defend themselves. For example, some had horns and some could run very fast.

Directions:

Look at the plant-eating dinosaurs below. Find the features of their bodies that gave them protection from their enemies. Explain in the space provided.

Stegosaurus
(steg-uh-SAWR-us)

Answers will vary.
Possible answers include:
The ridges on its back made it appear larger and more frightening.

Ankylosaurus
(ang-KILE-uh-sawr-us)

It may have defended itself with the sharp spikes on its back and bulb on its tail.

Lesothosaurus
(leh-SOTH-uh-sawr-us)

Its legs look long and powerful to help it escape from its enemies by running fast.

Triceratops
(try-SAIR-uh-tops)

Its sharp horns could have speared enemies. Also, its size and tough skin could have helped it.

© 1998 Tribune Education. All Rights Reserved.
7

Name _____

Dinosaurs

Dino-Find

Directions: Find the hidden words in the puzzle below. The words may be written forward, backward, up, down or diagonally. Circle the words. When you have located all the words, write the remaining letters at the bottom of the page to spell out a message.

ALLOSAURUS	BIRD HIP	FOSSIL	PLANT-EATER
APATOSAURUS	COELURUS	JURASSIC	PLATED
ARMORED	DINOSAUR	MEAT-EATER	SAUROPOD
ARCHAEOPTERYX	DIPLODOCUS	PALEONTOLOGIST	STEGOSAURUS

Hidden message: *During this period, shallow seas covered much of North America and Europe and rains came to the deserts.*

© 1998 Tribune Education. All Rights Reserved.
8

Name _____

Dinosaurs

Get a Clue!

Directions: Read the 16 clues below about a certain dinosaur. Use a science book or other resource materials and your own logical thinking to guess the name of the dinosaur. When you are finished, write your own clues about another dinosaur. Give it to someone else to see if he/she can guess the answer.

I am a dinosaur.

1. My name means "three-horned face."
2. My skull was 7 or 8 feet long.
3. I had a beaked mouth like a parrot.
4. I ate plants.
5. I walked on all four legs.
6. I was 30 feet long.
7. I weighed up to 10 tons.
8. I was one of the last dinosaurs to live.
9. I had 3 claws on my front feet.
10. I lived in Canada and the U.S.
11. I had a thick neck frill.
12. I had 3 horns on my skull.
13. I am the best-known horned dinosaur.
14. I used my horns for protection.
15. I had a small hoof on each toe.
16. I was named by O.C. Marsh in 1889.

I am a _Triceratops_.

- -

I am a dinosaur.

1. _____ 6. _____
2. _____ 7. _____
3. _____ 8. _____
4. _____ 9. _____
5. _____ 10. _____

I am a _____.

© 1998 Tribune Education. All Rights Reserved.
12

Name _____

Dinosaurs

The End of the Dinosaurs

What could have killed all the dinosaurs? Scientists are not really sure. They have many different theories, or explanations, for why the dinosaurs died out.

Several theories are listed below. Each theory has a **cause** and an **effect**. A cause is a change that happened on Earth and an effect is what resulted from the change on Earth.

Directions: Draw a line from each cause to its effect.

Cause

- A huge meteor hit the Earth, starting fires and making a thick cloud of dust and smoke that covered the Earth.

- Small, fast mammals that liked to eat eggs quickly spread around the world.

- New kinds of flowering plants started to grow on the earth. These plants had poison in them that the dinosaurs could not taste.

- When dinosaurs were living, the earth was warm all year long. Suddenly the earth became cooler with cold winter months.

Effect

Dinosaurs were cold-blooded. They couldn't find places to hibernate. They had no fur or feathers to keep themselves warm. They froze to death.

The sunlight was blocked and plants couldn't grow. The dinosaurs starved to death.

Fewer and fewer baby dinosaurs were born.

The dinosaurs ate poison without even knowing it and they died.

© 1998 Tribune Education. All Rights Reserved.
13

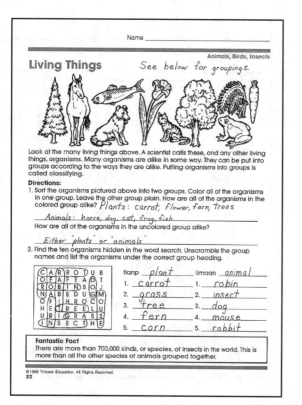

Name _____

Living Things   *See below for groupings.*

Animals, Birds, Insects

Look at the many living things above. A scientist calls these, and any other living things, organisms. Many organisms are alike in some way. They can be put into groups according to the ways they are alike. Putting organisms into groups is called classifying.

Directions:

1. Sort the organisms pictured above into two groups. Color all of the organisms in one group. Leave the other group plain. How are all of the organisms in the colored group alike? *Plants: carrot, flower, fern, trees*

   Animals: horse, dog, cat, frog, fish

   How are all of the organisms in the uncolored group alike?

   Either "plants" or "animals"

2. Find the ten organisms hidden in the word search. Unscramble the group names and list the organisms under the correct group heading.

tlanp *plant*   limaan *animal*

1. *carrot*	1. *robin*
2. *grass*	2. *insect*
3. *tree*	3. *dog*
4. *fern*	4. *mouse*
5. *corn*	5. *rabbit*

Fantastic Fact
There are more than 700,000 kinds, or species, of insects in the world. This is more than all the other species of animals grouped together.

©1998 Tribune Education. All Rights Reserved.
22

Name _____

Backbone or No Backbone?

Animals, Birds, Insects

Which part of your body helps you stand tall or sit up straight? It is your backbone. You are a member of a large group of animals that all have backbones. Animals with backbones are called vertebrates. Birds, fish, reptiles, amphibians and mammals are all vertebrates.

Some animals do not have backbones. These animals are called invertebrates. Worms, centipedes and insects are all invertebrates.

Directions:

Find the names of five vertebrates and five invertebrates hidden in the word search. Then, write them in the correct group.

Invertebrates		Vertebrates
1. *beetle*		1. *rabbit*
2. *worms*		2. *giraffe*
3. *fly*		3. *frog*
4. *moth*		4. *lion*
5. *spider*		5. *whale*

Your neighborhood has many animals in or near it. Add their names to the lists.

Invertebrates *Answers will vary.*   Vertebrates

6. *Possible answers*	6. *include:*
7. *bees*	7. *dogs*
8. *caterpillars*	8. *cats*
9. *ants*	9. *people*
10.	10.

Investigate
There are many more invertebrates than vertebrates. Nine out of ten animals is an invertebrate. Which group has the largest animals? Which group has the smallest animals?

©1998 Tribune Education. All Rights Reserved.
24

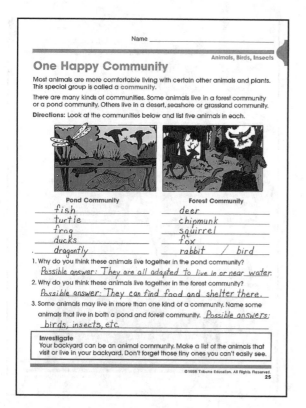

Name _____

One Happy Community

Animals, Birds, Insects

Most animals are more comfortable living with certain other animals and plants. This special group is called a community.

There are many kinds of communities. Some animals live in a forest community or a pond community. Others live in a desert, seashore or grassland community.

Directions: Look at the communities below and list five animals in each.

Pond Community	Forest Community
fish	*deer*
turtle	*chipmunk*
frog	*squirrel*
ducks	*fox*
dragonfly	*rabbit / bird*

1. Why do you think these animals live together in the pond community? *Possible answer: They are all adapted to live in or near water.*

2. Why do you think these animals live together in the forest community? *Possible answer: They can find food and shelter there.*

3. Some animals may live in more than one kind of a community. Name some animals that live in both a pond and forest community. *Possible answers: birds, insects, etc.*

Investigate
Your backyard can be an animal community. Make a list of the animals that visit or live in your backyard. Don't forget those tiny ones you can't easily see.

©1998 Tribune Education. All Rights Reserved.
25

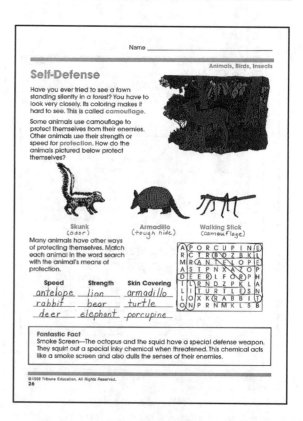

Name _____

Self-Defense

Animals, Birds, Insects

Have you ever tried to see a fawn standing silently in a forest? You have to look very closely. Its coloring makes it hard to see. This is called camouflage.

Some animals use camouflage to protect themselves from their enemies. Other animals use their strength or speed for protection. How do the animals pictured below protect themselves?

Skunk (odor)   **Armadillo** (tough hide)   **Walking Stick** (camouflage)

Many animals have other ways of protecting themselves. Match each animal in the word search with the animal's means of protection.

Speed	Strength	Skin Covering
antelope	*lion*	*armadillo*
rabbit	*bear*	*turtle*
deer	*elephant*	*porcupine*

Fantastic Fact
Smoke Screen—The octopus and the squid have a special defense weapon. They squirt out a special inky chemical when threatened. This chemical acts like a smoke screen and also dulls the senses of their enemies.

©1998 Tribune Education. All Rights Reserved.
26

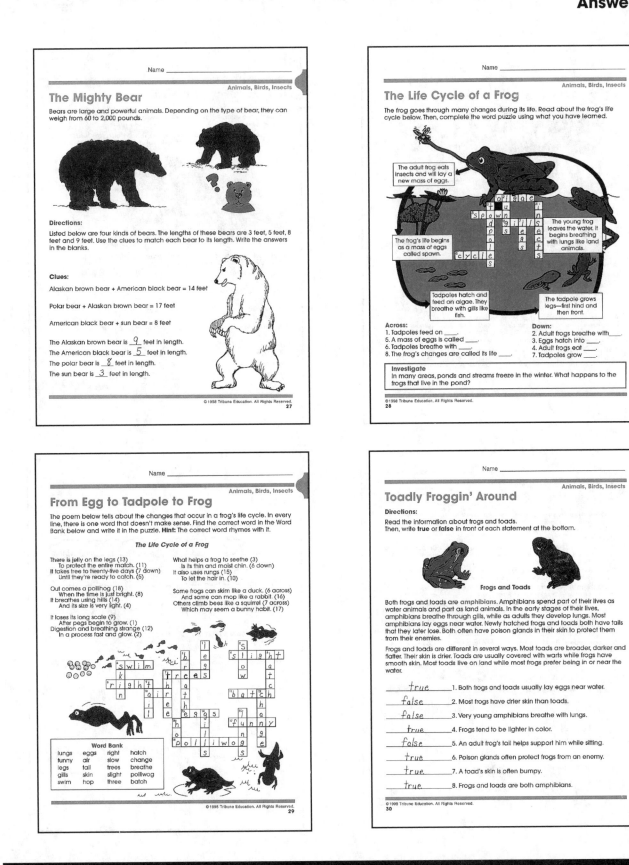

Name _____

Animals, Birds, Insects

The Mighty Bear

Bears are large and powerful animals. Depending on the type of bear, they can weigh from 60 to 2,000 pounds.

Directions:

Listed below are four kinds of bears. The lengths of these bears are 3 feet, 5 feet, 8 feet and 9 feet. Use the clues to match each bear to its length. Write the answers in the blanks.

Clues:

Alaskan brown bear + American black bear = 14 feet

Polar bear + Alaskan brown bear = 17 feet

American black bear + sun bear = 8 feet

The Alaskan brown bear is _9_ feet in length.
The American black bear is _5_ feet in length.
The polar bear is _8_ feet in length.
The sun bear is _3_ feet in length.

© 1998 Tribune Education. All Rights Reserved.
27

Name _____

Animals, Birds, Insects

The Life Cycle of a Frog

The frog goes through many changes during its life. Read about the frog's life cycle below. Then, complete the word puzzle using what you have learned.

The adult frog eats insects and will lay a new mass of eggs.

The young frog leaves the water. It begins breathing with lungs like land animals.

The frog's life begins as a mass of eggs called spawn.

Tadpoles hatch and feed on algae. They breathe with gills like fish.

The tadpole grows legs—first hind and then front.

Across:
1. Tadpoles feed on ____.
5. A mass of eggs is called ____.
6. Tadpoles breathe with ____.
8. The frog's changes are called its life ____.

Down:
2. Adult frogs breathe with____.
3. Eggs hatch into ____.
4. Adult frogs eat ____.
7. Tadpoles grow ____.

Investigate
In many areas, ponds and streams freeze in the winter. What happens to the frogs that live in the pond?

© 1998 Tribune Education. All Rights Reserved.
28

Name _____

Animals, Birds, Insects

From Egg to Tadpole to Frog

The poem below tells about the changes that occur in a frog's life cycle. In every line, there is one word that doesn't make sense. Find the correct word in the Word Bank below and write it in the puzzle. **Hint:** The correct word rhymes with it.

The Life Cycle of a Frog

There is jelly on the legs (13)
    To protect the entire match. (11)
It takes tree to twenty-five days (7 down)
    Until they're ready to catch. (5)

Out comes a polihog (18)
    When the time is just bright. (8)
It breathes using hills (14)
    And its size is very light. (4)

It loses its long scale (9)
    After pegs begin to grow. (1)
Digestion and breathing strange (12)
    In a process fast and glow. (2)

What helps a frog to seethe (3)
    Is its thin and moist chin. (6 down)
It also uses rungs (15)
    To let the hair in. (10)

Some frogs can skim like a duck. (6 across)
    And some can mop like a rabbit. (16)
Others climb bees like a squirrel (7 across)
    Which may seem a bunny habit. (17)

Word Bank			
lungs	eggs	right	hatch
funny	air	slow	change
legs	tail	trees	breathe
gills	skin	slight	polliwog
swim	hop	three	batch

© 1998 Tribune Education. All Rights Reserved.
29

Name _____

Animals, Birds, Insects

Toadly Froggin' Around

Directions:

Read the information about frogs and toads.
Then, write **true** or **false** in front of each statement at the bottom.

Frogs and Toads

Both frogs and toads are amphibians. Amphibians spend part of their lives as water animals and part as land animals. In the early stages of their lives, amphibians breathe through gills, while as adults they develop lungs. Most amphibians lay eggs near water. Newly hatched frogs and toads both have tails that they later lose. Both often have poison glands in their skin to protect them from their enemies.

Frogs and toads are different in several ways. Most toads are broader, darker and flatter. Their skin is drier. Toads are usually covered with warts while frogs have smooth skin. Most toads live on land while most frogs prefer being in or near the water.

__true__ 1. Both frogs and toads usually lay eggs near water.
__false__ 2. Most frogs have drier skin than toads.
__false__ 3. Very young amphibians breathe with lungs.
__true__ 4. Frogs tend to be lighter in color.
__false__ 5. An adult frog's tail helps support him while sitting.
__true__ 6. Poison glands often protect frogs from an enemy.
__true__ 7. A toad's skin is often bumpy.
__true__ 8. Frogs and toads are both amphibians.

© 1998 Tribune Education. All Rights Reserved.
30

Name _____

A Re-Appearing Act

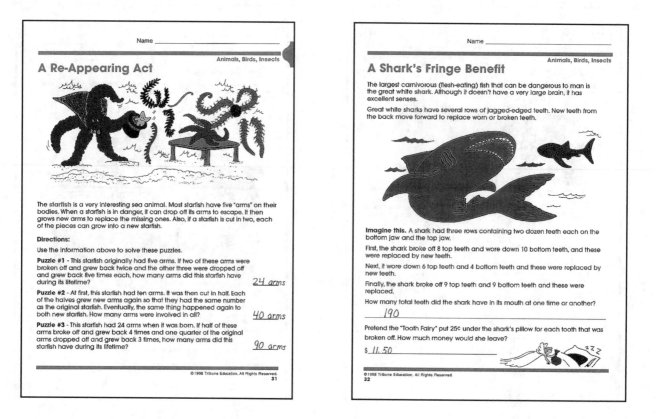

The starfish is a very interesting sea animal. Most starfish have five "arms" on their bodies. When a starfish is in danger, it can drop off its arms to escape. It then grows new arms to replace the missing ones. Also, if a starfish is cut in two, each of the pieces can grow into a new starfish.

Directions:

Use the information above to solve these puzzles.

Puzzle #1 - This starfish originally had five arms. If two of these arms were broken off and grew back twice and the other three were dropped off and grew back five times each, how many arms did this starfish have during its lifetime? _24 arms_

Puzzle #2 - At first, this starfish had ten arms. It was then cut in half. Each of the halves grew new arms again so that they had the same number as the original starfish. Eventually, the same thing happened again to both new starfish. How many arms were involved in all? _40 arms_

Puzzle #3 - This starfish had 24 arms when it was born. If half of these arms broke off and grew back 4 times and one quarter of the original arms dropped off and grew back 3 times, how many arms did this starfish have during its lifetime? _90 arms_

31

Name _____

A Shark's Fringe Benefit

The largest carnivorous (flesh-eating) fish that can be dangerous to man is the great white shark. Although it doesn't have a very large brain, it has excellent senses.

Great white sharks have several rows of jagged-edged teeth. New teeth from the back move forward to replace worn or broken teeth.

Imagine this. A shark had three rows containing two dozen teeth each on the bottom jaw and the top jaw.

First, the shark broke off 8 top teeth and wore down 10 bottom teeth, and these were replaced by new teeth.

Next, it wore down 6 top teeth and 4 bottom teeth and these were replaced by new teeth.

Finally, the shark broke off 9 top teeth and 9 bottom teeth and these were replaced.

How many total teeth did the shark have in its mouth at one time or another?

_190_

Pretend the "Tooth Fairy" put 25¢ under the shark's pillow for each tooth that was broken off. How much money would she leave?

$ _11.50_

32

Name _____

A Sampling of Snakes

The Snake House is a very popular place to visit at the zoo. There are many different types and sizes of snakes. Some snakes are poisonous while others are not. Some snakes are harmless to most creatures, and some are very dangerous.

Directions:

The five snakes described here are held in the cages below. Decide which snake belongs in each cage by using the clues given here and beneath the boxes. Then, write each name in the correct cage.

The King Cobra is the longest poisonous snake in the world. One measured almost 19 feet long. It lives in southeast Asia, Indonesia and the Philippines.

The Gaboon Viper, a very poisonous snake, has the longest fangs of all snakes (nearly 2 inches). It lives in tropical Africa.

The Reticulated Python is the longest snake of all. One specimen measured 32 feet, 9½ inches. It crushes its prey to death. It lives in southeast Asia, Indonesia and the Philippines.

The Black Mamba, the fastest-moving land snake, can move at speeds of 10-12 miles per hour. It lives in the eastern part of tropical Africa.

The Anaconda is almost twice as heavy as a reticulated python of the same length. One anaconda that was almost 28 feet long weighed nearly 500 pounds. It lives in tropical South America.

#1 ANACONDA   #2 KING-COBRA   #3 Reticulated Python   #4 GABOON VIPER   #5 BLACK MAMBA

Clues:

- The snake in cage #5 moves the fastest on land.
- The longest snake of all is between the snake that comes from tropical Africa and the longest poisonous snake.
- The very heavy snake is to the left of the longest poisonous snake.

33

Name _____

Secret Code for Worm Lovers

Directions:

To decode the secret words, use the code below.

A	B	C	D	E	F	G	H	I	J	K	L	M
1	2	3	4	5	6	7	8	9	10	11	12	13

N	O	P	Q	R	S	T	U	V	W	X	Y	Z
14	15	16	17	18	19	20	21	22	23	24	25	26

1. Earthworms can also be called _N i g h t   c r a w l e r s_.
   14 9 7 8 20   3 18 1 23 12 5 18 19

2. Earthworms have no _e a r s_ or _e y e s_.
   5 1 18 19   5 25 5 19

3. Sections of an earthworm are called _S e g m e n t s_.
   19 5 7 13 5 14 20 19

4. Earthworms _b r e a t h e_ through their _s k i n_.
   2 18 5 1 20 8 5   19 11 9 14

5. Earthworms eat _s o i l_.
   19 15 9 12

6. As they _b u r r o w_ through the soil, they give plants the _a i r_
   2 21 18 18 15 23   1 9 18
   that they need.

34

Name _____

Hibernation

Have you ever wondered why some animals hibernate? Some animals sleep all winter. This sleep is called hibernation.

Animals get their warmth and energy from food. Some animals cannot find enough food in the winter. They must eat large amounts of food in the autumn. Their bodies store this food as fat. Then, in winter, they hibernate. Their bodies live on the stored fat. Since their bodies need much less food during hibernation, they can stay alive without eating anymore food during the winter.

Some animals that hibernate are bats, chipmunks, bears, snakes and turtles.

Directions:

Match:
Animals that hibernate . . .

eat and store food — in the winter.
go to sleep — in the autumn.

Underline:

Hibernation . . . _is a sleep that some animals go into for the winter._
is the time of year to gather food for the winter.

Circle Yes or No:

Animals get their warmth and energy from food.	(Yes) No
Some animals cannot find enough food in the winter.	(Yes) No
Animals hibernate because they are lazy.	Yes (No)
Animals need less food while they are hibernating.	(Yes) No

Color the animals that hibernate.

(Child should color bear, bat, chipmunk, turtle and snake.)

Name _____

Food Chains

Did you ever wonder where the food you eat comes from? The hamburger you eat comes from a cow. The cow eats the green grass in the pasture. The cow eats the grass and you eat the cow. This is a food chain. It can be written like this:

grass ⟶ cow ⟶ person

Each arrow between an animal and its food is called a strand. How many strands are in the food chain above?
2

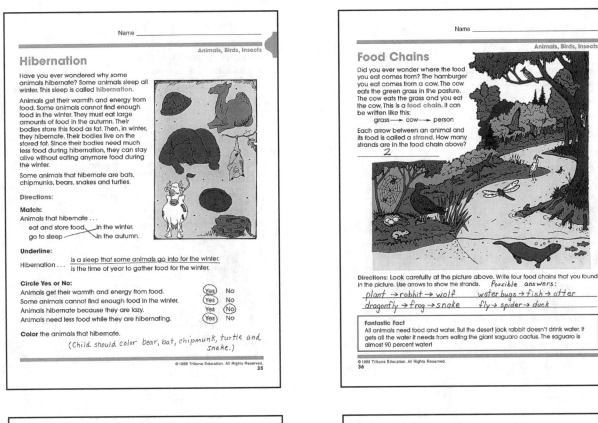

Directions: Look carefully at the picture above. Write four food chains that you found in the picture. Use arrows to show the strands. *Possible answers:*

plant → rabbit → wolf   water bugs → fish → otter
dragonfly → frog → snake   fly → spider → duck

Fantastic Fact
All animals need food and water. But the desert jack rabbit doesn't drink water. It gets all the water it needs from eating the giant saguaro cactus. The saguaro is almost 90 percent water!

Name _____

Endangered Animals

You will never see a dodo bird or a saber-tooth tiger. These animals are gone forever. They are extinct.

The animals on this page are not extinct, but they are in danger of becoming extinct. They are endangered. There may not be enough of them to reproduce.

There are many reasons why some animals are endangered. The signs on this page give clues to three main reasons.

Look at the signs. What do you think the three reasons are? Write them below.

1. _Cutting down trees can eliminate shelter for wildlife._
2. _Hunters kill too many animals and disrupt food chains._
3. _Trash pollutes environments and kills animals._

Directions: Unscramble the names of these endangered animals.

dalb gleae	nereg teltur	lueb laweh	bremit lofw
bald eagle	green turtle	blue whale	timber wolf

Investigate
There are more than 100 endangered animals in North America. Find the name of one that lives near your area. Make a poster to help people become aware of this animal and the danger it is in.

Name _____

Endangered Animal Acrostic

Directions: Using the animal names in the Word Bank and the clues below, fill in the blanks in the spaces provided. The circled letters are used as clues for your answers.

WORD BANK	blue whale	jaguar	pronghorn
	cheetah	okapi	polar bear
	vicuna	yak	giant panda

1. p(O)lar bear
2. p(R)onghorn
3. ok(A)pi
4. gia(N)t panda
5. ja(G)uar
6. bl(U)e whale
7. chee(T)ah
8. y(A)k
9. vicu(N)a

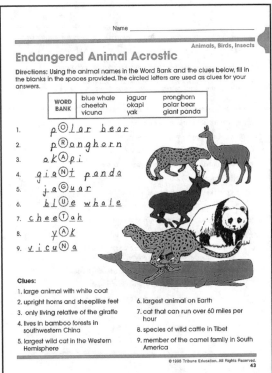

Clues:
1. large animal with white coat
2. upright horns and sheeplike feet
3. only living relative of the giraffe
4. lives in bamboo forests in southwestern China
5. largest wild cat in the Western Hemisphere
6. largest animal on Earth
7. cat that can run over 60 miles per hour
8. species of wild cattle in Tibet
9. member of the camel family in South America

Endangered Animals

Many of the earth's animals are endangered or extinct. Use the names of the animals to build a puzzle. Only use the **bold-faced** words.

Word Bank

brown **hyena**	Darwin's **rhea**	red **wolf**	black-footed **ferret**
Spanish **lynx**	Philippine **eagle**	**gavial**	ring-tailed **lemur**
giant **panda**	blue **whale**	**numbat**	resplendent **quetzal**
Arabian **oryx**	Grevy's **zebra**	**dugong**	Galapagos **penguin**
Indian **python**	wild **yak**	**kakapo**	

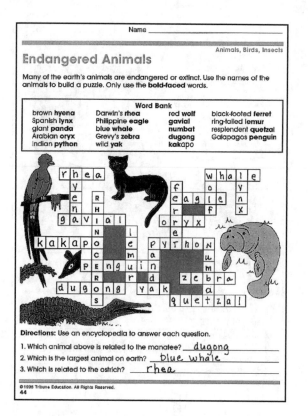

Directions: Use an encyclopedia to answer each question.

1. Which animal above is related to the manatee? _dugong_
2. Which is the largest animal on earth? _blue whale_
3. Which is related to the ostrich? _rhea_

Animal Magic Challenge

Directions: Read Column A. Choose an answer from Column B that matches. Write the number of the answer in the Magic Square. The first one has been done for you. You may need to research some of these animals on your own!

Column A	Column B
A. grizzly bear	1. large bear of the American grasslands
B. koala	2. lives on dry grasslands of South Africa
C. peregrine falcon	3. the most valuable reptile in the world
D. California condor	4. largest soaring bird of North America
E. black-footed ferret	5. the tallest American bird
F. cheetah	6. the fastest animal on land
G. orangutan	7. the only great ape outside Africa
H. giant panda	8. large aquatic seal-like animal
I. Florida manatee	9. large black and white mammal of China
J. kit fox	10. small, fast mammal; nocturnal predator
K. blue whale	11. largest animal in the world
L. whooping crane	12. member of the weasel family
M. red wolf	13. has interbred with coyotes in some areas
N. green sea turtle	14. also called a duck hawk; size of a crow
O. brown hyena	15. eats leaves of the eucalyptus tree
P. jaguar	16. known as *el tigre* in Spanish

A	B	C	D
1	15	14	4
E	**F**	**G**	**H**
12	6	7	9
I	**J**	**K**	**L**
8	10	11	5
M	**N**	**O**	**P**
13	3	2	16

Add the numbers across, down and diagonally. What answer do you get? _34_
Why do you think this is called a magic square?

Bald Eagle Puzzler

Directions: Research the bald eagle. Read each statement about the bald eagle. If the statement is false, darken the letter in the circle to the left of that statement. The letters not darkened spell out the name of the chemical that affected the bald eagle's food supply.

(P) Because of federal protection, the bald eagle population is increasing.

● It is legal to shoot this bird today.

(E) This bird has keen eyesight and strong wings.

● The wingspan of this bird is about 3 feet.

● The nest of a bald eagle is made of mud and rocks.

(S) This bird eats mainly fish.

● This bird likes to eat only berries and seeds.

(T) The bald eagle is found only in North America.

● Only four bald eagles exist today in the United States.

● An injured bald eagle may be kept as a pet.

(I) Chemical poisons in the bald eagle's food caused its eggs to crack before incubation could be completed.

(C) The nest of a bald eagle is built high on a cliff or in a tree.

(I) This bird is the national symbol of the United States.

● The bald eagle is noted for its bright orange head.

(D) The bald eagle has a hooked beak.

(E) The nest of a bald eagle is called an aerie.

What is the type of chemical? _P e s t i c i d e_

Going Places

Looking at a bird's feet can tell you a lot about how they are used. Look at the birds' feet below. Unscramble each bird's name. Write the bird's name by the sentence that best describes it.

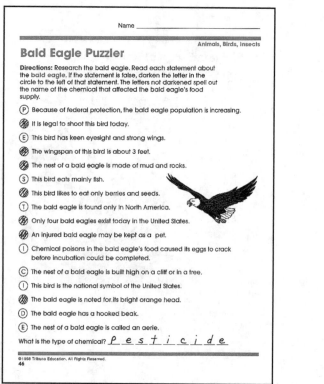

duck "My webbed feet are great for swimming."

woodpecker "My feet are great for walking up trees."

heron "I use my feet with long toes to wade in the water and mud."

hawk "I use my strong, powerful feet to catch small animals."

kawh _hawk_   noreh _heron_
ckud _duck_   reckwoodep _woodpecker_

Can the shape of a bird's bill tell you anything about what it eats? Look closely at the bills below. Unscramble each bird's name. Write the bird's name by the sentence that best describes it.

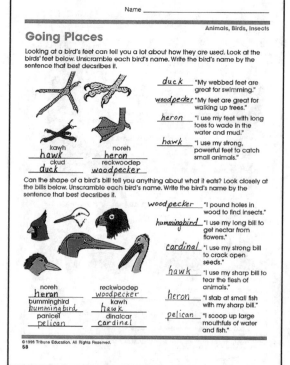

woodpecker "I pound holes in wood to find insects."

hummingbird "I use my long bill to get nectar from flowers."

cardinal "I use my strong bill to crack open seeds."

hawk "I use my sharp bill to tear the flesh of animals."

heron "I stab at small fish with my sharp bill."

pelican "I scoop up large mouthfuls of water and fish."

noreh _heron_   reckwoodep _woodpecker_
bumminghird _hummingbird_   kawh _hawk_
panicel _pelican_   dinalcar _cardinal_

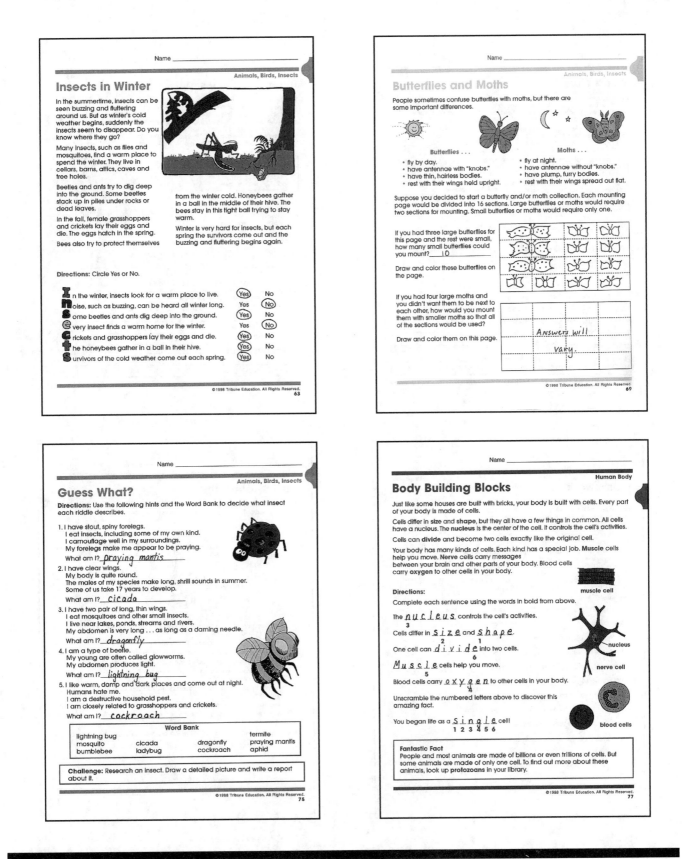

Name _____

Animals, Birds, Insects

Insects in Winter

In the summertime, insects can be seen buzzing and fluttering around us. But as winter's cold weather begins, suddenly the insects seem to disappear. Do you know where they go?

Many insects, such as flies and mosquitoes, find a warm place to spend the winter. They live in cellars, barns, attics, caves and tree holes.

Beetles and ants try to dig deep into the ground. Some beetles stack up in piles under rocks or dead leaves.

In the fall, female grasshoppers and crickets lay their eggs and die. The eggs hatch in the spring.

Bees also try to protect themselves

from the winter cold. Honeybees gather in a ball in the middle of their hive. The bees stay in this tight ball trying to stay warm.

Winter is very hard for insects, but each spring the survivors come out and the buzzing and fluttering begins again.

Directions: Circle Yes or No.

I n the winter, insects look for a warm place to live. **(Yes)** No

N oise, such as buzzing, can be heard all winter long. Yes **(No)**

S ome beetles and ants dig deep into the ground. **(Yes)** No

E very insect finds a warm home for the winter. Yes **(No)**

C rickets and grasshoppers lay their eggs and die. **(Yes)** No

T he honeybees gather in a ball in their hive. **(Yes)** No

S urvivors of the cold weather come out each spring. **(Yes)** No

63

Name _____

Animals, Birds, Insects

Butterflies and Moths

People sometimes confuse butterflies with moths, but there are some important differences.

Butterflies . . .
- fly by day.
- have antennae with "knobs."
- have thin, hairless bodies.
- rest with their wings held upright.

Moths . . .
- fly at night.
- have antennae without "knobs."
- have plump, furry bodies.
- rest with their wings spread out flat.

Suppose you decided to start a butterfly and/or moth collection. Each mounting page would be divided into 16 sections. Large butterflies or moths would require two sections for mounting. Small butterflies or moths would require only one.

If you had three large butterflies for this page and the rest were small, how many small butterflies could you mount? **10**

Draw and color these butterflies on the page.

If you had four large moths and you didn't want them to be next to each other, how would you mount them with smaller moths so that all of the sections would be used?

Draw and color them on this page.

Answers will vary.

69

Name _____

Animals, Birds, Insects

Guess What?

Directions: Use the following hints and the Word Bank to decide what insect each riddle describes.

1. I have stout, spiny forelegs.
   I eat insects, including some of my own kind.
   I camouflage well in my surroundings.
   My forelegs make me appear to be praying.
   What am I? *praying mantis*

2. I have clear wings.
   My body is quite round.
   The males of my species make long, shrill sounds in summer.
   Some of us take 17 years to develop.
   What am I? *cicada*

3. I have two pair of long, thin wings.
   I eat mosquitoes and other small insects.
   I live near lakes, ponds, streams and rivers.
   My abdomen is very long . . . as long as a darning needle.
   What am I? *dragonfly*

4. I am a type of beetle.
   My young are often called glowworms.
   My abdomen produces light.
   What am I? *lightning bug*

5. I like warm, damp and dark places and come out at night.
   Humans hate me.
   I am a destructive household pest.
   I am closely related to grasshoppers and crickets.
   What am I? *cockroach*

Word Bank			
lightning bug			termite
mosquito	cicada	dragonfly	praying mantis
bumblebee	ladybug	cockroach	aphid

Challenge: Research an insect. Draw a detailed picture and write a report about it.

75

Name _____

Human Body

Body Building Blocks

Just like some houses are built with bricks, your body is built with cells. Every part of your body is made of cells.

Cells differ in **size** and **shape**, but they all have a few things in common. All cells have a **nucleus**. The **nucleus** is the center of the cell. It controls the cell's activities.

Cells can **divide** and become two cells exactly like the original cell.

Your body has many kinds of cells. Each kind has a special job. **Muscle** cells help you move. **Nerve** cells carry messages between your brain and other parts of your body. Blood cells carry **oxygen** to other cells in your body.

muscle cell

Directions:

Complete each sentence using the words in bold from above.

The **nucleus** controls the cell's activities.
          3

Cells differ in **size** and **shape**.
                2   1

One cell can **divide** into two cells.
                     6

Muscle cells help you move.
     5

Blood cells carry **oxygen** to other cells in your body.
                       4

nucleus

nerve cell

Unscramble the numbered letters above to discover this amazing fact.

You began life as a **single** cell.
                    1 2 3 4 5 6

blood cells

Fantastic Fact
People and most animals are made of billions or even trillions of cells. But some animals are made of only one cell. To find out more about these animals, look up **protozoans** in your library.

77

Name _____

Human Body

Blood Work

If you could look at a drop of your blood under a microscope, you would see some odd-shaped cells floating around in a liquid called **plasma**. These are the **white blood cells**. White blood cells are "soldiers" that fight germs which cause disease.

You would also see many smaller, saucer-shaped cells called **red blood cells**. Red blood cells give your blood its red color. They also have the important job of carrying **oxygen** to all of the cells in your body.

Blood **platelets** go to work when you have a cut. They form a plug, called a clot, that stops the bleeding.

Blood travels throughout your whole body. It goes to the **lungs** to pick up oxygen and to the intestines to pick up digested food. It carries the oxygen and food nutrients to all part of your body. It also takes away carbon dioxide and other waste products.

Directions: Fill in the spaces with words from the Word Bank.

1. Red blood cells carry o x y g e n.
2. The blood gets oxygen from your l u n g s.
3. Blood carries f o o d nutrients from the intestines.
4. W h i t e blood cells fight germs.
5. Blood travels to all parts of your b o d y.
6. The liquid part of the blood is called p l a s m a.
7. R e d blood cells give blood its color.
8. P l a t e l e t s form blood clots.
9. Adults donate blood at a blood b a n k.

Word Bank
oxygen
platelets
red
white
bank
lungs
plasma
food
body

Challenge
Use the numbered letters to finish the sentence. "Dirty" blood is cleansed by two large bean-shaped organs. These organs are called k i d n e y s.

79

Name _____

Human Body

Ingenious Genes

Your body is made up of cells. Each cell holds threadlike structures called **chromosomes** that contain genes. Genes are inherited from your parents and determine how you will look. This is why we often look like our parents. Some genes are stronger, or **dominant**, and some are carried down through generations. Below is a table listing the characteristics of a mother and a father. See if you can find all of the possible combinations for their children and write them in the space provided. There are 16 possibilities!

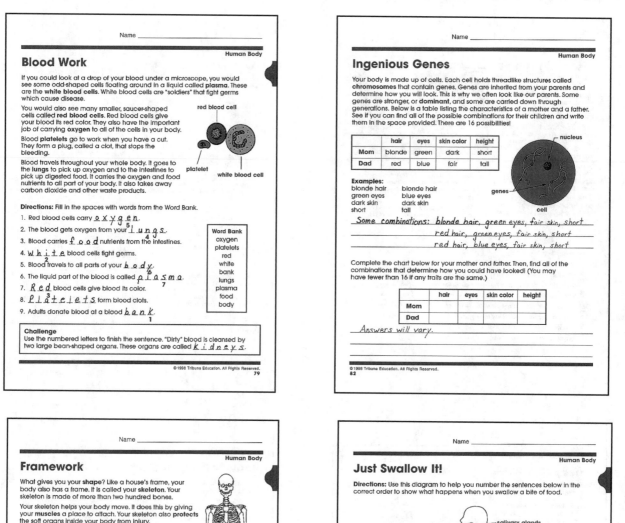

	hair	eyes	skin color	height
Mom	blonde	green	dark	short
Dad	red	blue	fair	tall

Examples:
blonde hair   blonde hair
green eyes   blue eyes
dark skin   dark skin
short   tall

Some combinations: blonde hair, green eyes, fair skin, short
red hair, green eyes, fair skin, short
red hair, blue eyes, fair skin, short

Complete the chart below for your mother and father. Then, find all of the combinations that determine how you could have looked! (You may have fewer than 16 if any traits are the same.)

	hair	eyes	skin color	height
Mom				
Dad				

Answers will vary.

82

Name _____

Human Body

Framework

What gives you your **shape**? Like a house's frame, your body also has a frame. It is called your **skeleton**. Your skeleton is made of more than two hundred bones.

Your skeleton helps your body move. It does this by giving your **muscles** a place to attach. Your skeleton also **protects** the soft organs inside your body from injury.

Bones have a hard, outer layer made of **calcium**. Inside each bone is a soft, **spongy** layer that looks like a honeycomb. The hollow spaces in the honeycomb are filled with **marrow**. Every minute, millions of **blood** cells die. But you don't need to worry. The bone marrow works like a little factory, making new blood cells for you.

Directions:

Use the highlighted words above to finish the sentences below.

1. Your skeleton p r o t e c t s your soft organs.
2. Bone m a r r o w makes new blood cells.
3. Inside the bone is a soft, s p o n g y layer.
4. Millions of b l o o d cells die every minute.
5. The hard, outer layer of bone is made from c a l c i u m.
6. More than two hundred bones are in your s k e l e t o n.
7. Your skeleton is a place for m u s c l e s to attach.
8. Your skeleton gives your body its s h a p e.

Challenge
What do you call a skeleton that won't get out of bed? Use the numbered letters above to find out. l a z y   b o n e s
1 2 3   4 5 6 7 8

83

Name _____

Human Body

Just Swallow It!

Directions: Use this diagram to help you number the sentences below in the correct order to show what happens when you swallow a bite of food.

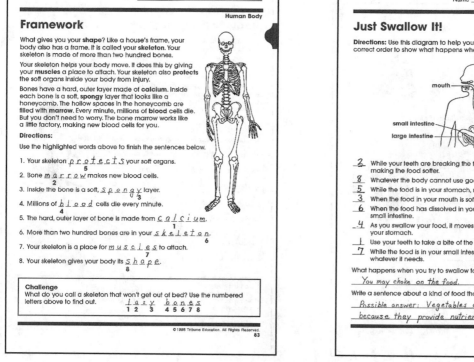

2 While your teeth are breaking the food into tiny pieces, saliva is making the food softer.

8 Whatever the body cannot use goes into the large intestine.

5 While the food is in your stomach, more juices help to dissolve it.

3 When the food in your mouth is soft enough, you swallow it.

6 When the food has dissolved in your stomach, it goes to your small intestine.

4 As you swallow your food, it moves down the esophagus to your stomach.

1 Use your teeth to take a bite of the sandwich.

7 While the food is in your small intestine, the body absorbs whatever it needs.

What happens when you try to swallow too big of a bite? Possible answer: You may choke on the food.

Write a sentence about a kind of food that is good for your body. Possible answer: Vegetables are good for your body because they provide nutrients and fiber.

87

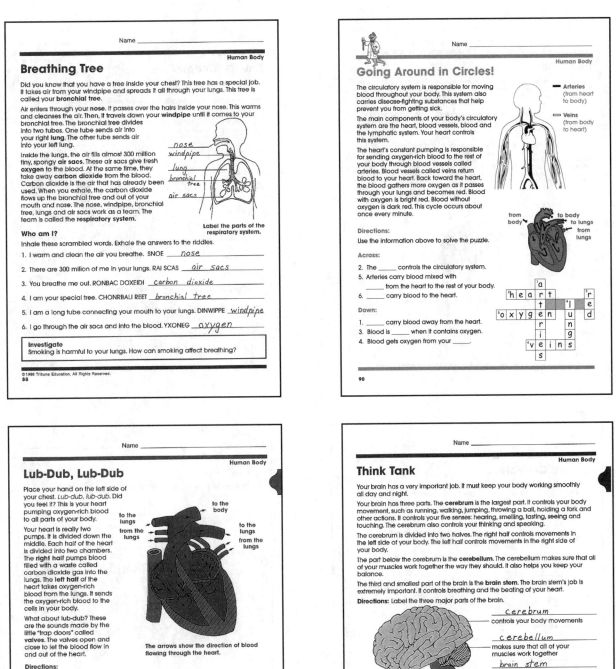

Name _____

Human Body

Breathing Tree

Did you know that you have a tree inside your chest? This tree has a special job. It takes air from your windpipe and spreads it all through your lungs. This tree is called your **bronchial tree**.

Air enters through your **nose**. It passes over the hairs inside your nose. This warms and cleanses the air. Then, it travels down your **windpipe** until it comes to your bronchial tree. The bronchial tree divides into two tubes. One tube sends air into your right **lung**. The other tube sends air into your left lung.

Inside the lungs, the air fills almost 300 million tiny, spongy **air sacs**. These air sacs give fresh **oxygen** to the blood. At the same time, they take away **carbon dioxide** from the blood. Carbon dioxide is the air that has already been used. When you exhale, the carbon dioxide flows up the bronchial tree and out of your mouth and nose. The nose, windpipe, bronchial tree, lungs and air sacs work as a team. The team is called the **respiratory system**.

nose
windpipe
lung
bronchial tree
air sacs

Label the parts of the respiratory system.

Who am I?
Inhale these scrambled words. Exhale the answers to the riddles.

1. I warm and clean the air you breathe. SNOE ___nose___

2. There are 300 million of me in your lungs. RAI SCAS ___air sacs___

3. You breathe me out. RONBAC DOXEIDI ___carbon dioxide___

4. I am your special tree. CHONRBALI REET ___bronchial tree___

5. I am a long tube connecting your mouth to your lungs. DINWIPPE ___windpipe___

6. I go through the air sacs and into the blood. YXONEG ___oxygen___

Investigate
Smoking is harmful to your lungs. How can smoking affect breathing?

Name _____

Human Body

Going Around in Circles!

The circulatory system is responsible for moving blood throughout your body. This system also carries disease-fighting substances that help prevent you from getting sick.

The main components of your body's circulatory system are the heart, blood vessels, blood and the lymphatic system. Your heart controls this system.

The heart's constant pumping is responsible for sending oxygen-rich blood to the rest of your body through blood vessels called arteries. Blood vessels called veins return blood to your heart. Back toward the heart, the blood gathers more oxygen as it passes through your lungs and becomes red. Blood with oxygen is bright red. Blood without oxygen is dark red. This cycle occurs about once every minute.

Arteries (from heart to body)
Veins (from body to heart)

from body / to body / to lungs / from lungs

Directions:
Use the information above to solve the puzzle.

Across:
2. The _____ controls the circulatory system.
5. Arteries carry blood mixed with _____ from the heart to the rest of your body.
6. _____ carry blood to the heart.

Down:
1. _____ carry blood away from the heart.
3. Blood is _____ when it contains oxygen.
4. Blood gets oxygen from your _____.

Crossword answers: heart / oxygen / veins / arteries / red / lungs

---

Name _____

Human Body

Lub-Dub, Lub-Dub

Place your hand on the left side of your chest. *Lub-dub, lub-dub.* Did you feel it? This is your heart pumping oxygen-rich blood to all parts of your body.

Your heart is really two pumps. It is divided down the middle. Each half of the heart is divided into two chambers. The **right half** pumps blood filled with a waste called carbon dioxide gas into the lungs. The **left half** of the heart takes oxygen-rich blood from the lungs. It sends the oxygen-rich blood to the cells in your body.

What about lub-dub? These are the sounds made by the little "trap doors" called **valves**. The valves open and close to let the blood flow in and out of the heart.

to the lungs / from the lungs / to the body / to the lungs / from the lungs

The arrows show the direction of blood flowing through the heart.

Directions:
Answer the questions below, using the information from above.

1. How many pumps does your heart have? ___2___

2. Where does the right half pump its blood? ___into the lungs___

3. Where does the left half pump its blood? ___to the body's cells___

4. Which part of the heart makes the lub-dub sound? ___valves___

Name _____

Human Body

Think Tank

Your brain has a very important job. It must keep your body working smoothly all day and night.

Your brain has three parts. The **cerebrum** is the largest part. It controls your body movement, such as running, walking, jumping, throwing a ball, holding a fork and other actions. It controls your five senses: hearing, smelling, tasting, seeing and touching. The cerebrum also controls your thinking and speaking.

The cerebrum is divided into two halves. The right half controls movements in the left side of your body. The left half controls movements in the right side of your body.

The part below the cerebrum is the **cerebellum**. The cerebellum makes sure that all of your muscles work together the way they should. It also helps you keep your balance.

The third and smallest part of the brain is the **brain stem**. The brain stem's job is extremely important. It controls breathing and the beating of your heart.

Directions: Label the three major parts of the brain.

___cerebrum___
controls your body movements

___cerebellum___
makes sure that all of your muscles work together

___brain stem___
controls breathing and the beating of your heart

1. Which part of the skeleton protects the brain from injury?
2. Give the common name and the scientific name.
   common name: ___skull___   scientific name: ___cranium___

Fantastic Fact
In order to function properly, the brain must have a constant supply of blood. The blood provides oxygen and other vitamins and nutrients needed by the brain to stay healthy.

Name _____

Think Tank

Your body's **central nervous system** includes your brain, spinal cord and nerves that transmit information. It receives information from your senses, analyzes this information and decides how your body should respond. Once it has decided, it sends instructions triggering the required actions.

The central nervous system makes some simple decisions about your body's actions within the spinal cord. These **spinal reflexes** include actions like pulling your hand away from a hot object. However, the brain still makes the majority of the decisions.

Your brain weighs about three pounds and is made up of three major parts: the cerebrum, the cerebellum and the brain stem. The **cerebrum** is divided into two hemispheres which are responsible for all thought and learning processes. The **cerebellum** is also divided into two parts, which control all voluntary muscle movement. The **brain stem**, which is about the size of your thumb, takes care of all involuntary functions.

Directions:

Fill in the jobs of each part of the brain. Then, answer the questions below.

cerebrum
(thinking and
learning)
brain stem
(involuntary functions)

cerebellum
(muscle movement)

1. Name someone in your family who is using his/her cerebellum. _Answers will vary._
2. What is he/she doing? _____
3. Name someone who is using his/her brain stem. _____
4. What is he/she doing? _____
5. Name someone in your home who is using his/her cerebrum. _____
6. What is he/she doing? _____

96

Name _____

Round Windows

"Oh, what beautiful brown eyes you have!" Whether you know it or not, those eyes are not totally brown. Only the iris is colored brown.

Your eye is shaped like a ball. It has a clear, round window in front called the **cornea**. The colored **iris** controls the amount of light that enters the eye. Light enters through an opening called the **pupil**. In bright light, your pupil is a small dot. In dim light, it is much larger. Behind the pupil is the **lens**. It focuses the light onto the back wall of your eye. This back wall is called the **retina**. The retina changes the light into nerve messages. These messages are sent to the brain along the **optic nerve**. Close your eyes. Gently touch them. They are firm because they are filled with a clear jelly called **vitreous humor**.

Directions:
Label the parts of the eye using the words in bold from above.

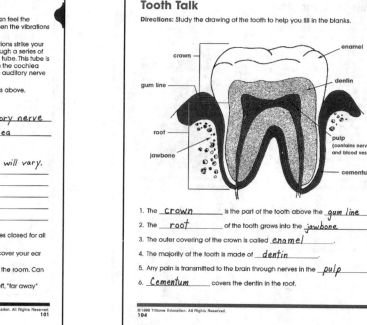

What am I?

I focus the light. _l e n s_
         2   4

I become smaller in bright light. _p u p i l_
                    11   1

I am the clear window. _c o r n e a_
            3   6

I am the colored part of the eye. _i r i s_
                  10

I send pictures to the brain. _o p t i c   n e r v e_
               12 5   7

I am the clear jelly. _v i t r e o u s   h u m o r_
            9   13   8

What did the teacher say when his glass eye went down the drain? Use the numbered letters to find out.

_I l o s t   a n o t h e r   p u p i l_!
1 2 3 4 5   6 7 3 5 8 9 10 11 13 12 1 2

99

Name _____

Sound Collectors

A large jet plane rumbles as it takes off down the runway. You can feel the ground vibrate. The plane is also filling the air with vibrations. When the vibrations reach your ear, you hear them as sound.

Your **outer ear** collects the vibrations just like a funnel. The vibrations strike your **eardrum**, making it vibrate too. These vibrations are passed through a series of three small bones. The last bone vibrates against a snail-shaped tube. This tube is called the **cochlea**. It is filled with liquid. Small hair-like sensors in the cochlea pick up the vibrations and send them to the **auditory nerve**. The auditory nerve sends the sound message to your brain.

Directions: Label the parts of the ear using the highlighted words above.

outer ear

eardrum

auditory nerve

cochlea

Sounds Around Us

Answers will vary.

1. What is the loudest sound you have ever heard? _____
2. What is the softest sound you have ever heard? _____
3. What sound wakes you up in the morning? _____
4. What sound relaxes you? _____
5. What sound frightens you? _____

Extensions:
Try some of these sound experiments with a friend. Keep your eyes closed for all of the experiments!

1. Cover one ear and listen for the sounds around you. Then, uncover your ear and listen again. What is the difference?
2. Choose a friend to make several sounds with objects found in the room. Can you identify the sounds?
3. We usually hear the loudest sounds around us. Listen for the soft, "far away" sounds. List the sounds. Try this experiment outside.

101

Name _____

Tooth Talk

Directions: Study the drawing of the tooth to help you fill in the blanks.

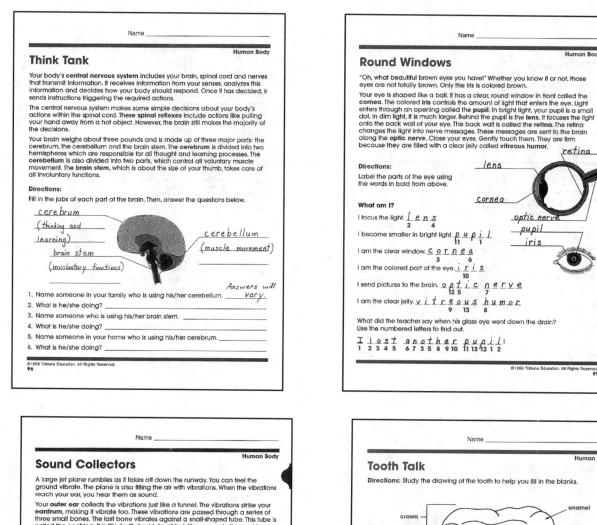

enamel
crown
gum line
dentin
root
pulp (contains nerves and blood vessels)
jawbone
cementum

1. The _crown_ is the part of the tooth above the _gum line_
2. The _root_ of the tooth grows into the _jawbone_.
3. The outer covering of the crown is called _enamel_
4. The majority of the tooth is made of _dentin_.
5. Any pain is transmitted to the brain through nerves in the _pulp_
6. _Cementum_ covers the dentin in the root.

104

Name _____

Nutrition

Energy Savers

Fats give you twice as much energy as proteins or carbohydrates. Your body uses fats to save energy for future use. The fats we eat come from animals in the form of meat, eggs, milk and much more. We also get fats from some plants like beans, peanuts and corn. But not all plants give us fats in our diet.

Directions:
Circle the foods which are rich in fat. Then, list them on the chart.

Fat Food Sources	
Animal	**Plant**
chicken	olive oil
eggs	beans
ice cream	nuts
cheese	
steak	
butter	

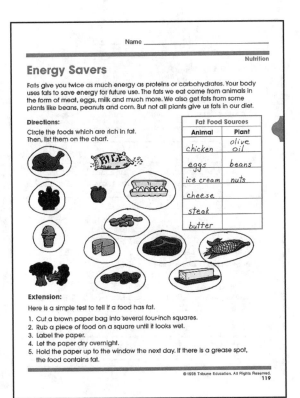

Extension:

Here is a simple test to tell if a food has fat.

1. Cut a brown paper bag into several four-inch squares.
2. Rub a piece of food on a square until it looks wet.
3. Label the paper.
4. Let the paper dry overnight.
5. Hold the paper up to the window the next day. If there is a grease spot, the food contains fat.

119

Name _____

Nutrition

Protein: The Body Builder

Protein is the nutrient that repairs and builds new body tissue. Most of the foods we eat contain some protein. We call these "high protein foods."

Directions: Circle all of the high protein foods.

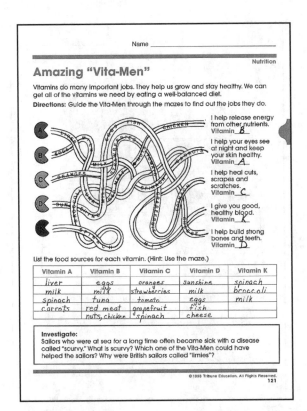

Did you notice that most of the foods you circled belong to two food groups? Name these groups and list the circled foods under the correct group. Add two more high protein foods to each list.

Group: _Meat_

1. eggs
2. nuts
3. steak
4. fish
5. chicken
6. hamburger

Group: _Dairy_

1. cheese
2. yogurt
3.
4. (add 2 more)
5.
6.

Investigate:
Legumes (dry peas and beans) are an important protein source in many countries around the world. List as many kinds of legumes as you can think of. (Hint: A trip to your favorite grocery store will help you answer this.)

120

Name _____

Nutrition

Amazing "Vita-Men"

Vitamins do many important jobs. They help us grow and stay healthy. We can get all of the vitamins we need by eating a well-balanced diet.

Directions: Guide the Vita-Men through the mazes to find out the jobs they do.

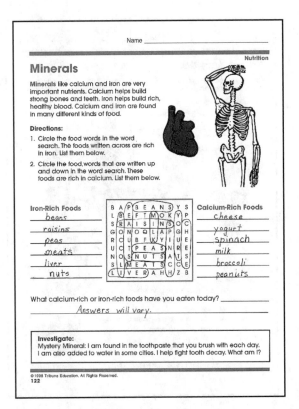

I help release energy from other nutrients.
Vitamin _B_

I help your eyes see at night and keep your skin healthy.
Vitamin _A_

I help heal cuts, scrapes and scratches.
Vitamin _C_

I give you good, healthy blood.
Vitamin _K_

I help build strong bones and teeth.
Vitamin _D_

List the food sources for each vitamin. (Hint: Use the maze.)

Vitamin A	Vitamin B	Vitamin C	Vitamin D	Vitamin K
liver	eggs	oranges	sunshine	spinach
milk	milk	strawberries	milk	broccoli
spinach	tuna	tomato	eggs	milk
carrots	red meat	grapefruit	fish	
	nuts, chicken	spinach	cheese	

Investigate:
Sailors who were at sea for a long time often became sick with a disease called "scurvy." What is scurvy? Which one of the Vita-Men could have helped the sailors? Why were British sailors called "limies"?

121

Name _____

Nutrition

Minerals

Minerals like calcium and iron are very important nutrients. Calcium helps build strong bones and teeth. Iron helps build rich, healthy blood. Calcium and iron are found in many different kinds of food.

Directions:

1. Circle the food words in the word search. The foods written across are rich in iron. List them below.

2. Circle the food words that are written up and down in the word search. These foods are rich in calcium. List them below.

Iron-Rich Foods

beans
raisins
peas
meats
liver
nuts

B	A	P	B	E	A	N	S	Y	S
L	B	E	F	T	M	O	K	Y	P
S	R	A	I	S	I	N	S	O	C
G	O	N	O	Q	L	A	P	G	H
R	C	U	B	F	K	Y	I	U	E
U	C	T	P	E	A	S	N	E	E
N	O	S	N	U	T	S	A	T	S
S	L	M	E	A	T	S	C	R	I
L	I	V	E	R	A	H	H	Z	B

Calcium-Rich Foods

cheese
yogurt
spinach
milk
broccoli
peanuts

What calcium-rich or iron-rich foods have you eaten today? _____
Answers will vary.

Investigate:
Mystery Mineral: I am found in the toothpaste that you brush with each day. I am also added to water in some cities. I help fight tooth decay. What am I?

122

You Are What You Eat!

You are not made out of pickles and carrots. The food you eat must be digested before your body can use it. Digested food is changed into nutrients which help your body grow and give you energy.

Unscramble the names of the six nutrient groups. Use the Word Bank.

Word Bank
proteins
vitamins
minerals
carbohydrates
water
fats

netroips _proteins_
ralmenis _minerals_
afts _fats_
ratew _water_
timnivas _vitamins_
droracbaytesh _carbohydrates_

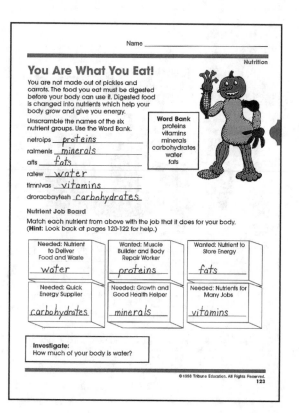

Nutrient Job Board

Match each nutrient from above with the job that it does for your body.
(**Hint:** Look back at pages 120-122 for help.)

Needed: Nutrient to Deliver Food and Waste	Wanted: Muscle Builder and Body Repair Worker	Wanted: Nutrient to Store Energy
water	proteins	fats

Needed: Quick Energy Supplier	Needed: Growth and Good Health Helper	Needed: Nutrients for Many Jobs
carbohydrates	minerals	vitamins

Investigate:
How much of your body is water?

123

You Are What You Eat!

A nutritious diet helps your body fight diseases. Write the foods from the Word Bank in their correct category(s). Use references if necessary.

Word Bank				
tomatoes	bread	eggs	milk	potatoes
oranges	sugar	fish	cereal	green beans
chicken	margarine	cheese	noodles	rice
apples	red meat	butter		

Carbohydrates
tomatoes   cereal
oranges   noodles
bread   potatoes
sugar   green beans
apples   rice

Proteins
chicken   milk
eggs   fish
cheese   red meat

Fats
butter   cheese
margarine   chicken
eggs   red meat

Minerals
Answers will vary; many of these items contain minerals.

Directions: Write what you ate yesterday in each group. Did you get enough servings of each?

Milk Group
(2-3 servings a day)
(Answers will vary.)

Meat-Egg-Nut-Bean Group
(2-3 servings a day)
(Answers will vary.)

Grain Group
(6-11 servings a day)
(Answers will vary.)

Fruit & Vegetable Groups
(5-9 servings a day)
(Answers will vary.)

124

Tasty Plant Parts

All of the fruits and vegetables you eat come from plant parts. Some parts are much tastier than others. Carrot roots probably taste better than walnut tree roots.

Directions: Unscramble the names of the plant parts and label the pictures.

ealt _leaf_   fruit _fruit_   frowel _flower_
smet _stem_   toors _roots_   eseds _seeds_

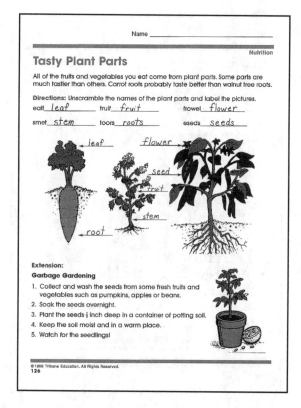

leaf
flower
seed
fruit
stem
root

Extension:

Garbage Gardening

1. Collect and wash the seeds from some fresh fruits and vegetables such as pumpkins, apples or beans.
2. Soak the seeds overnight.
3. Plant the seeds ½ inch deep in a container of potting soil.
4. Keep the soil moist and in a warm place.
5. Watch for the seedlings!

126

Vegetable Stand

Help Leon sort all of his produce. List the letter of each of the fruits and vegetables under the correct plant part.

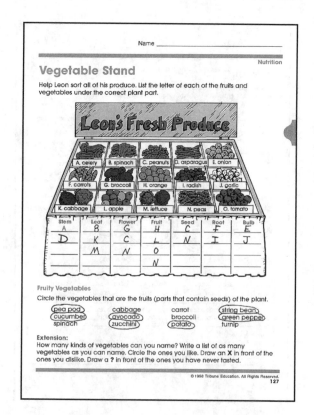

Leon's Fresh Produce

A. celery B. spinach C. peanuts D. asparagus E. onion
F. carrots G. broccoli H. orange I. radish J. garlic
K. cabbage L. apple M. lettuce N. peas O. tomato

Stem	Leaf	Flower	Fruit	Seed	Root	Bulb
A	B	G	H	C	F	E
D	K	C	L	N	I	J
	M		O			
			N			

Fruity Vegetables

Circle the vegetables that are the fruits (parts that contain seeds) of the plant.

(pea pod)   cabbage   carrot   (string bean)
(cucumber)   (avocado)   broccoli   (green pepper)
spinach   (zucchini)   (potato)   turnip

Extension:
How many kinds of vegetables can you name? Write a list of as many vegetables as you can name. Circle the ones you like. Draw an **X** in front of the ones you dislike. Draw a **?** in front of the ones you have never tasted.

127

Labels

Nutrition

Labels give us all kinds of information about the foods we eat. The ingredients of a food are listed in a special order. The ingredient with the largest amount is listed first, the one with the next largest amount is listed second and so on.

Directions:

Complete the "Breakfast Table Label Survey" using the information from the label on this page.

Breakfast Table Label Survey

1. What does R.D.A. mean? _Recommended Daily Allowance_
2. Calories per serving with milk _190_
3. Calories per serving without milk _110_
4. Calories per ½ cup serving of milk _80_
5. Protein per serving with milk _8_ %
6. Protein per serving without milk _2_ %
7. Protein in ½ cup serving of milk _6_%
8. Percentage U.S. R.D.A. of Vitamin C _>2%_
9. First ingredient _Corn flour_
10. Is sugar a listed ingredient? _yes_
    If yes, in what place is it listed? _2nd_
11. Were any vitamins added? _yes_
12. What preservative was added? _BHA_

Investigate
What food product has this ingredient label? Carbonated water, sugar, corn sweetener, natural flavorings, caramel color, phosphoric acid, caffeine.

Nutrition Information Per Serving

Serving Size: 1 OZ. (About 1 1/3 Cups) (28.35 g)

Servings Per Package: 14

	1 OZ. (28.35 g) Cereal	with 1/2 Cup (118 mL) Vitamin D Fortified Whole Milk
Calories	110	190
Protein	2 g	5 g
Carbohydrate	25 g	31 g
Fat	1 g	5 g
Sodium	195 mg	255 mg

Percentages of U.S. Recommended Daily Allowances (U.S. RDA)

Protein	2%	8%
Vitamin A	25%	30%
Vitamin C	*	*
Thiamine	25%	30%
Riboflavin	25%	35%
Niacin	25%	25%
Calcium	*	15%
Iron	10%	10%
Vitamin D	10%	25%
Vitamin B6	25%	30%
Folic Acid	25%	25%
Vitamin B12	25%	30%
Phosphorus	2%	10%
Magnesium	2%	6%
Zinc	10%	15%
Copper	2%	4%

*Contains less than 2% of the U.S. RDA for these nutrients.

Ingredients: Corn Flour, Sugar, Oat Flour, Salt, Hydrogenated Coconut and/or Palm Kernel Oil, Corn Syrup, Honey and fortified with the following nutrients: Vitamin A Palmitate, Niacinamide, Iron, Zinc Oxide (Source of Zinc), Vitamin B6, Riboflavin (Vitamin B2), Thiamine Mononitrate (Vitamin B1), Vitamin B12, Folic Acid and Vitamin D2. BHA added to packaging material to preserve freshness.

Carbohydrate Information

	1 OZ. (28.35 g) Cereal	with 1/2 Cup (118 mL) Whole Milk
Starch and Related Carbohydrates	14 g	14 g
Sucrose and Other Sugars	11 g	17 g
Total Carbohydrates	25 g	31 g

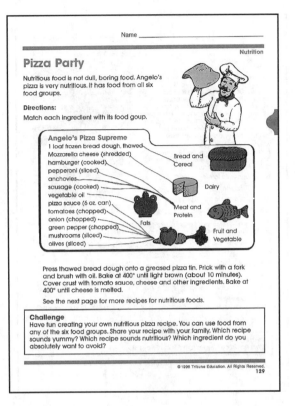

Pizza Party

Nutrition

Nutritious food is not dull, boring food. Angelo's pizza is very nutritious. It has food from all six food groups.

Directions:

Match each ingredient with its food group.

Angelo's Pizza Supreme
1 loaf frozen bread dough, thawed
Mozzarella cheese (shredded)
hamburger (cooked)
pepperoni (sliced)
anchovies
sausage (cooked)
vegetable oil
pizza sauce (6 oz. can)
tomatoes (chopped)
onion (chopped)
green pepper (chopped)
mushrooms (sliced)
olives (sliced)

Bread and Cereal
Dairy
Meat and Protein
Fats
Fruit and Vegetable

Press thawed bread dough onto a greased pizza tin. Prick with a fork and brush with oil. Bake at 400° until light brown (about 10 minutes). Cover crust with tomato sauce, cheese and other ingredients. Bake at 400° until cheese is melted.

See the next page for more recipes for nutritious foods.

Challenge
Have fun creating your own nutritious pizza recipe. You can use food from any of the six food groups. Share your recipe with your family. Which recipe sounds yummy? Which recipe sounds nutritious? Which ingredient do you absolutely want to avoid?

Plant Parts

Plants

Green, flowering plants grow all around you. Beautiful red roses, tall cornstalks or prickly thistle weeds are all green, flowering plants. Green, flowering plants have six parts: stem, root, leaf, flower, fruit and seeds.

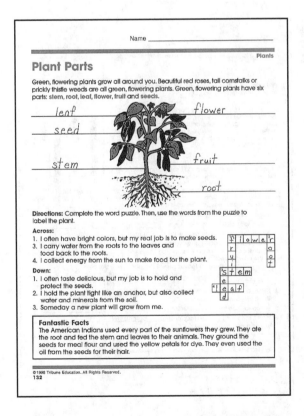

leaf
seed
stem
flower
fruit
root

Directions: Complete the word puzzle. Then, use the words from the puzzle to label the plant.

Across:
1. I often have bright colors, but my real job is to make seeds.
3. I carry water from the roots to the leaves and food back to the roots.
4. I collect energy from the sun to make food for the plant.

Down:
1. I often taste delicious, but my job is to hold and protect the seeds.
2. I hold the plant tight like an anchor, but also collect water and minerals from the soil.
3. Someday a new plant will grow from me.

Crossword answers: flower, root, fruit, stem, seed, leaf

Fantastic Facts
The American Indians used every part of the sunflowers they grew. They ate the root and fed the stem and leaves to their animals. They ground the seeds for meal flour and used the yellow petals for dye. They even used the oil from the seeds for their hair.

Garden Fresh Produce

Plants

Plants give us all the fruits, vegetables, grains, spices and herbs we eat. Amy has just planted her garden. List all of the fruits and vegetables in Amy's garden under the correct plant part that can be eaten.

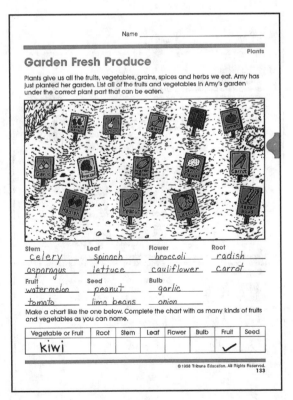

Stem	Leaf	Flower	Root
celery	spinach	broccoli	radish
asparagus	lettuce	cauliflower	carrot

Fruit	Seed	Bulb
watermelon	peanut	garlic
tomato	lima beans	onion

Make a chart like the one below. Complete the chart with as many kinds of fruits and vegetables as you can name.

Vegetable or Fruit	Root	Stem	Leaf	Flower	Bulb	Fruit	Seed
kiwi						✓	

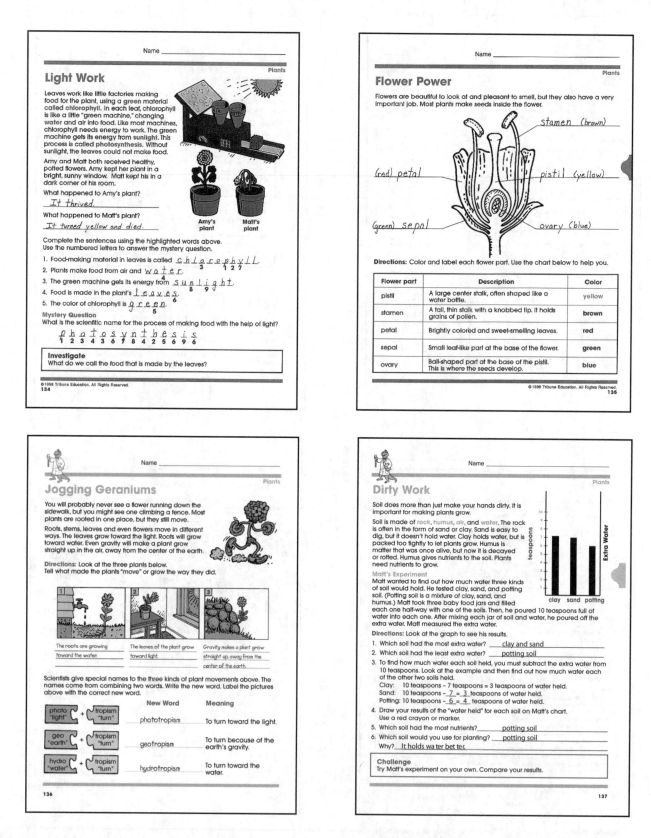

Light Work

Leaves work like little factories making food for the plant, using a green material called chlorophyll. In each leaf, chlorophyll is like a little "green machine," changing water and air into food. Like most machines, chlorophyll needs energy to work. The green machine gets its energy from sunlight. This process is called photosynthesis. Without sunlight, the leaves could not make food.

Amy and Matt both received healthy, potted flowers. Amy kept her plant in a bright, sunny window. Matt kept his in a dark corner of his room.

What happened to Amy's plant?

It thrived.

What happened to Matt's plant?

It turned yellow and died.

Amy's plant **Matt's plant**

Complete the sentences using the highlighted words above. Use the numbered letters to answer the mystery question.

1. Food-making material in leaves is called _c h l o r o p h y l l_
2. Plants make food from air and _w a t e r_
3. The green machine gets its energy from _s u n l i g h t_
4. Food is made in the plant's _l e a v e s_
5. The color of chlorophyll is _g r e e n_

Mystery Question
What is the scientific name for the process of making food with the help of light?

_p h o t o s y n t h e s i s_
1 2 3 4 3 6 7 8 4 2 5 6 9 6

Investigate
What do we call the food that is made by the leaves?

134

Flower Power

Flowers are beautiful to look at and pleasant to smell, but they also have a very important job. Most plants make seeds inside the flower.

stamen (brown)

(red) petal

pistil (yellow)

(green) sepal

ovary (blue)

Directions: Color and label each flower part. Use the chart below to help you.

Flower part	Description	Color
pistil	A large center stalk, often shaped like a water bottle.	yellow
stamen	A tall, thin stalk with a knobbed tip. It holds grains of pollen.	brown
petal	Brightly colored and sweet-smelling leaves.	red
sepal	Small leaf-like part at the base of the flower.	green
ovary	Ball-shaped part at the base of the pistil. This is where the seeds develop.	blue

135

Jogging Geraniums

You will probably never see a flower running down the sidewalk, but you might see one climbing a fence. Most plants are rooted in one place, but they still move.

Roots, stems, leaves and even flowers move in different ways. The leaves grow toward the light. Roots will grow toward water. Even gravity will make a plant grow straight up in the air, away from the center of the earth.

Directions: Look at the three plants below. Tell what made the plants "move" or grow the way they did.

1	2	3
The roots are growing toward the water.	The leaves of the plant grow toward light.	Gravity makes a plant grow straight up, away from the center of the earth.

Scientists give special names to the three kinds of plant movements above. The names come from combining two words. Write the new word. Label the pictures above with the correct new word.

	New Word	Meaning
photo "light" + tropism "turn"	phototropism	To turn toward the light.
geo "earth" + tropism "turn"	geotropism	To turn because of the earth's gravity.
hydro "water" + tropism "turn"	hydrotropism	To turn toward the water.

136

Dirty Work

Soil does more than just make your hands dirty. It is important for making plants grow.

Soil is made of rock, humus, air, and water. The rock is often in the form of sand or clay. Sand is easy to dig, but it doesn't hold water. Clay holds water, but is packed too tightly to let plants grow. Humus is matter that was once alive, but now it is decayed or rotted. Humus gives nutrients to the soil. Plants need nutrients to grow.

Extra Water
teaspoons
clay sand potting

Matt's Experiment
Matt wanted to find out how much water three kinds of soil would hold. He tested clay, sand, and potting soil. (Potting soil is a mixture of clay, sand, and humus.) Matt took three baby food jars and filled each one half-way with one of the soils. Then, he poured 10 teaspoons full of water into each one. After mixing each jar of soil and water, he poured off the extra water. Matt measured the extra water.

Directions: Look at the graph to see his results.

1. Which soil had the most extra water? _clay and sand_
2. Which soil had the least extra water? _potting soil_
3. To find how much water each soil held, you must subtract the extra water from 10 teaspoons. Look at the example and then find out how much water each of the other two soils held.
   Clay: 10 teaspoons - 7 teaspoons = 3 teaspoons of water held.
   Sand: 10 teaspoons - _7_ = _3_ teaspoons of water held.
   Potting: 10 teaspoons - _6_ = _4_ teaspoons of water held.
4. Draw your results of the "water held" for each soil on Matt's chart. Use a red crayon or marker.
5. Which soil had the most nutrients? _potting soil_
6. Which soil would you use for planting? _potting soil_
   Why? _It holds water better._

Challenge
Try Matt's experiment on your own. Compare your results.

137

Name _____

Plants

Slurp, Slurp

Slurp, slurp! On a hot summer day, a cherry soda is cool and refreshing. Plants like to drink, too. The plant's root system slurps water and minerals from the ground. There are two kinds of root systems. Some plants have one main root that grows deep into the ground. This is called a tap root. Other plants have shallow roots with many branches. These roots are called fibrous roots. Attached to both root systems are tiny root hairs that do all the work of absorbing water.

fibrous roots

Directions: Color the tap root orange. Color the fibrous roots **brown.** Write the name of the root system in the blank space. Label the root hairs.

root hairs

tap root

Use the highlighted words to complete the word puzzle. Then, find the mystery word in the puzzle.

1. The _____ root grows deep into the ground.
2. Roots "slurp" water and _____ .
3. Fibrous roots have many _____ .
4. Tiny root _____ absorb water.
5. There are _____ types of root systems.
6. _____ roots grow shallow.

1. t a p
2. m i n e r a l s
3. b r a n c h e s
4. h a i r s
5. t w o
6. F i b r o u s

Use the mystery word in the puzzle to solve the riddle.

A ship's is made of iron,
To hold it fast at berth.
A plant's roots work like one,
To hold it firm in the earth.   **What is it?** _anchor_

Fantastic Fact
The American Indians boiled the balsam root to make tea. They drank the tea when they had a sore throat, cough, pneumonia or hay fever.

138

Name _____

Plants

Tree-mendous Plant

What is the largest plant growing near your home? It is probably a tree. It may be a maple, oak, pine or palm. All trees have many of the same parts as the plants that grow in your garden—only much larger.

Word Bank
seed
trunk
leaves
roots
bark

The riddles below tell about the jobs of the tree parts. Use the tree parts listed in the Word Bank to solve each riddle. Then, label the parts of the tree.

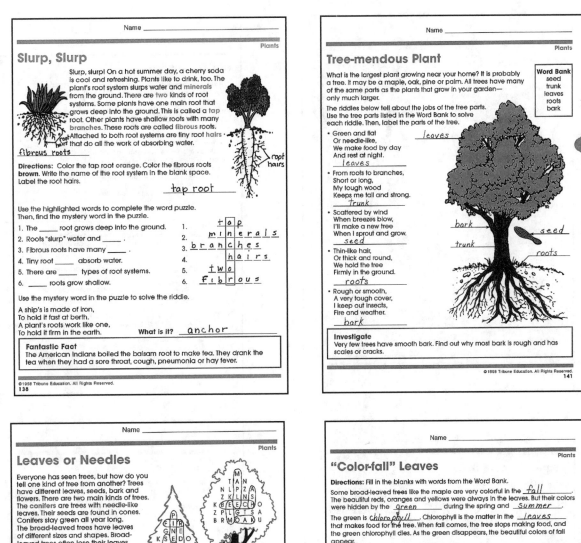

leaves

- Green and flat
  Or needle-like,
  We make food by day
  And rest at night.
  leaves
- From roots to branches,
  Short or long,
  My tough wood
  Keeps me tall and strong.
  trunk
- Scattered by wind
  When breezes blow,
  I'll make a new tree
  When I sprout and grow.
  seed
- Thin-like hair,
  Or thick and round,
  We hold the tree
  Firmly in the ground.
  roots
- Rough or smooth,
  A very tough cover,
  I keep out insects,
  Fire and weather.
  bark

bark   _seed_   _trunk_   _roots_

Investigate
Very few trees have smooth bark. Find out why most bark is rough and has scales or cracks.

141

Name _____

Plants

Leaves or Needles

Everyone has seen trees, but how do you tell one kind of tree from another? Trees have different leaves, seeds, bark and flowers. The conifers are trees with needle-like leaves. Their seeds are found in cones. Conifers stay green all year long. The broad-leaved trees have leaves of different sizes and shapes. Broad-leaved trees often lose their leaves in the fall. In warm regions, some broad-leaved trees keep their leaves all year long.

Find the hidden names of conifer trees in the conifer tree. Find the hidden names of broad-leaved trees in the broad-leaved tree. Use the Word Bank to help you.

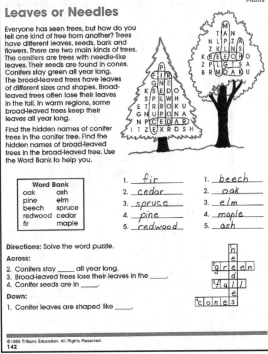

Word Bank	
oak	ash
pine	elm
beech	spruce
redwood	cedar
fir	maple

1. _fir_
2. _cedar_
3. _spruce_
4. _pine_
5. _redwood_

1. _beech_
2. _oak_
3. _elm_
4. _maple_
5. _ash_

Directions: Solve the word puzzle.

Across:
2. Conifers stay _____ all year long.
3. Broad-leaved trees lose their leaves in the _____ .
4. Conifer seeds are in _____ .

Down:
1. Conifer leaves are shaped like _____ .

2. g r e e n
3. f a l l
4. c o n e s
(down: n e e d l e)

142

Name _____

Plants

"Color-fall" Leaves

Directions: Fill in the blanks with words from the Word Bank.

Some broad-leaved trees like the maple are very colorful in the _fall_ . The beautiful reds, oranges and yellows were always in the leaves. But their colors were hidden by the _green_ during the spring and _summer_ .
The green is _chlorophyll_ . Chlorophyll is the matter in the _leaves_ that makes food for the tree. When fall comes, the tree stops making food, and the green chlorophyll dies. As the green disappears, the beautiful colors of fall appear.

Complete the word puzzle using words from the Word Bank. Find the hidden word in the puzzle. Use it to answer the riddle at the bottom.

1. Food is made in the _____ .
2. Trees make food in the spring and _____ .
3. Fall colors are hidden by the _____ .
4. Leaves stop making food in the _____ .
5. The green matter that makes food is _____ .

1. l e a v e s
2. s u m m e r
3. g r e e n
4. f a l l
5. c h l o r o p h y l l

Word Bank	
fall	green
leaves	summer
chlorophyll	

Kids really like me,
I'm food for the trees.
My taste is really sweet,
And I'm made by the leaves.
What am I? _sugar_

143

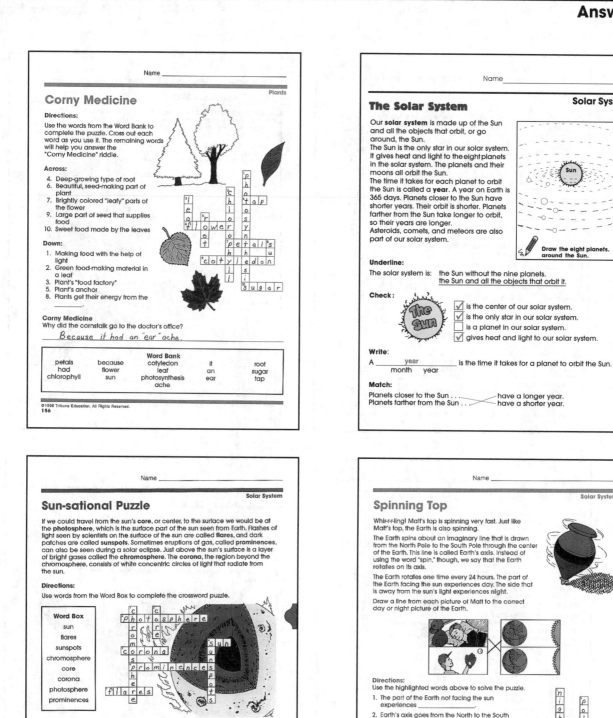

Name _____

Corny Medicine

Plants

Directions:
Use the words from the Word Bank to complete the puzzle. Cross out each word as you use it. The remaining words will help you answer the "Corny Medicine" riddle.

Across:
4. Deep-growing type of root
6. Beautiful, seed-making part of plant
7. Brightly colored "leafy" parts of the flower
9. Large part of seed that supplies food
10. Sweet food made by the leaves

Down:
1. Making food with the help of light
2. Green food-making material in a leaf
3. Plant's "food factory"
5. Plant's anchor
8. Plants get their energy from the ___

Corny Medicine
Why did the cornstalk go to the doctor's office?
Because it had an "ear" ache.

	Word Bank			
petals	because	cotyledon	it	root
had	flower	leaf	an	sugar
chlorophyll	sun	photosynthesis	ear	tap
		ache		

©1998 Tribune Education. All Rights Reserved.
156

Name _____

The Solar System

Solar System

Our **solar system** is made up of the Sun and all the objects that orbit, or go around, the Sun.
The Sun is the only star in our solar system. It gives heat and light to the eight planets in the solar system. The planets and their moons all orbit the Sun.
The time it takes for each planet to orbit the Sun is called a **year**. A year on Earth is 365 days. Planets closer to the Sun have shorter years. Their orbit is shorter. Planets farther from the Sun take longer to orbit, so their years are longer.
Asteroids, comets, and meteors are also part of our solar system.

Draw the eight planets around the Sun.

Underline:
The solar system is: the Sun without the nine planets.
the Sun and all the objects that orbit it.

Check:
The Sun
☑ is the center of our solar system.
☑ is the only star in our solar system.
☐ is a planet in our solar system.
☑ gives heat and light to our solar system.

Write:
A ___year___ is the time it takes for a planet to orbit the Sun.
month   year

Match:
Planets closer to the Sun . . . — have a longer year.
Planets farther from the Sun . . . — have a shorter year.

Name _____

Sun-sational Puzzle

Solar System

If we could travel from the sun's **core**, or center, to the surface we would be at the **photosphere**, which is the surface part of the sun seen from Earth. Flashes of light seen by scientists on the surface of the sun are called **flares**, and dark patches are called **sunspots**. Sometimes eruptions of gas, called **prominences**, can also be seen during a solar eclipse. Just above the sun's surface is a layer of bright gases called the **chromosphere**. The **corona**, the region beyond the chromosphere, consists of white concentric circles of light that radiate from the sun.

Directions:
Use words from the Word Box to complete the crossword puzzle.

Word Box
sun
flares
sunspots
chromosphere
core
corona
photosphere
prominences

Across:
3. the part of the sun you can see
4. huge glowing ball of gases at the center of our solar system
5. the region of the sun's atmosphere above the chromosphere
6. big, bright eruptions of gas
7. flashes of light on the sun's surface

Down:
1. the middle part of the sun's atmosphere
2. the center of the sun
4. dark patches that sometimes appear on the sun

©1998 Tribune Education. All Rights Reserved.
159

Name _____

Spinning Top

Solar System

Whir-r-r-ling! Matt's top is spinning very fast. Just like Matt's top, the Earth is also spinning.
The Earth spins about an imaginary line that is drawn from the North Pole to the South Pole through the center of the Earth. This line is called Earth's axis. Instead of using the word "spin," though, we say that the Earth rotates on its axis.
The Earth rotates one time every 24 hours. The part of the Earth facing the sun experiences day. The side that is away from the sun's light experiences night.

Draw a line from each picture of Matt to the correct day or night picture of the Earth.

Directions:
Use the highlighted words above to solve the puzzle.

1. The part of the Earth not facing the sun experiences _____.
2. Earth's axis goes from the North to the South _____.
3. The Earth spins, or _____.
4. Number of times the Earth rotates in 24 hours.
5. Imaginary line on which the Earth rotates.

Fantastic Fact
At the Equator, the Earth is spinning at a speed of almost 1,000 miles per hour. At a point halfway between the poles and the Equator, the speed is about 800 miles per hour. Spin a globe and you will see how this happens.

©1998 Tribune Education. All Rights Reserved.
160

Name _____

Lo-o-o-ng Trip

What is the longest trip you have ever taken? Was it 100 miles? 500 miles? Maybe it was more than 1,000 miles. You probably didn't know it, but last year you traveled 620 million miles.

The Earth travels in a path around the sun called its **orbit**. Earth's orbit is almost 620 million miles. It takes 1 year, or 365 days, for the Earth to orbit or **revolve** around the sun.

Earth's orbit is not a perfect circle. It is a special shape called an **ellipse**.

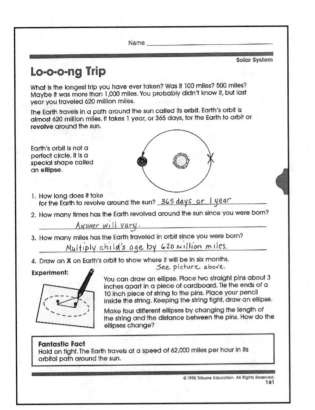

1. How long does it take for the Earth to revolve around the sun? _365 days or 1 year_

2. How many times has the Earth revolved around the sun since you were born?
   Answer will vary.

3. How many miles has the Earth traveled in orbit since you were born?
   Multiply child's age by 620 million miles.

4. Draw an **X** on Earth's orbit to show where it will be in six months.
   See picture above.

Experiment:

You can draw an ellipse. Place two straight pins about 3 inches apart in a piece of cardboard. Tie the ends of a 10 inch piece of string to the pins. Place your pencil inside the string. Keeping the string tight, draw an ellipse.

Make four different ellipses by changing the length of the string and the distance between the pins. How do the ellipses change?

Fantastic Fact
Hold on tight. The Earth travels at a speed of 62,000 miles per hour in its orbital path around the sun.

161

Name _____

How Big?

Planets vary greatly in size. Look at the list of planets and their **diameters**.

Planet	Diameter
Mercury	3,000 miles
Venus	7,500 miles
Earth	7,900 miles
Mars	4,200 miles
Jupiter	88,700 miles
Saturn	74,600 miles
Uranus	31,600 miles
Neptune	30,200 miles

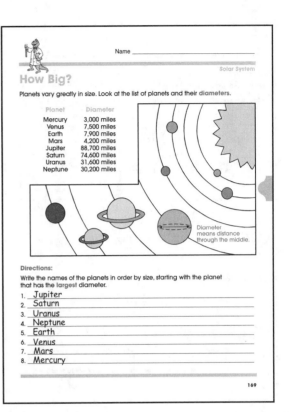

Diameter means distance through the middle.

Directions:
Write the names of the planets in order by size, starting with the planet that has the **largest** diameter.

1. _Jupiter_
2. _Saturn_
3. _Uranus_
4. _Neptune_
5. _Earth_
6. _Venus_
7. _Mars_
8. _Mercury_

169

Name _____

Mercury

Mercury is the smallest of the eight planets in our solar system. It is also the nearest planet to the sun.

Mercury spins very slowly. The side next to the sun gets very hot before it turns away from the sun. The other side freezes while away from the sun. As the planet slowly spins, the frozen side then becomes burning hot and the hot side becomes freezing cold.

Even though Mercury spins slowly, it moves around the sun very quickly. That is why it was named Mercury—after the Roman messenger for the gods.

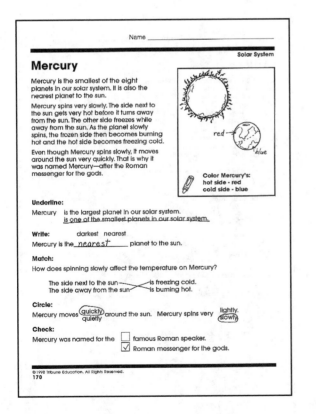

Color Mercury's:
hot side - red
cold side - blue

Underline:

Mercury is the largest planet in our solar system.
         is one of the smallest planets in our solar system.

Write: darkest nearest
Mercury is the _nearest_ planet to the sun.

Match:
How does spinning slowly affect the temperature on Mercury?

The side next to the sun ⟍ is freezing cold.
The side away from the sun ⟍ is burning hot.

Circle:
Mercury moves (quickly) around the sun.   Mercury spins very lightly.
          quietly   (slowly).

Check:
Mercury was named for the ☐ famous Roman speaker.
                            ☑ Roman messenger for the gods.

170

Name _____

Venus

Venus is the planet nearest to Earth. Because it is the easiest planet to see in the sky, it has been called the **Morning Star** and **Evening Star**. The Romans named Venus after their goddess of love and beauty. Venus is sometimes called "Earth's twin."

Venus is covered with thick clouds. The sun's heat is trapped by the clouds. The temperature on Venus is nearly 900°F!

Space probes have been sent to study Venus. They have reported information to scientists. But they can only last a few hours on Venus because of the high temperature.

Venus turns in the opposite direction from Earth. So, on Venus, the sun rises in the west and sets in the east!

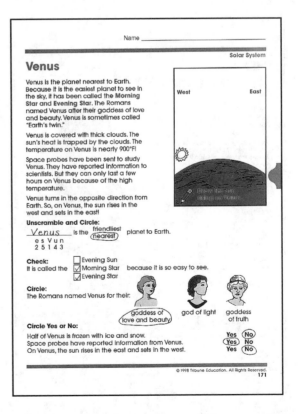

West   East

Unscramble and Circle:
Venus is the friendliest (nearest) planet to Earth.
e s V u n
2 5 1 4 3

Check:
It is called the ☐ Evening Sun
                  ☑ Morning Star   because it is so easy to see.
                  ☑ Evening Star

Circle:
The Romans named Venus for their:

(goddess of love and beauty)   god of light   goddess of truth

Circle Yes or No:
Half of Venus is frozen with ice and snow.   Yes (No)
Space probes have reported information from Venus.   (Yes) No
On Venus, the sun rises in the east and sets in the west.   Yes (No)

171

Name _____

Jupiter

Jupiter is the largest planet in our solar system. It has sixteen moons. Jupiter is the second-brightest planet—only Venus is brighter.

Jupiter is bigger and heavier than all of the other planets together. It is covered with thick clouds. Many loose rocks and dust particles form a single, thin, flat ring around Jupiter.

One of the most fascinating things about Jupiter is its Great Red Spot. The Great Red Spot of Jupiter is a huge storm in the atmosphere. It looks like a red ball. This giant storm is larger than Earth! Every six days it goes completely around Jupiter.

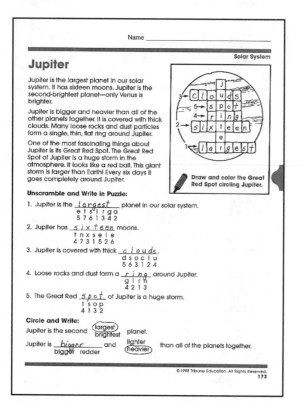

Draw and color the Great Red Spot circling Jupiter.

Unscramble and Write in Puzzle:

1. Jupiter is the __largest__ planet in our solar system.
   e t s' l r g a
   5 7 6 1 3 4 2

2. Jupiter has __s i x t e e n__ moons.
   t n x s e i e
   4 7 3 1 5 2 6

3. Jupiter is covered with thick __c l o u d s__.
   d s o c l u
   5 6 3 1 2 4

4. Loose rocks and dust form a __r i n g__ around Jupiter.
   g i r h
   4 2 1 3

5. The Great Red __s p o t__ of Jupiter is a huge storm.
   t s o p
   4 1 3 2

Circle and Write:

Jupiter is the second (largest) brightest planet.

Jupiter is __bigger__ and (heavier) than all of the planets together.
bigger redder / lighter

Name _____

Saturn

Saturn is probably most famous for its rings. These rings are made of billions of tiny pieces of ice and dust. Although these rings are very wide, they are very thin. If you look at the rings from the side, they are almost too thin to be seen.

Saturn is the second-largest planet in our solar system. It is so big that 758 Earths could fit inside it!

Saturn is covered by clouds. Strong, fast winds move the clouds quickly across the planet.

Saturn has 18 moons! Its largest moon is called Titan.

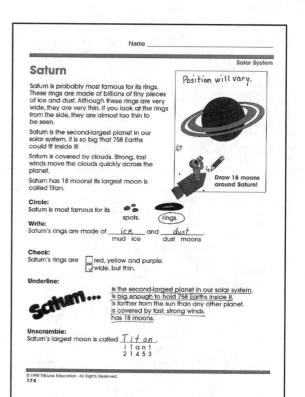

Position will vary.

Draw 18 moons around Saturn!

Circle:
Saturn is most famous for its spots. (rings.)

Write:
Saturn's rings are made of __ice__ and __dust__.
mud ice / dust moons

Check:
Saturn's rings are ☐ red, yellow and purple.
☑ wide, but thin.

Underline:

Saturn...
is the second-largest planet in our solar system.
is big enough to hold 758 Earths inside it.
is farther from the sun than any other planet.
is covered by fast, strong winds.
has 18 moons.

Unscramble:
Saturn's largest moon is called __T i t a n__
l T a n t
2 1 4 5 3

Name _____

Uranus

Did you know that Uranus was first thought to be a comet? Many scientists studied the mystery comet. It was soon decided that Uranus was a planet. It was the first planet to be discovered through a telescope.

Scientists believe that Uranus is made of rock and metal with gas and ice surrounding it.

Even through a telescope, Uranus is not easy to see. That is because it is almost two billion miles from the sun that lights it. It takes Uranus 84 Earth years to orbit the sun! Scientists know that Uranus has fifteen moons and is circled by ten thin rings. But there are still many mysteries about this faraway planet.

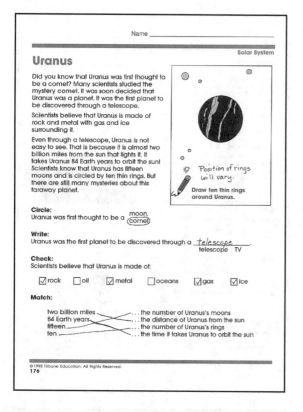

Position of rings will vary.

Draw ten thin rings around Uranus.

Circle:
Uranus was first thought to be a moon. (comet)

Write:
Uranus was the first planet to be discovered through a __telescope__.
telescope TV

Check:
Scientists believe that Uranus is made of:

☑ rock ☐ oil ☑ metal ☐ oceans ☑ gas ☑ ice

Match:

two billion miles ..... the number of Uranus's moons
84 Earth years ..... the distance of Uranus from the sun
fifteen ..... the number of Uranus's rings
ten ..... the time it takes Uranus to orbit the sun

Name _____

Neptune

Neptune is the eighth planet from the sun. It is difficult to see Neptune—even through a telescope. It is almost three billion miles from Earth.

Scientists believe that Neptune is much like Uranus—made of rock, iron, ice and gases.

Neptune has eight moons. Scientists believe that it may also have several rings.

Neptune is so far away from the sun that it takes 164 Earth years for it to orbit the sun just once!

Scientists still know very little about this cold and distant planet.

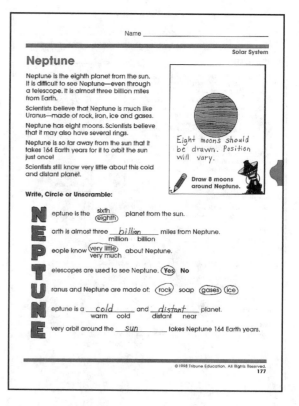

Eight moons should be drawn. Position will vary.

Draw 8 moons around Neptune.

Write, Circle or Unscramble:

N eptune is the sixth (eighth) planet from the sun.

E arth is almost three __billion__ miles from Neptune.
million billion

P eople know (very little) about Neptune.
very much

T elescopes are used to see Neptune. (Yes) No

U ranus and Neptune are made of: (rock) soap (gases) (ice)

N eptune is a __cold__ and __distant__ planet.
warm cold / distant near

E very orbit around the __sun__ takes Neptune 164 Earth years.

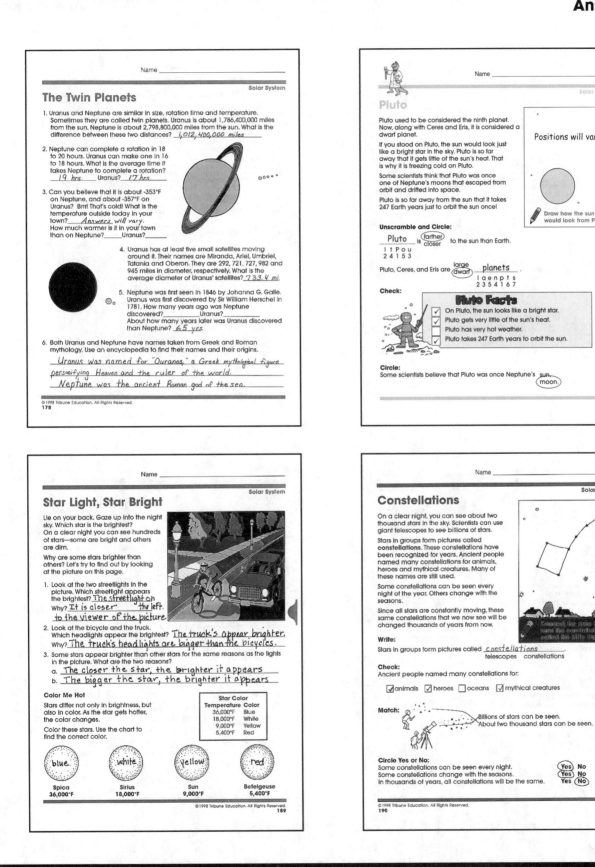

The Twin Planets

1. Uranus and Neptune are similar in size, rotation time and temperature. Sometimes they are called twin planets. Uranus is about 1,786,400,000 miles from the sun. Neptune is about 2,798,800,000 miles from the sun. What is the difference between these two distances? **1,012,400,000 miles**

2. Neptune can complete a rotation in 18 to 20 hours. Uranus can make one in 16 to 18 hours. What is the average time it takes Neptune to complete a rotation? **19 hrs.** Uranus? **17 hrs.**

3. Can you believe that it is about -353°F on Neptune, and about -357°F on Uranus? Brrr! That's cold! What is the temperature outside today in your town? **Answers will vary.** How much warmer is it in your town than on Neptune? **Uranus?**

4. Uranus has at least five small satellites moving around it. Their names are Miranda, Ariel, Umbriel, Tatania and Oberon. They are 292, 721, 727, 982 and 945 miles in diameter, respectively. What is the average diameter of Uranus' satellites? **733.4 mi.**

5. Neptune was first seen in 1846 by Johanna G. Galle. Uranus was first discovered by Sir William Herschel in 1781. How many years ago was Neptune discovered? _____ Uranus? _____ About how many years later was Uranus discovered than Neptune? **65 yrs.**

6. Both Uranus and Neptune have names taken from Greek and Roman mythology. Use an encyclopedia to find their names and their origins.
Uranus was named for "Ouranos," a Greek mythological figure personifying Heaven and the ruler of the world.
Neptune was the ancient Roman god of the sea.

©1998 Tribune Education. All Rights Reserved.
178

Pluto

Pluto used to be considered the ninth planet. Now, along with Ceres and Eris, it is considered a dwarf planet.

If you stood on Pluto, the sun would look just like a bright star in the sky. Pluto is so far away that it gets little of the sun's heat. That is why it is freezing cold on Pluto.

Some scientists think that Pluto was once one of Neptune's moons that escaped from orbit and drifted into space.

Pluto is so far away from the sun that it takes 247 Earth years just to orbit the sun once!

Positions will vary.

Draw how the sun would look from Pluto.

Unscramble and Circle:

Pluto is (farther) closer to the sun than Earth.
l t P o u
2 4 1 5 3

Pluto, Ceres, and Eris are large (dwarf) **planets**.
l a e n p t s
2 3 5 4 1 6 7

Check:

Pluto Facts
- ✓ On Pluto, the sun looks like a bright star.
- ✓ Pluto gets very little of the sun's heat.
- ✓ Pluto has very hot weather.
- ✓ Pluto takes 247 Earth years to orbit the sun.

Circle:
Some scientists believe that Pluto was once Neptune's **sun.** (moon.)

179

Star Light, Star Bright

Lie on your back. Gaze up into the night sky. Which star is the brightest? On a clear night you can see hundreds of stars—some are bright and others are dim.

Why are some stars brighter than others? Let's try to find out by looking at the picture on this page.

1. Look at the two streetlights in the picture. Which streetlight appears the brightest? **The streetlight on** Why? **It is closer the left. to the viewer of the picture.**

2. Look at the bicycle and the truck. Which headlights appear the brightest? **The truck's appear brighter.** Why? **The truck's headlights are bigger than the bicycle's.**

3. Some stars appear brighter than other stars for the same reasons as the lights in the picture. What are the two reasons?
a. **The closer the star, the brighter it appears**
b. **The bigger the star, the brighter it appears**

Color Me Hot

Stars differ not only in brightness, but also in color. As the star gets hotter, the color changes.

Color these stars. Use the chart to find the correct color.

Star Color	
Temperature	Color
36,000°F	Blue
18,000°F	White
9,000°F	Yellow
5,400°F	Red

blue — Spica 36,000°F
white — Sirius 18,000°F
yellow — Sun 9,000°F
red — Betelgeuse 5,400°F

©1998 Tribune Education. All Rights Reserved.
189

Constellations

On a clear night, you can see about two thousand stars in the sky. Scientists can use giant telescopes to see billions of stars.

Stars in groups form pictures called **constellations**. These constellations have been recognized for years. Ancient people named many constellations for animals, heroes and mythical creatures. Many of these names are still used.

Some constellations can be seen every night of the year. Others change with the seasons.

Since all stars are constantly moving, these same constellations that we now see will be changed thousands of years from now.

Write:
Stars in groups form pictures called **constellations**.
telescopes   constellations

Check:
Ancient people named many constellations for:
- ✓ animals
- ✓ heroes
- ☐ oceans
- ✓ mythical creatures

Match:
Billions of stars can be seen.
About two thousand stars can be seen.

Circle Yes or No:
Some constellations can be seen every night. (Yes) No
Some constellations change with the seasons. (Yes) No
In thousands of years, all constellations will be the same. Yes (No)

©1998 Tribune Education. All Rights Reserved.
190

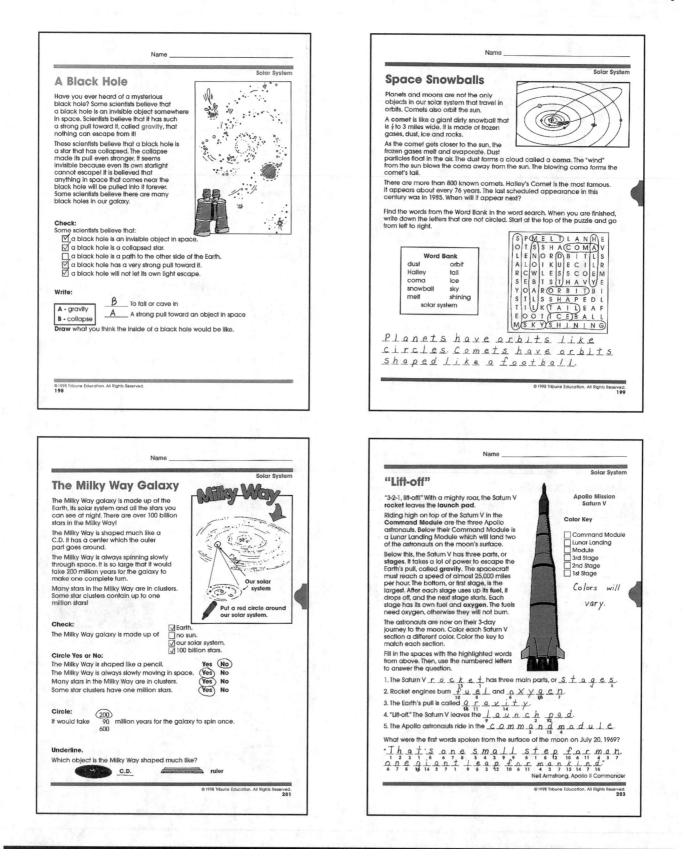

Name _____

A Black Hole

Solar System

Have you ever heard of a mysterious black hole? Some scientists believe that a black hole is an invisible object somewhere in space. Scientists believe that it has such a strong pull toward it, called **gravity**, that nothing can escape from it!

These scientists believe that a black hole is a star that has collapsed. The collapse made its pull even stronger. It seems invisible because even its own starlight cannot escape! It is believed that anything in space that comes near the black hole will be pulled into it forever. Some scientists believe there are many black holes in our galaxy.

Check:
Some scientists believe that:
☑ a black hole is an invisible object in space.
☑ a black hole is a collapsed star.
☐ a black hole is a path to the other side of the Earth.
☑ a black hole has a very strong pull toward it.
☑ a black hole will not let its own light escape.

Write:

A - gravity
B - collapse

__B__ To fall or cave in
__A__ A strong pull toward an object in space

Draw what you think the inside of a black hole would be like.

© 1998 Tribune Education. All Rights Reserved.
198

Name _____

Space Snowballs

Solar System

Planets and moons are not the only objects in our solar system that travel in orbits. Comets also orbit the sun.

A **comet** is like a giant dirty snowball that is ⅓ to 3 miles wide. It is made of frozen gases, dust, ice and rocks.

As the comet gets closer to the sun, the frozen gases melt and evaporate. Dust particles float in the air. The dust forms a cloud called a **coma**. The "wind" from the sun blows the coma away from the sun. The blowing coma forms the comet's tail.

There are more than 800 known comets. Halley's Comet is the most famous. It appears about every 76 years. The last scheduled appearance in this century was in 1985. When will it appear next?

Find the words from the Word Bank in the word search. When you are finished, write down the letters that are not circled. Start at the top of the puzzle and go from left to right.

Word Bank

dust	orbit
Halley	tail
coma	ice
snowball	sky
melt	shining
solar system	

```
S P M E L T L A N H E
O T S S H A C O M A V
L E N O R D B I T L S
A L O I K U E C I L R
R C W L E S S C O E M
Y O A R O R B I T B I
S T L S S H A P E D L
T I U K T A I L E A F
E O O T I C E B A L L
M S K Y S H I N I N G
```

Planets have orbits like
circles. Comets have orbits
shaped like a football.

© 1998 Tribune Education. All Rights Reserved.
199

Name _____

The Milky Way Galaxy

Solar System

The Milky Way galaxy is made up of the Earth, its solar system and all the stars you can see at night. There are over 100 billion stars in the Milky Way!

The Milky Way is shaped much like a C.D. It has a center which the outer part goes around.

The Milky Way is always spinning slowly through space. It is so large that it would take 200 million years for the galaxy to make one complete turn.

Many stars in the Milky Way are in clusters. Some star clusters contain up to one million stars!

Put a red circle around our solar system.

Our solar system

Check:
The Milky Way galaxy is made up of
☑ Earth.
☐ no sun.
☑ our solar system.
☑ 100 billion stars.

Circle Yes or No:
The Milky Way is shaped like a pencil. Yes **No**
The Milky Way is always slowly moving in space. **Yes** No
Many stars in the Milky Way are in clusters. **Yes** No
Some star clusters have one million stars. **Yes** No

Circle:
It would take (200) 90 600 million years for the galaxy to spin once.

Underline.
Which object is the Milky Way shaped much like?

__C.D.__   ruler

© 1998 Tribune Education. All Rights Reserved.
201

Name _____

"Lift-off"

Solar System

"3-2-1, lift-off!" With a mighty roar, the Saturn V **rocket** leaves the **launch pad**.

Riding high on top of the Saturn V in the **Command Module** are the three Apollo astronauts. Below their Command Module is a Lunar Landing Module which will land two of the astronauts on the moon's surface.

Below this, the Saturn V has three parts, or **stages**. It takes a lot of power to escape the Earth's pull, called **gravity**. The spacecraft must reach a speed of almost 25,000 miles per hour. The bottom, or first stage, is the largest. After each stage uses up its **fuel**, it drops off, and the next stage starts. Each stage has its own fuel and **oxygen**. The fuels need oxygen, otherwise they will not burn.

The astronauts are now on their 3-day journey to the moon. Color each Saturn V section a different color. Color the key to match each section.

Fill in the spaces with the highlighted words from above. Then, use the numbered letters to answer the question.

Apollo Mission Saturn V

Color Key
☐ Command Module
☐ Lunar Landing Module
☐ 3rd Stage
☐ 2nd Stage
☐ 1st Stage

Colors will vary.

1. The Saturn V _r o c k e t_ has three main parts, or _s t a g e s_.
2. Rocket engines burn _f u e l_ and _o x y g e n_.
3. The Earth's pull is called _g r a v i t y_.
4. "Lift-off." The Saturn V leaves the _l a u n c h   p a d_.
5. The Apollo astronauts ride in the _c o m m a n d   m o d u l e_.

What were the first words spoken from the surface of the moon on July 20, 1969?

"_That's one small step for man,_
one giant leap for mankind."

Neil Armstrong, Apollo 11 Commander

© 1998 Tribune Education. All Rights Reserved.
203

"Live Via Satellite"

Solar System

"This program is brought to you live via satellite from halfway around the world." Satellites are very helpful in sending TV messages from the other side of the world. But this is only one of the special jobs that satellites can do.

Most satellites are placed into orbit around the Earth by riding on top of giant rockets. More recently some satellites have been carried into orbit by a space shuttle. While orbiting the Earth, the giant doors of the shuttle are opened, and the satellite is pushed into orbit.

This satellite relays TV signals from halfway around the world.

Satellites send information about many things. Use the code to find the different kinds of messages and information satellites send.

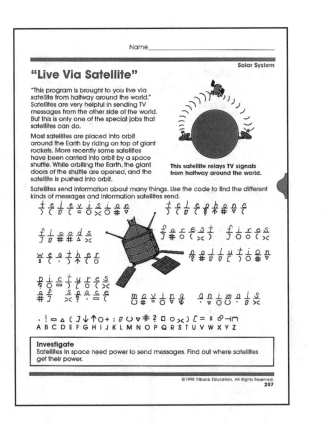

television   telephone

floods   forest fires

weather   pollution

pictures
of space   moving animals

· ! = △ (⅃ ↓ ↑ ○ + : ♂ ∪ ▽ # ? □ ○ ×) ⌐ = з ♂ ⌐⌐
A B C D E F G H I J K L M N O P Q R S T U V W X Y Z

Investigate
Satellites in space need power to send messages. Find out where satellites get their power.

© 1998 Tribune Education. All Rights Reserved.
207

Rain in the Rainforest

Weather

At least 80 inches of rain falls, and thundershowers may occur for 200 or more days each year in a rainforest. **Rainforests** need a lot of rain so that the plants native to them do not dry out. Fill in the precipitation graph below with the average rainfall of a typical tropical rainforest. The amounts are listed beneath the graph.

	J	F	M	A	M	J	J	A	S	O	N	D
	24"	20"	13"	11"	10"	7"	8"	9"	9"	11"	14"	18"

What was the total rainfall for the year in this rainforest? __154 "__

What is the total rainfall for a year in your area? __Answers will vary.__

© 1998 Tribune Education. All Rights Reserved.
232

Lightning

Weather

Lightning is a flash of light caused by electricity in the sky. Clouds are made of many water droplets. All of these droplets together contain a large electrical charge. Sometimes these clouds set off a large spark of electricity called **lightning**. Lightning travels very fast. As it cuts through the air, it can cause thunder.

Lightning takes various forms. Some lightning looks like a zigzag in the sky. Sheet lightning spreads and lights the sky. Ball lightning looks like a ball of fire.

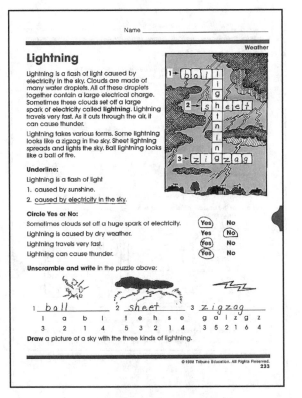

1 → b a l l
2 → s h e e t
3 → z i g z a g

Underline:

Lightning is a flash of light
1. caused by sunshine.
2. caused by electricity in the sky.

Circle Yes or No:

Sometimes clouds set off a huge spark of electricity.   (Yes)   No
Lightning is caused by dry weather.   Yes   (No)
Lightning travels very fast.   (Yes)   No
Lightning can cause thunder.   (Yes)   No

Unscramble and write in the puzzle above:

1 b a l l   2 s h e e t   3 z i g z a g
  l a b l   t e h s e   g a i z g z
  3 2 1 4   5 3 2 1 4   3 5 2 1 6 4

Draw a picture of a sky with the three kinds of lightning.

© 1998 Tribune Education. All Rights Reserved.
233

The Eye of the Storm

Weather

A **hurricane** is a powerful storm that forms over some parts of an ocean. A hurricane can be several hundred miles wide.

A hurricane has two main parts: the **eye** and the **wall cloud**. The eye is the center of the storm. In the eye, the weather is calm. The storm around the eye is called the wall cloud. It has strong winds and heavy rain. In some hurricanes, the wind can blow 150 miles an hour!

As the storm moves across the water, it causes giant waves in the ocean. As the storm moves over land, it can cause floods, destroy buildings and kill people who have not taken shelter.

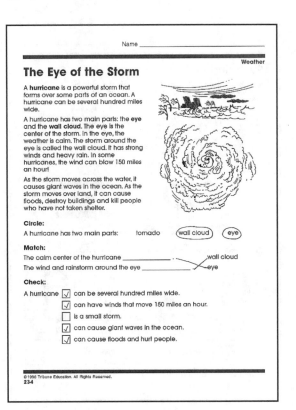

Circle:

A hurricane has two main parts: tornado   (wall cloud)   (eye)

Match:

The calm center of the hurricane _____ wall cloud
The wind and rainstorm around the eye _____ eye

Check:

A hurricane ☑ can be several hundred miles wide.
☑ can have winds that move 150 miles an hour.
☐ is a small storm.
☑ can cause giant waves in the ocean.
☑ can cause floods and hurt people.

© 1998 Tribune Education. All Rights Reserved.
234

A Funnel Cloud—Danger!

Weather

Did you know that a tornado is the most violent windstorm on Earth? A **tornado** is a whirling, twisting storm that is shaped like a funnel.

A tornado usually occurs in the spring on a hot day. It begins with thunderclouds and thunder. A cloud becomes very dark. The bottom of the cloud begins to twist and form a funnel. Rain and lightning begin. The funnel cloud drops from the dark storm clouds. It moves down toward the ground.

A tornado is very dangerous. It can destroy almost everything in its path.

Circle:

A ~~thunder~~ / **(tornado)** is the most violent windstorm on Earth.

Check:

Which words describe a tornado?

☑ whirling ☑ twisting ☐ icy ☑ funnel-shaped ☑ dangerous

Underline:

A funnel shape is: ◯ ▢ ⬭ **⬭(circled)** 〰

Write and Circle:

A tornado usually occurs in the _spring_ (autumn / spring) on a **(cool / hot)** day.

Write 1 - 2 - 3 below and in the picture above.

(3) The funnel cloud drops down to the ground.

(1) A tornado begins with dark thunder clouds.

(2) The dark clouds begin to twist and form a funnel.

©1998 Tribune Education. All Rights Reserved.
237

The Invisible Force

Magnets

Hold a magnet close to a piece of metal. Do you feel a pulling force? Magnets are attracted to certain metals. The invisible force is called **magnetism**.

What kinds of objects will a magnet pull? The best and the most fun way to find out is to experiment. Gather some of the objects listed below. Hold a small magnet next to these objects. Which objects will the magnet pull? Add some of your own objects to the list.

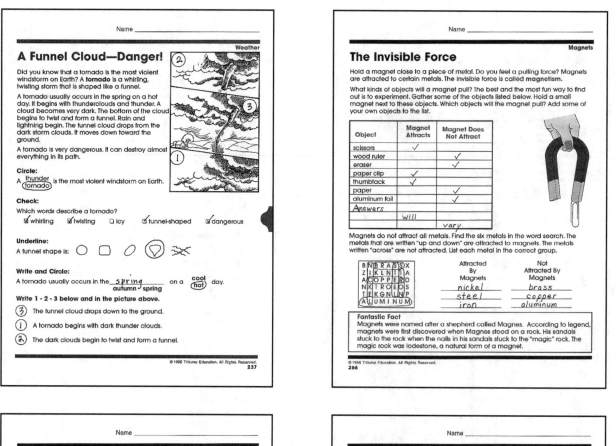

Object	Magnet Attracts	Magnet Does Not Attract
scissors	✓	
wood ruler		✓
eraser		✓
paper clip	✓	
thumbtack	✓	
paper		✓
aluminum foil		✓
Answers	will	
		vary.

Magnets do not attract all metals. Find the six metals in the word search. The metals that are written "up and down" are attracted to magnets. The metals written "across" are not attracted. List each metal in the correct group.

```
B N B R A S S X
Z I K L N T I A
A C O P P E R D
N K T R O E O S
T E K G N L U P
A L U M I N U M
```

Attracted By Magnets	Not Attracted By Magnets
nickel	brass
steel	copper
iron	aluminum

Fantastic Fact

Magnets were named after a shepherd called Magnes. According to legend, magnets were first discovered when Magnes stood on a rock. His sandals stuck to the rock when the nails in his sandals stuck to the "magic" rock. The magic rock was lodestone, a natural form of a magnet.

©1998 Tribune Education. All Rights Reserved.
266

Push and Pull

Magnets

The ends of a magnet are called its poles. One pole is called the north-seeking pole or north pole; the other is the south-seeking pole, or south pole.

When the poles of two bar magnets are put near each other, they have a force that will either pull them together or push them apart. If the poles are different, then they will pull together, or attract each other. (One pole is a south pole and one pole is a north pole.) If the poles are the same, then they will push apart, or repel each other. (They are either both south poles or both north poles.) The push and pull force of a magnet is called **magnetism**.

1. If these magnets are brought toward each other, will they attract or repel each other?

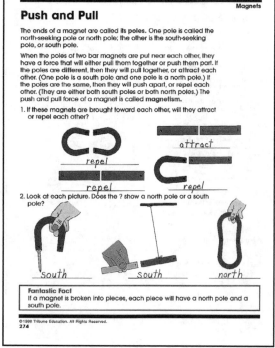

repel   _attract_

repel   _repel_

2. Look at each picture. Does the ? show a north pole or a south pole?

south   _south_   _north_

Fantastic Fact

If a magnet is broken into pieces, each piece will have a north pole and a south pole.

©1998 Tribune Education. All Rights Reserved.
274

Electromagnets

Magnets

Some of the most powerful magnets are made with electricity. These magnets are called **electromagnets**. A strong magnet can be made by winding wire around an iron bar. As soon as the current from a battery is switched on, the bar becomes a strong electromagnet. The magnet can be switched off by stopping the flow of current.

Larry and Eddie each made an electromagnet. Only one of them worked.

Larry   Eddie

1. Whose electromagnet worked? _Larry's_

2. Why wouldn't the other electromagnet work? _It is switched off._

3. Electromagnets have many uses and can be found in many places.

Circle and list the objects in the word search which use electromagnets.

1. _doorbell_
2. _tape recorder_
3. _telephone_
4. _television_
5. _motor_
6. _stereo_
7. _radio_
8. _refrigerator_

```
D O O R B E L L T
E T A B E K J S R A
L X O L F V R E P
E S T E R E O T R E
V A E L I T H O N C
I M L O G U A R B O
S P E R E N O G L R
I X P L R K A M I D
O R H R A D I O T E
N B A N M O T O R K R
A S H E L L R M U S L
```

Investigate

Make an electromagnet like the one in the picture above.

1. What happens to the strength of your electromagnet if you use more turns of wire?

2. Is your electromagnet still magnetic when you disconnect it from the battery?

©1998 Tribune Education. All Rights Reserved.
279

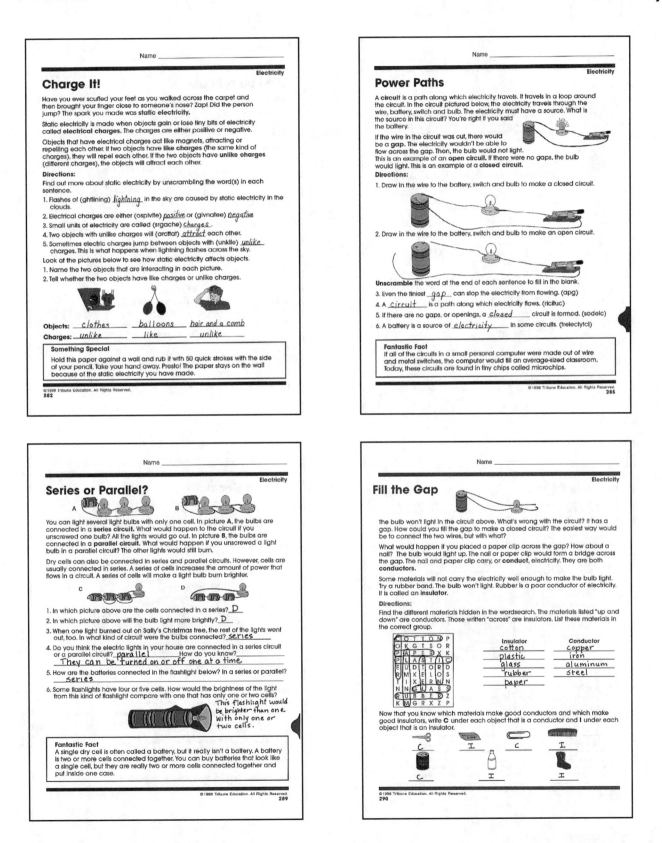

Name _____

Electricity

Charge It!

Have you ever scuffed your feet as you walked across the carpet and then brought your finger close to someone's nose? Zap! Did the person jump? The spark you made was **static electricity.**

Static electricity is made when objects gain or lose tiny bits of electricity called **electrical charges.** The charges are either positive or negative.

Objects that have electrical charges act like magnets, attracting or repelling each other. If two objects have **like charges** (the same kind of charges), they will repel each other. If the two objects have **unlike charges** (different charges), the objects will attract each other.

Directions:

Find out more about static electricity by unscrambling the word(s) in each sentence.

1. Flashes of (ghtlining) _lightning_ in the sky are caused by static electricity in the clouds.

2. Electrical charges are either (osplvite) _positive_ or (glvnatee) _negative_.

3. Small units of electricity are called (srgache) _charges_.

4. Two objects with unlike charges will (arcttat) _attract_ each other.

5. Sometimes electric charges jump between objects with (unkile) _unlike_ charges. This is what happens when lightning flashes across the sky.

Look at the pictures below to see how static electricity affects objects.

1. Name the two objects that are interacting in each picture.
2. Tell whether the two objects have like charges or unlike charges.

Objects: _clothes_ _balloons_ _hair and a comb_
Charges: _unlike_ _like_ _unlike_

Something Special

Hold this paper against a wall and rub it with 50 quick strokes with the side of your pencil. Take your hand away. Presto! The paper stays on the wall because of the static electricity you have made.

Name _____

Electricity

Power Paths

A **circuit** is a path along which electricity travels. It travels in a loop around the circuit. In the circuit pictured below, the electricity travels through the wire, battery, switch and bulb. The electricity must have a source. What is the source in this circuit? You're right if you said the battery.

If the wire in the circuit was cut, there would be a **gap**. The electricity wouldn't be able to flow across the gap. Then, the bulb would not light. This is an example of an **open circuit.** If there were no gaps, the bulb would light. This is an example of a **closed circuit.**

Directions:

1. Draw in the wire to the battery, switch and bulb to make a closed circuit.

2. Draw in the wire to the battery, switch and bulb to make an open circuit.

Unscramble the word at the end of each sentence to fill in the blank.

3. Even the tiniest _gap_ can stop the electricity from flowing. (apg)

4. A _circuit_ is a path along which electricity flows. (rlcituc)

5. If there are no gaps, or openings, a _closed_ circuit is formed. (sodelc)

6. A battery is a source of _electricity_ in some circuits. (trelectytcl)

Fantastic Fact

If all of the circuits in a small personal computer were made out of wire and metal switches, the computer would fill an average-sized classroom. Today, these circuits are found in tiny chips called microchips.

Name _____

Electricity

Series or Parallel?

You can light several light bulbs with only one cell. In picture **A,** the bulbs are connected in a **series circuit.** What would happen to the circuit if you unscrewed one bulb? All the lights would go out. In picture **B,** the bulbs are connected in a **parallel circuit.** What would happen if you unscrewed a light bulb in a parallel circuit? The other lights would still burn.

Dry cells can also be connected in series and parallel circuits. However, cells are usually connected in series. A series of cells increases the amount of power that flows in a circuit. A series of cells will make a light bulb burn brighter.

1. In which picture above are the cells connected in a series? _D_

2. In which picture above will the bulb light more brightly? _D_

3. When one light burned out on Sally's Christmas tree, the rest of the lights went out, too. In what kind of circuit were the bulbs connected? _series_

4. Do you think the electric lights in your house are connected in a series circuit or a parallel circuit? _parallel_ How do you know? _They can be turned on or off one at a time._

5. How are the batteries connected in the flashlight below? In a series or parallel? _series_

6. Some flashlights have four or five cells. How would the brightness of the light from this kind of flashlight compare with one that has only one or two cells? _This flashlight would be brighter than one with only one or two cells._

Fantastic Fact

A single dry cell is often called a battery, but it really isn't a battery. A battery is two or more cells connected together. You can buy batteries that look like a single cell, but they are really two or more cells connected together and put inside one case.

Name _____

Electricity

Fill the Gap

The bulb won't light in the circuit above. What's wrong with the circuit? It has a gap. How could you fill the gap to make a closed circuit? The easiest way would be to connect the two wires, but with what?

What would happen if you placed a paper clip across the gap? How about a nail? The bulb would light up. The nail or paper clip would form a bridge across the gap. The nail and paper clip carry, or **conduct**, electricity. They are both **conductors.**

Some materials will not carry the electricity well enough to make the bulb light. Try a rubber band. The bulb won't light. Rubber is a poor conductor of electricity. It is called an **insulator.**

Directions:

Find the different materials hidden in the wordsearch. The materials listed "up and down" are conductors. Those written "across" are insulators. List these materials in the correct group.

Insulator	Conductor
cotton	copper
plastic	iron
glass	aluminum
rubber	steel
paper	

Now that you know which materials make good conductors and which make good insulators, write **C** under each object that is a conductor and **I** under each object that is an insulator.

_C_ _I_ _C_ _I_

_C_ _I_ _I_

W A T S O N
• — • —   • — •••   — — — •   — •

In 1877, Samuel Morse used electricity to make the first telegraph. This invention allowed people to communicate directly with one another over long distances.

Study the picture of the simple telegraph. Notice how the switch, light bulb, battery and wire form a circuit. Use the symbols in the key to draw a diagram of the telegraph.

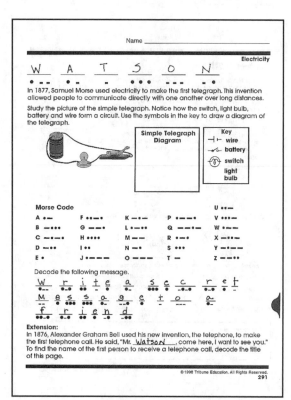

Simple Telegraph Diagram	Key
	⊣⊢ **wire**
	⊸⊢ **battery**
	⊸⊶ **switch**
	light bulb

Morse Code

A • —		F ••—•		K —•—		P •——•		V •••—
B —•••		G ——•		L •—••		Q ——•—		W •——
C —•—•		H ••••		M ——		R •—•		X —••—
D —••		I ••		N —•		S •••		Y —•——
E •		J •———		O ———		T —		Z ——••

Decode the following message.

W r i t e   a   s e c r e t
•— •—• •• — • •— ••• • —•—• •—• • —

M e s s a g e   t o   a
—— • ••• ••• •— ——• • — ——— •—

f r i e n d
••—• •—• •• • —• —••

Extension:
In 1876, Alexander Graham Bell used his new invention, the telephone, to make the first telephone call. He said, "Mr. _Watson_, come here, I want to see you." To find the name of the first person to receive a telephone call, decode the title of this page.

Light Up Your Life

A light bulb changes electricity into light. Electricity passes through the very thin wire, called a **filament**, inside the bulb. As electricity flows through the filament, the wire gets hot and gives off light.

Look very closely at the filament in a light bulb. It is made of tiny coils of wire. By using coils, more wire can be put in the bulb—so more light can be made.

Directions: Label the parts of the light bulb using the words from the Word Bank.

Word Bank
coil filament
glass bulb
wire support
glass support
base

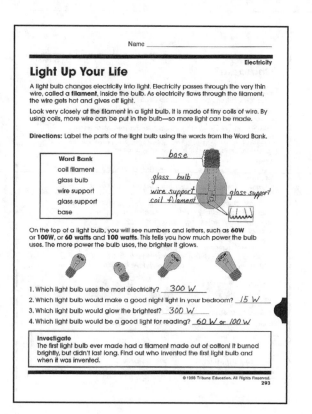

base
glass bulb
wire support
coil filament
glass support

On the top of a light bulb, you will see numbers and letters, such as **60W** or **100W**, or **60 watts** and **100 watts**. This tells you how much power the bulb uses. The more power the bulb uses, the brighter it glows.

1. Which light bulb uses the most electricity? _300 W_
2. Which light bulb would make a good night light in your bedroom? _15 W_
3. Which light bulb would glow the brightest? _300 W_
4. Which light bulb would be a good light for reading? _60 W or 100 W_

Investigate
The first light bulb ever made had a filament made out of cotton! It burned brightly, but didn't last long. Find out who invented the first light bulb and when it was invented.

Portable Power

Steve and Lenny really enjoyed listening to the radio while they fished. Radios need electricity to work. Where did Steve's radio get its power? From a **dry cell battery**, of course. Dry cells are sources of portable power.

Most portable radios use dry cells. A dry cell makes electricity by changing chemical energy into electrical energy. Chemicals in the dry cell act on each other and make **electrons** flow. The flow of electrons is called **electricity**.

Directions:

Use the words from the Word Bank to label the parts of the dry cell. You can use a science book to help, but first try to figure out each part by yourself.

Word Bank
chemical paste
carbon rod
zinc case
terminal

zinc case
terminal
chemical paste
carbon rod

Portable Power Inventory

List the appliances, tools or toys in your house that are powered with dry cells.

Possible answers include: _tape recorder_
flashlight   _clock_
"boom box"

Investigate
Before batteries were invented, scientists did all their experiments with static electricity. Find out who made the first battery and when it was made.

Making Electricity

Where does the electricity that is in your house come from? It all begins at a large **power plant**. The power plant has a large **turbine generator**. High-pressure steam spins the turbines and the generator that is attached to the turbine shaft. As the generator spins, it produces hundreds of megawatts of electricity.

Directions:

Below is a picture of a power plant where electricity is generated. Label each part using the terms found in the Power Bank below.

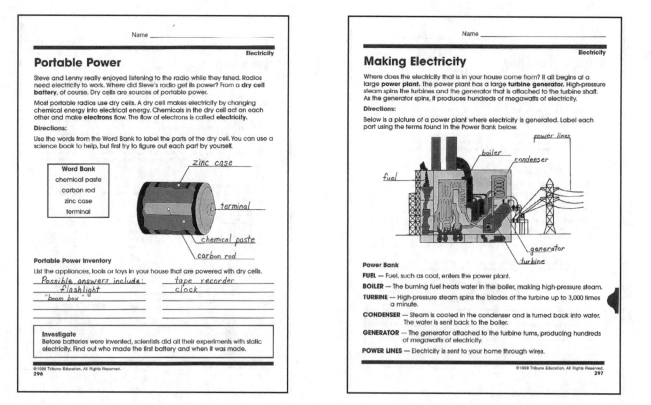

power lines
boiler
condenser
fuel
generator
turbine

Power Bank

FUEL — Fuel, such as coal, enters the power plant.

BOILER — The burning fuel heats water in the boiler, making high-pressure steam.

TURBINE — High-pressure steam spins the blades of the turbine up to 3,000 times a minute.

CONDENSER — Steam is cooled in the condenser and is turned back into water. The water is sent back to the boiler.

GENERATOR — The generator attached to the turbine turns, producing hundreds of megawatts of electricity.

POWER LINES — Electricity is sent to your home through wires.

Name _____

Electricity

Conserving Electricity

"Jane, did you remember to turn off the TV?" Jane's parents want Jane to remember to conserve electricity. It takes a lot of fuel to make electricity. We have to be careful not to waste electricity.

Your house has an **electric meter** that measures the amount of electricity your family uses. The meter measures the electricity in **kilowatt hours**. It would take one kilowatt hour to light ten light bulbs (100 watts each) for one hour. Would a 75-watt light bulb use more or less power than the 100-watt light bulb?

Look carefully at Jane's home. How could Jane conserve electricity?

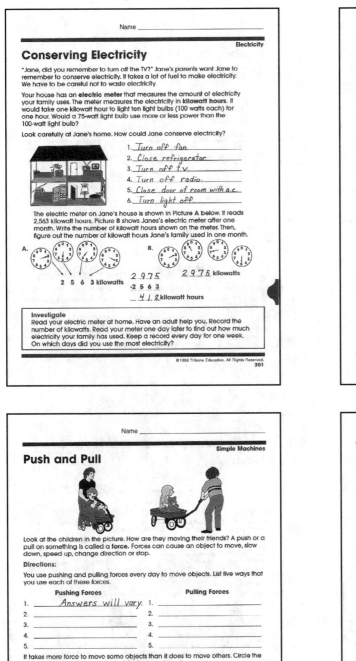

1. Turn off fan.
2. Close refrigerator.
3. Turn off t.v.
4. Turn off radio.
5. Close door of room with a.c.
6. Turn light off.

The electric meter on Jane's house is shown in Picture A below. It reads 2,563 kilowatt hours. Picture B shows Jane's electric meter after one month. Write the number of kilowatt hours shown on the meter. Then, figure out the number of kilowatt hours Jane's family used in one month.

A.   B.

2 5 6 3 kilowatts   2 9 7 5 kilowatts

2 9 7 5
-2 5 6 3
_____
4 1 2 kilowatt hours

Investigate
Read your electric meter at home. Have an adult help you. Record the number of kilowatts. Read your meter one day later to find out how much electricity your family has used. Keep a record every day for one week. On which days did you use the most electricity?

© 1998 Tribune Education. All Rights Reserved.
301

Name _____

Electricity

Energy

Do you feel tired after raking the lawn? You feel tired then because work takes a lot of energy. **Energy** is the ability to do work.

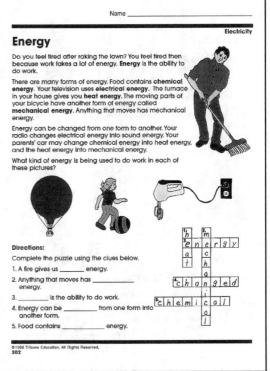

There are many forms of energy. Food contains **chemical energy**. Your television uses **electrical energy**. The furnace in your house gives you **heat energy**. The moving parts of your bicycle have another form of energy called **mechanical energy**. Anything that moves has mechanical energy.

Energy can be changed from one form to another. Your radio changes electrical energy into sound energy. Your parents' car may change chemical energy into heat energy, and the heat energy into mechanical energy.

What kind of energy is being used to do work in each of these pictures?

Directions:

Complete the puzzle using the clues below.

1. A fire gives us _____ energy.
2. Anything that moves has _____ energy.
3. _____ is the ability to do work.
4. Energy can be _____ from one form into another form.
5. Food contains _____ energy.

© 1998 Tribune Education. All Rights Reserved.
302

Name _____

Simple Machines

Push and Pull

Look at the children in the picture. How are they moving their friends? A push or a pull on something is called a **force**. Forces can cause an object to move, slow down, speed up, change direction or stop.

Directions:

You use pushing and pulling forces every day to move objects. List five ways that you use each of these forces.

Pushing Forces	Pulling Forces
1. Answers will vary.	1.
2.	2.
3.	3.
4.	4.
5.	5.

It takes more force to move some objects than it does to move others. Circle the object in each picture which would take *more* force to move.

© 1998 Tribune Education. All Rights Reserved.
304

Name _____

Simple Machines

Around and Around

A doorknob is a simple machine you use every day. It is a **wheel and axle machine**. The wheel is connected to the axle. The axle is a center post. When the wheel moves, the axle does, too.

Opening a door by turning the axle with your fingers is very hard. But by turning the doorknob, which is the "wheel," you use much less force. The doorknob turns the axle for you. The doorknob makes it easy because it is much bigger than the axle. You turn the doorknob a greater distance, but with much less force.

Sometimes the "wheel" of a wheel-and-axle machine doesn't look like a wheel. But look at the path the doorknob makes when it is turned. The path makes a circle, just like a wheel.

Directions:

Color only the wheels of the wheel-and-axle machines below.

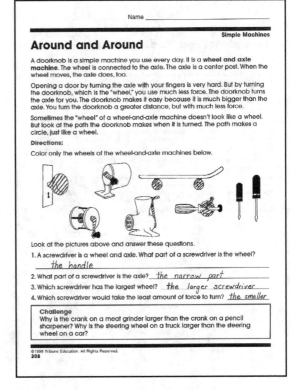

Look at the pictures above and answer these questions.

1. A screwdriver is a wheel and axle. What part of a screwdriver is the wheel?
   the handle
2. What part of a screwdriver is the axle? the narrow part
3. Which screwdriver has the largest wheel? the larger screwdriver
4. Which screwdriver would take the least amount of force to turn? the smaller

Challenge
Why is the crank on a meat grinder larger than the crank on a pencil sharpener? Why is the steering wheel on a truck larger than the steering wheel on a car?

© 1998 Tribune Education. All Rights Reserved.
308

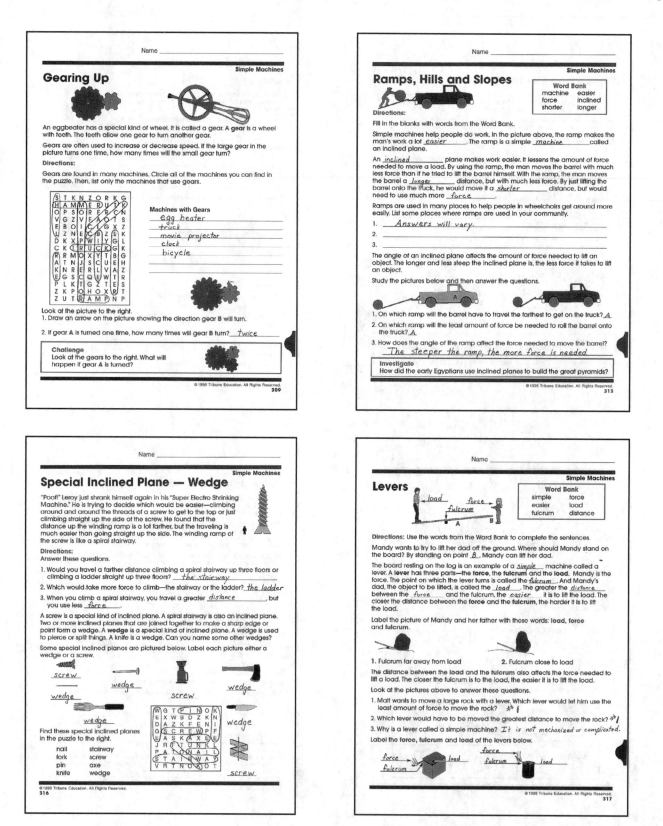

Gearing Up

An eggbeater has a special kind of wheel. It is called a gear. A **gear** is a wheel with teeth. The teeth allow one gear to turn another gear.

Gears are often used to increase or decrease speed. If the large gear in the picture turns one time, how many times will the small gear turn?

Directions:

Gears are found in many machines. Circle all of the machines you can find in the puzzle. Then, list only the machines that use gears.

Machines with Gears

egg beater
truck
movie projector
clock
bicycle

Look at the picture to the right.
1. Draw an arrow on the picture showing the direction gear B will turn.

2. If gear A is turned one time, how many times will gear B turn? _twice_

Challenge
Look at the gears to the right. What will happen if gear A is turned?

© 1998 Tribune Education. All Rights Reserved.
309

Ramps, Hills and Slopes

Word Bank
machine   easier
force   inclined
shorter   longer

Directions:
Fill in the blanks with words from the Word Bank.

Simple machines help people do work. In the picture above, the ramp makes the man's work a lot _easier_. The ramp is a simple _machine_ called an inclined plane.

An _inclined_ plane makes work easier. It lessens the amount of force needed to move a load. By using the ramp, the man moves the barrel with much less force than if he tried to lift the barrel himself. With the ramp, the man moves the barrel a _longer_ distance, but with much less force. By just lifting the barrel onto the truck, he would move it a _shorter_ distance, but would need to use much more _force_.

Ramps are used in many places to help people in wheelchairs get around more easily. List some places where ramps are used in your community.
1. _Answers will vary._
2. _____
3. _____

The angle of an inclined plane affects the amount of force needed to lift an object. The longer and less steep the inclined plane is, the less force it takes to lift an object.

Study the pictures below and then answer the questions.

1. On which ramp will the barrel have to travel the farthest to get on the truck? _A_
2. On which ramp will the least amount of force be needed to roll the barrel onto the truck? _A_
3. How does the angle of the ramp affect the force needed to move the barrel?
The steeper the ramp, the more force is needed.

Investigate
How did the early Egyptians use inclined planes to build the great pyramids?

© 1998 Tribune Education. All Rights Reserved.
313

Special Inclined Plane — Wedge

"Poof!" Leroy just shrank himself again in his "Super Electro Shrinking Machine." He is trying to decide which would be easier—climbing around and around the threads of a screw to get to the top or just climbing straight up the side of the screw. He found that the distance up the winding ramp is a lot farther, but the traveling is much easier than going straight up the side. The winding ramp of the screw is like a spiral stairway.

Directions:
Answer these questions.

1. Would you travel a farther distance climbing a spiral stairway up three floors or climbing a ladder straight up three floors? _the stairway_
2. Which would take more force to climb—the stairway or the ladder? _the ladder_
3. When you climb a spiral stairway, you travel a greater _distance_, but you use less _force_.

A screw is a special kind of inclined plane. A spiral stairway is also an inclined plane. Two or more inclined planes that are joined together to make a sharp edge or point form a wedge. A **wedge** is a special kind of inclined plane. A wedge is used to pierce or split things. A knife is a wedge. Can you name some other wedges?

Some special inclined planes are pictured below. Label each picture either a wedge or a screw.

screw   _wedge_   _wedge_
wedge   _screw_   _screw_
wedge   _wedge_

Find these special inclined planes in the puzzle to the right.

nail   stairway
fork   screw
pin   axe
knife   wedge

© 1998 Tribune Education. All Rights Reserved.
316

Levers

load   force
fulcrum

Word Bank
simple   force
easier   load
fulcrum   distance

Directions: Use the words from the Word Bank to complete the sentences.

Mandy wants to try to lift her dad off the ground. Where should Mandy stand on the board? By standing on point _B_, Mandy can lift her dad.

The board resting on the log is an example of a _simple_ machine called a lever. A **lever** has three parts—the **force**, the **fulcrum** and the **load**. Mandy is the force. The point on which the lever turns is called the _fulcrum_. And Mandy's dad, the object to be lifted, is called the _load_. The greater the _distance_ between the _force_ and the fulcrum, the _easier_ it is to lift the load. The closer the distance between the **force** and the **fulcrum**, the harder it is to lift the load.

Label the picture of Mandy and her father with these words: **load, force** and **fulcrum**.

1. Fulcrum far away from load   2. Fulcrum close to load

The distance between the **load** and the **fulcrum** also affects the force needed to lift a load. The closer the fulcrum is to the load, the easier it is to lift the load.

Look at the pictures above to answer these questions.

1. Matt wants to move a large rock with a lever. Which lever would let him use the least amount of force to move the rock? _#1_
2. Which lever would have to be moved the greatest distance to move the rock? _#1_
3. Why is a lever called a simple machine? _It is not mechanized or complicated._
Label the **force, fulcrum** and **load** of the levers below.

force   _load_
fulcrum

force   _load_
fulcrum

© 1998 Tribune Education. All Rights Reserved.
317